MATH EDUCATION AT ITS BEST:
The Potsdam Model

THE CENTER FOR TEACHING/LEARNING OF

MATHEMATICS

— SERIES ON IMPROVING MATHEMATICS EDUCATION

Under the editorship of

MAHESH SHARMA

**1. MATH EDUCATION AT ITS BEST:
The Potsdam Model**
by Dilip K. Datta

Published by

THE CENTER FOR TEACHING/LEARNING OF
MATHEMATICS
P.O. Box 3149, Framingham, MA 01701

and

RHODE ISLAND DESKTOP ENTERPRISES
P.O. Box 353, Kingston, R.I. 02881

MATH EDUCATION AT ITS BEST:
The Potsdam Model

Dilip K. Datta

Department of Mathematics
University of Rhode Island

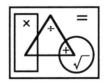

CENTER FOR TEACHING/LEARNING OF MATHEMATICS
FRAMINGHAM

© Copyright, 1993, by Dilip K. Datta

Consulting Editor: Sandra Wall

Cover design by Suzanne Langelier Lebeda.

Suzanne is a native of upstate NewYork. She is an award winning artist, whose posters and cover designs promoting Potsdam College's publications have been receiving national attention. Recently, she was awarded a silver medal by the Council for the Advancement and Support of Education (CASE), a non-profit organization of College and University advancement professionals throughout the nation, in the category of individual in-house publications. In 1992, one of her watercolor originals was selected as the Adirondack Park Centennial Poster Exhibit. At present, Suzanne is the coordinator of publications, Potsdam College, and many say that her eye-catching cover and poster designs for Potsdam College have been instrumental in attracting the attention of potential students to Potsdam College.

Library of Congress Catalog Card Number: 93-85952

ISBN 0-9638605-1-8 9.95

Manufactured in the United States of America

DEDICATED TO

PROFESSOR CLARENCE F. STEPHENS,

a great math teacher who exemplifies the definition:

"A good mathematics teacher is one who uses his knowledge of math as well as his love and respect for his pupils to lead them to an enjoyment of the study of mathematics."

[John Egsgard, President National Council of Teachers of Mathematics, 1976]

CONTENTS

Preface
Acknowledgements
Introduction

THE BACKGROUND

THE STRATEGIES

THE VISION AND PRESENT REALITIES

APPENDIXES

PREFACE

During the last decade, numerous reports have cited how poorly our students, both in schools and colleges, are performing in mathematics. But the number of students graduating from institutions of higher education with mathematics major or with adequate training in mathematics teaching is also a matter of concern. Only through a dedicated and concerned effort, at all levels, can this trend be turned around. The Center for Teaching/Learning of Mathematics and its publications: *Focus on Learning Problems of Mathematics* and the *Math Notebook* are dedicated to improving mathematics education at all levels. They have been helpful in bringing important information to the nation on how to improve mathematics education. With the publication of *Math Education at its Best: The Potsdam Model,* we begin a series of publications on mathematics education bringing proven practices.

Most reform efforts have dealt with improving mathematics education at the school level. At the higher education level, the effort has focussed on changing the content and infusion of technology. In order to bring lasting change the focus should be on all aspects of math education: content, teaching methodology, environment, and the quality of student-teacher interaction.

Math Education at Its Best: The Potsdam Model gives a fascinating account of how a dedicated band of math teachers at Potsdam has shaped into reality the vision of creating a humanistic environment for learning and teaching mathematics. This has evolved into a method of teaching that prepares an excellent cadre of mathematics students. Many of them have become accomplished mathematicians, scientists, and teachers of mathematics. The method provides an approach to meet the crucial challenge of supplying mathematicians, scientists, and mathematically educated workers. This book, first in our series, understands the major challenge, the undersupply of mathematicians poses for the country's needs and is an answer to this critical condition. This work is a blueprint for rebuilding the mathematics education at all levels. It contains a thorough account of how Potsdam College achieved the goal of educating a large number of men and women in mathematics.

"For nearly two decades mathematics has dominated this regional public college of 4000 students, both in terms of quality and quantity of students. In 1985 the college graduated 184 mathematics majors, a total exceeded only by two campuses of the University of California. Approximately 24 percent of the bachelor's degrees at SUNY Potsdam are in mathematics and over 40 percent of the college's honor students are mathematics majors." [1]

The book discusses the all inclusive and comprehensive methods of teaching and provides strategies for how others can emulate Potsdam in establishing a successful mathematics program.

Mahesh Sharma
Series Editor
September 15, 1993   Improving Mathematics Education

---

[1] National Research Council's report to the nation:
Moving Beyond Myths, Revitalizing Undergraduate Mathematics.

ACKNOWLEDGEMENTS

I would like to thank Professor Clarence Stephens, Professor Charles Smith and the present members of the math department of Potsdam College for their kind cooperation in furnishing me details of their work, their strategies and their views. Special thanks to the department's present chairman Vasily C. Cateforis for his consistent help and for all the hours he spent enlightening me about various details and insights about the Potsdam program.

Many thanks to the following persons for going through the manuscript and pointing out mistakes and inaccuracies: Professor Clarence Stephens, Vasily C. Cateforis, Armond C. Spencer and James T. Lewis. Special thanks to Patricia A. Beaulieu for typing the major portion of this book and for all the help she gave me in finding old papers and other materials.

I would like to express my appreciation to Matt Kaplan of the Center for Teaching and Learning Mathematics, University of North Carolina for organizing the workshop on teaching Mathematics the Potsdam Way and to all the participants who so enthusiastically came to share the ideas that now forms the core of the material in chapter 10.

I would like to thank the consulting editor Sandra Wall for her careful and critical reading of the manuscript. I am also grateful to Suzane Langelier-Lebeda for the beautiful cover design. Special thanks to Mahesh C. Sharma, Lillian E. Travaglini and Bush Chaudhary for their enthusiastic support in producing the book.

I appreciate the courtesy of the following organizations who allowed us to reproduce material in this book: The National Academy Press, Washington, DC, Addison-Wesley Publishing Company, Department of Mathematics, Potsdam College, and the Office of Educational Research and Improvement, U.S. Department of Education.

Last but not the least I would like to thank the University of Rhode Island for granting me a sabbatical leave to carry on the study and the Potsdam College for its hospitality in providing me with everything I needed to fulfill my task.

D.K.D

Kingston, Rhode Island
September, 1993

INTRODUCTION

The tradition of teaching and learning mathematics that Clarence Stephens and a band of dedicated teachers have established at SUNY Potsdam is unique in many ways. It is one of the most successful undergraduate programs in the country. In addition to producing a very high percentage of accomplished math majors, it is very simple and stable and can easily be duplicated elsewhere. At a time when the experts are declaring, "..deficiencies in mathematics education are pervasive throughout the U.S. system of education," and at a time when the country is looking for tested and proven models of success, a simple and stable model like that of SUNY Potsdam is one that we can turn to. Therefore, we need to take a very close look at the Potsdam model and find why it works and how we can duplicate it. This account of the Potsdam model is based on a year-long study made during the academic year 1991 - 92.

Ever since I read John Poland's article, "A Modern Fairy Tale", Potsdam College attracted my attention. Then after listening to a lecture about the Potsdam program in a Northeastern Section meeting of the Mathematical Association of America, I got a strong urge to make definite plans to find out what they were doing at Potsdam. So, in August 1991, I ended up in Potsdam to begin my year-long sabbatical leave.

This study contains a truthful account of what I observed and what I found out during my stay at Potsdam. The curriculum at Potsdam is no different from those of others; the students that come to study at Potsdam are not any different from the kind of students that come to a state college or state school anywhere else in the country; the program is not significantly different from those at other similar institution. So, what can be the secret of Potsdam's success?

It did not take me long to realize that the teachers constitute the key element behind Potsdam college's math-power. The math teachers at Potsdam represent diverse background as seen anywhere else in America --- people from Greece, India, Iran, Taiwan, and various regions of the country have filtered into the Potsdam math department. They were carefully selected by its leader Clarence Stephens, an American of African heritage. Somehow or other they all nicely fit into the Potsdam mold of dedicated teachers, who love math, who enjoy teaching math, who care about their students and who seek their rewards in the achievements of their students. So I decided to focus my study on the teachers.

A few words concerning my method of observation will be in order. During my stay at Potsdam, I was appointed as an adjunct Professor and as such I enjoyed all the rights and privileges of a department member. I had free access to the department files and records, I was free to attend department meetings, I could sit in the paper presentations of the students in advanced courses, and above all I was invited to all the social events organized by the department or by the local chapter of Pi Mu Epsilon.

Within a few days, it became clear to me that to know more about the Potsdam program, it was necessary to know more about the background, the views, the experiments, the experiences of Clarence Stephens, and the background leading to his appointment as the Chairman of the mathematics department. After clearing these areas, I held formal interviews with every member of the department -- in these interviews I tried to gather as much information about the policies of the teachers regarding class preparations, student participations, office hours, homework, syllabus, textbooks etc. These were followed by informal chats. Then I attended a few classes to find out how they do what they say they do in class. I was also able to take a few classes of a teacher when she was in the hospital. To get a clear idea about the time the teachers spent on various duties like correcting homework, preparing lectures, helping students in office and research work, I had the teachers fill out time charts for a whole week, once during the middle of the semester and once during the later part of the semester. More than two-thirds of the teachers returned the time-charts. In addition, I stayed long enough to start a close friendship with several members of the department with whom I had frequent discussions about pedagogical matters. In short, the emphasis of my study is on the teachers. I have deliberately avoided the students. Whatever I have written about the students at Potsdam are based on casual contacts.

I have also studied, quite thoroughly, the documents available in the department and listed in the references. Unfortunately, most of the papers written by Stephens were presented as lectures and were not published. Some of them are not available in the department office. I had to dig them out of private folders of some members. Hopefully, Professor Stephens or the department will collect and print them. In my opinion, these papers are pure gems and are very important to understand the Potsdam model.

Most of the mathematics teachers at Potsdam do their things very naturally. Many of them perhaps do not see their activities from the same angle as I have outlined here. This is clear from the response I received from Professor Stephens after I sent him the first draft of this book, "From your paper I learned, for the first time, some interesting historical facts about the SUNY at Potsdam Mathematics Program and Department. Also, I learned from reading your paper more about the teaching strategies of the SUNY Potsdam Mathematics faculty than I had learned during my 18 years as Chair of the Mathematics Department." What I have tried to do here is to single out the striking characteristics of the Potsdam teachers and to analyze why the Potsdam program has been so successful in winning the hearts of students, and in teaching mathematics to undegraduates.

It should also be pointed out that many, including the authors of *Moving Beyond Myths*, emphasize the need to improve the quality of undergraduate mathematics education to achieve "Prosperity in today's global economy" or to achieve worldwide "preeminence in mathematics education" because they hold the view "mathematics forms the core of the qualitative skills needed by our nation's scientific, technical, and managerial work force, including the nation's mathematics teachers."

However, the Potsdam mathgurus are not motivated by such material considerations as prosperity in today's global economy or such vain glory as supremacy or preeminence in mathematics education. At Potsdam, the emphasis is on mathematics as mental nourishment and cultural enrichment, that is, learning mathematics for the sake of learning. Therefore, it will be vain to emulate the Potsdam model with the goal of oiling the machines of prosperity or of establishing supremacy over other nations. These of course, may come as a byproduct of successful undergraduate math programs.

September, 1993   Dilip K. Datta

Chapter 1

POTSDAM'S MATH POWER

Some call it a modern fairy tale, some call it an experience, and many refer to it as an experiment in teaching. Be it what it may, the percentage of math graduates produced by Potsdam College during the last decade has defied all national trends. Figure 1 presents a comparative picture of the percentage of math graduates of Potsdam and the national percentage of math graduates for the years 1978 - 89.

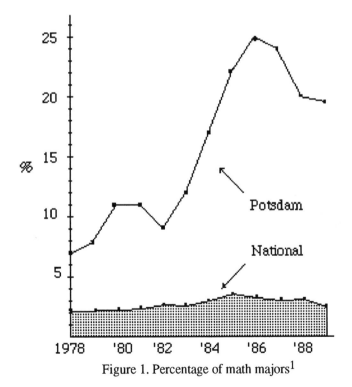

Figure 1. Percentage of math majors[1]

1

The number of female math graduates produced by Potsdam is even more impressive because nationally the number of females earning a bachelor's degree in math has always been far less than the number of males earning the same degree [Figure 2]. Whereas in the case of Potsdam College in recent years it has been just the opposite, that is, the number of females earning a bachelor's degree in math has usually been higher than the number of males earning the same degree [Figure 3]. The data for the graph in figure 2 is by courtesy of the Office of Educational Research and Improvement, U.S. Department of Education.

To get a better idea, we may point out that Potsdam College (an institution of just over 4,000 students) produced more math graduates in 1985 than the University of Rhode Island (an institution of 15,000 students) in the last five years.

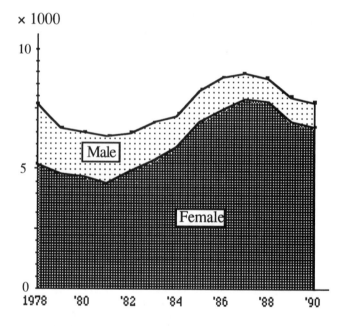

Figure 2. The number of undergraduates majoring in mathematics and statistics in the United States

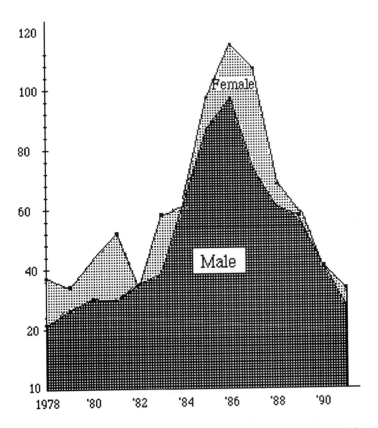

Figure 3. Number of male and female math graduates produced by
SUNY Potsdam

Impressive as they are, these comparative figures do not reflect the
quality of math graduates produced by Potsdam. Because, in their love
of math, their ability to appreciate mathematical knowledge and their
sense of accomplishments, the math graduates of Potsdam are a
different breed. For example, the MAA Panel that prepared the
recommendations for a general mathematical sciences program noted,
"The most striking feature to a visitor to the Potsdam State
Mathematics Department is the great enthusiasm among the students

and the sense of pride students have in their ability to think mathematically" [3].

Yet, the impressive number of math graduates produced and the quality of the math graduates do not tell the whole story - the whole story of how one man's vision of creating a humanistic academic environment for learning undergraduate mathematics was shaped into reality by a team of dedicated teachers.

Here we will try to give a good view of that vision and some nitty gritty details about the attitudes, efforts, and strategies of the members of that team of dedicated teachers who made it all possible. It is my sincere belief that every math teacher, whether he or she be teaching in elementary school, high school, a college or a university has a lot to learn from this story.

Historical Background

Potsdam College traces its origin back to the St. Lawrence Academy, founded in 1816. Accordingly, in 1991 the college celebrated its 175th year of existence. The St. Lawrence Academy, which prepared public school teachers, deeded its properties and assets in 1866 to the Potsdam Normal School. Potsdam remained a normal school till 1942, when it became a teachers college. As a teachers college, it became a part of the State University of New York in 1948 and it remained a teachers college until 1962, when it became a college of arts and sciences of the State University of New York.

So, until 1962, Potsdam was a teachers college and it had about 7 math teachers who taught mostly elementary math courses. The most advanced course taught was Introductory Calculus. The courses were so-so, but the course assignments and the teaching load of the math teachers were at best terrible. Sometimes one had to teach five sections of trigonometry, and a teaching load of 18 hours a week was regarded as normal. The pay was low and the teachers tried to supplement their incomes by working on other campuses like the Clarkson campus and the Watertown campus. Until 1966, when the math department was moved to the present MacVicar Hall, the department was moved from place to place. For a while, four of the math teachers shared the same office. The preparation and teaching of undergraduate math courses had brought additional hardships on the handful of math teachers, most of whom had degrees in math education, and none of them had any experience of teaching math at a liberal arts college. To make matters worse, the college administration appointed a chairman of the math department in 1967 without consulting any member of the math department. Even though the chairman appointed had a Ph.D. in math, that appointment was like letting a wolf loose among a herd of sheep or like feeding a sheep to a pack of hungry wolves. In any case, the scenario was such that after a year, he was happy to leave the department and the department was happy to see him go. However, the math program was badly shattered and the morale of the department was low. Yet Potsdam College had a band of math teachers, who were very dedicated to teaching math and who were looking for an opportunity to make their profession meaningful and worthwhile.

This opportunity came in the spring of 1969, when the campus was visited by Clarence F. Stephens, who was then teaching at the Geneseo campus of SUNY, to give a talk sponsored by the Seaway Section of the MAA. His talk on math and math teaching opened the eyes of the math teachers at Potsdam College and they felt that if they could persuade him to chair the department, he would be able to provide them with good leadership. Of course, Stephens was not looking for a job, nor was he seeking the chairmanship, even then they approached him and started a dialogue. Stephens was impressed by the sincerity of their purpose to establish a good math program there and he saw the possibility of testing the reality of a vision about a math program that he had been formulating in his mind for years; so, he expressed a desire to take the responsibility. The math teachers there felt that he was the right man, and they were so overwhelmed by his vision of creating a humanistic environment for learning undergraduate mathematics that they approached the administration to give him the best possible offer because "he is worth more than we can pay him."

Clarence F. Stephens took charge as the Chairman of the Mathematics Department of Potsdam College in the fall of 1969, and he retired from that position in 1987. How the math program at Potsdam was transformed during that period into an exemplary math program and how it continues to draw praise from the mathematical community of the country after that period is the subject matter of this report.

[1] To make the comparison meaningful, in calculating the national percentage we have considered the total number of bachelor's degrees awarded in the following disciplines: area and ethnic studies, computer and information sciences, education, foreign languages, home economics, letters, liberal/general studies, life sciences (includes degrees in anatomy, bacteriology, biochemistry, biology, botany, entomology, physiology, zoology, and other biological sciences), mathematics (includes degrees in statistics), philosophy and religion, physical sciences (includes degrees in astronomy, chemistry, geology, metallurgy, meteorology, physics, science technologies and other physical sciences), psychology, social sciences (includes degrees in anthropology, archeology, economics, history, geography, political science and government, sociology, criminology, international relations, urban studies, demography and other social sciences), theology, and visual and performing arts. The data is by courtesy of the Office of Educational Research and Improvement, U.S. Department of Education.

Chapter 2

THE ENVIRONMENT

The success of the mathematics faculty at SUNY Potsdam in establishing a humanistic academic environment during the last two decades is now well-known:

> " ... Potsdam State College (in the economically depressed northeast corner of New York) has possibly the greatest percentage of mathematics graduates of any public institution in the country -- close to 10% -- despite competition from a popular computer science major [34]."
> "Clarence Stephens created at SUNY Potsdam an undergraduate mathematics program that is difficult to overlook. For nearly two decades mathematics has dominated this regional public college of 4000 students, both in terms of quality and quantity of students. In 1985 the college graduated 184 mathematics majors, a total exceeded only by two campuses of the University of California. Approximately 24 percent of the bachelor's degrees at SUNY Potsdam are in mathematics and over 40 percent of the college's honor students are mathematics majors [21]."

Therefore, instead of reiterating figures to describe the success story, we would like to point out the main ingredients of a humanistic academic environment for learning undergraduate mathematics as envisioned by Clarence Stephens and as established by the determined efforts of the team of math teachers that he gathered at Potsdam. After spending a year at SUNY Potsdam, extensive interviews with the math teachers there, and studying the various aspects of the program, I have come to observe the following main ingredients which have made the environment for learning undergraduate mathematics at Potsdam an outstanding one.

(1) The welfare of the students must be the most important consideration of the department.

7

(2)   A comfortable physical environment that fosters interaction between teachers and students.

(3)   Teaching mathematics as an important part of liberal education and not necessarily as a way of making a living using mathematics.

(4)   An undergraduate program that is simple and stable and that allows the better students to excel and take graduate courses early.

(5)   Easily available and accessible support system.

(6)   Creation of student role models.

(7)   Careful and considerate teaching by a well trained and dedicated faculty, who love and respect the students.

Now we shall discuss how these ingredients have been carefully refined and blended by the math department at SUNY Potsdam.

Students Come First. The members of the Potsdam math department do not pay lip service to the motto "students come first" but they go all out to put it into practice. In my interviews with the faculty members of the Math Department, I asked the question, "in what way the Potsdam environment is different from the math teaching and learning environments you have known as a student, as a teacher, or otherwise?" Almost all of them replied that the most important difference was the concern for students. Thus Professor A, who taught in several other places before coming here, says, "I never worked so hard in my life - here I spend a lot of time with my students and it is very rewarding." Professor B, who is a new comer to the department, says, "I found that teachers here care a lot for students. When I was an undergraduate, the chairman of the math department told me not to bother going to graduate school. We do not treat students like that here. There is a big difference in attitude towards students."

Indeed there is - whether it is the furniture in the offices, whether it is teaching assignments or whether it is examination or grading of homework, the motto of the math department at SUNY Potsdam is "students come first." As a matter of fact, from day one after he assumed the chairmanship, Clarence Stephens drove this motto hard into the hearts of every member of the department. He believed that if a student knows that his teacher cares for his well-being, the student will respond well to the math the teacher is trying to teach.

- He insisted that every faculty office must be furnished with comfortable cushioned chairs for the students.
- He would constantly make the teachers aware that students have other courses to study and they need to relax over the weekends.
- The first thing he would ask a teacher would be something like "Are your students enjoying math?" On the wall of the math department hangs a poster that says: ARE WE HAVING FUN YET?

Here are some of the things Steve used to say in this regard:
- You do not attract better students, you work with the ones you get and develop them.
- Believe in your students, everyone can do mathematics.
- Know your students well - their names, what they know, their hopes and fears.
- High standards do not mean having unrealistic expectations so students feel that they have failed.
- Go fast slowly.

The math teachers at Potsdam do care for their students and do their best to create an atmosphere where the students feel comfortable, where a student's self-esteem is protected and strengthened, and which provides "an intellectual climate where the mathematical potential of all students who elect to take mathematics courses in the Department can be identified and nurtured." The students' reactions to such a student-welfare-oriented department has been best described by John Poland, "The students say they feel that the faculty members really care about them, care that each one of them can develop to the maximum possible level. The faculty can be quite explicit about it: for example, the chairman (C.F. Stephens) tells his classes that he believes in each of them, and cares about them, that he is there to help them achieve their potential. He stresses that a mind is a terrible thing to waste. The faculty win the students over to enjoy and do mathematics. And it is simply the transforming power of love, love through encouragement, caring, and fostering of a supportive environment [22]."

Physical Environment that fosters closer interaction between students and teachers. The math classrooms of SUNY at Potsdam are like an extension of the faculty offices; this makes it very easy for the students to go and see their teachers before walking into or after walking out of a math class. Four of the classrooms are used only by math and three other adjacent classrooms are used mostly by the math department. In addition, the math lab is sandwiched between math classrooms. This makes the math lab very easily accessible and often students who were not planning to go there end up being there. Mingled with the faculty offices is a very pleasant reading room and a student/faculty coffee room. Both these rooms are open to teachers and students. This is another striking thing about Potsdam math - the students and faculty exist like a family. There is no separation between students and faculty. As a matter of fact, the students are regarded as members of the department. The restrooms in the area do not say 'Faculty only' as is the case in many other schools, and the defective doors of the toilets in the men's room trap students and faculty alike.

Even though the classrooms have their share of leaking roofs, lights that are barely hanging from the ceiling endangering the safety of students and teachers, and blackboards with glare etc., the proximity of the classrooms to the offices of the teachers and to the math lab adds to an advantageous physical environment. If a teacher finds himself/herself without his/her text notes in his/her classroom, he/she can easily run back to his/her office to pick them up or pick up anything that he/she forgot to take to class. The students also do not have far to go from their classroom to find their teacher whenever they need him/her or whenever he/she forgets, as many absent minded professors do, to show up in his/her classroom. In any case, this layout is very favorable for the intermixing of students and teachers of the math department at SUNY Potsdam. Even though they deny it, I cannot help thinking that the narrow corridor in the math building is rather by design than anything else, for you cannot pass a person coming from the otherside without rubbing "belly to belly or back to back" and saying "hello".

Teaching mathematics as an important part of a liberal arts education. Clarence Stephens wrote in 1981, "Most students enroll in mathematics courses on a voluntary basis and not as a requirement for a major or minor in some other subject. Our college has no mathematics requirement as a condition for graduation. For example, one year with a freshman class of less than 1000 students, more than 600 students enrolled in beginning calculus. No more than 100 of these students came from supply departments. The issue of teaching algorithms vs. teaching thinking or concrete vs. abstract in mathematics education is not a problem at Potsdam College. Students consider the study of mathematics as an important part of a liberal arts education and not necessarily as a way of making a living using mathematics primarily [31]." This explains why a large number of students chose to obtain a math degree at Potsdam. In addition, to the students who wanted to go for higher studies in math or to become math teachers, many students who came to Potsdam to have a degree or a liberal arts education, perhaps found the math program very meaningful and very attractive. I have met one such math graduate of Potsdam, who after getting her B.A. math degree, later decided to become an electrical engineer. But she has no regrets because she finds that her math training not only made the electrical engineering courses easier but also gave her a sense of accomplishment.

There is no doubt that among the math graduates of Potsdam there are many who would not have gone near the math department if they were at a different college or university. The emphasis on mathematics as an important part of a liberal arts education not only brings it closer to the humanities, but also helps to create a humanistic environment for the students.

There have been some changes at Potsdam since Stephens wrote that article. The big change is that nowadays a course in either statistical analysis and reasoning or problem solving and abstract reasoning is a compulsory requirement of the evolving general education component (of the B.A. degree). The statistical analysis requirement may be satisfied by an introductory course in discrete statistics which is normally offered in the department of mathematics, computer science and psychology. The problem solving and abstract reasoning requirement may be normally satisfied by courses in the departments of computer science, economics, mathematics and physics. So this 'math requirement' does not have to be satisfied in the mathematics department, but many students do opt to take it there. In any case, we can no longer say that a student takes every math course voluntarily. Because many of those who opt to take a math course see it as a math requirement.

In any case, the emphasis of the math department continues to be on pure math as can be seen from the position paper of the math department. "We believe that the study of mathematics, by students whose majors and career objectives are not close to mathematics, to be both liberal and liberating. We believe that we should provide courses that these students will continue to elect and that such students should be encouraged to explore the true nature of Mathematics, hence through understanding to overcome those prejudices or negative attitudes they may have toward the discipline."

Potsdam Programs

If we compare the Undergraduate Bulletin of Potsdam College for the year 1969-70 with that of the year 1970-71, we can clearly see how the math programs quickly changed after Steve, as Clarence Stephens is referred to by the math faculty, took over the chairmanship.

The core requirements for the regular major and honors major are not strong but minimum under the 30 credit hours limit. A student who completes these core requirements with high grades and good recommendations should be able to continue his studies successfully to the graduate level in mathematics. Each major is expected to be strengthened by electives. Honors mathematics majors are advised to include among their electives Linear Algebra II. Regular mathematics majors are advised to include among their electives at least one course from the following: Concepts of Geometry, Topology of the Real Line, Introduction to Topology, Differential Equations, Applied Mathematics I, Probability, Mathematical Statistics, Introduction to Complex Variables with Applications."

<u>1969-70</u>

"**Requirements for Majors**

	Credit Hours
Mathematics major	30
Calculus I, II	8
Set Theory and Logic	3
Topology of the Real Line	3
Additional mathematics courses	16

1970 - 71

Requirements for Majors

Regular Major ....30 credit hours

Calculus I, II, III 12
Set Theory and Logic 3
Introduction to Modern Algebra I 3
Linear Algebra I 3
Advanced Calculus I 3
Problem Seminar 3

One course from the following:

Introduction to Modern Algebra II
Linear Algebra II
Advanced Calculus II 3

Honors Major............................30 credit hours
Calculus I, II, III 12
Set Theory and Logic 3
Linear Algebra I 3
Advanced Calculus I and II 6
Abstract Algebra I (Graduate level) 3
Independent Study.............................3

The following year, Clarence, in spite of opposition from some members of the department and bitter opposition by some faculty members of other departments, was able to introduce the very innovative four-year B.A./M.A. program. Since then, the programs have changed a little but the main features of the programs remain the same [For a description of the present programs, please see *Why Mathematics ?* in Appendix 1]. Here are the main thrusts of the programs.

(1) The basic program is designed to give the students a liberal education through the study of mathematics. "The educated person,"

says Peter Hilton, "is characterized by a desire to learn and to understand, by an awarness of what he or she does not know and an appreciation of what is worth knowing -- and why. The study of mathematics contributes to the development of these characteristics, because it can only be learned effectively - learned so that it can be used - if it is understood and if its importance, both for rational thought and for significant application, is appreciated [12]". It seems that the B.A. math program at Potsdam is designed to produce educated persons as described by Hilton.

(2) The honors program is designed for better than average math students, who may or may not go to graduate school or even if they continue to graduate school, it may not be in math.

(3) The B.A./M.A. program is definitely for people who love math and who will perhaps go to graduate school for a Ph.D. degree in math.

The following are some important features of the Potsdam program. To enable bright entering freshmen, regardless of intended major, to satisfy their love for mathematics and realize their great potential the department provides for honors sections of the calculus courses. The enrollment in the honors sections is strictly by invitation. The entering freshman are normally screened by the teacher of the Honors Calculus sections using established objective criteria, and invitation letters are sent to selected students without regard to their intended major in college. The percentage of invitees who elect to take honors calculus has ranged from over twenty to over fifty. It is made clear to the students invited that they will not be penalized by the grades they will receive as a result of electing the honors calculus course rather than the regular calculus course. All students enrolled in calculus are given the same final examination. Also, the teachers who teach an honors calculus section teach a regular calculus section and are well able to compare the achievement of students in different calculus sections. The honors program does not require Honors Calculus.

Able students with advanced placement credit in calculus are allowed to enroll in Calculus II or to complete the courses in Linear Algebra I, and Theory of Sets during the first semester of their freshman year.

Students who have been highly successful in Set Theory and Logic, and Linear Algebra I during their freshmen or sophomore year are promising candidates for the B.A./M.A. program. The mathematics faculty will recommend these promising candidates to the Chair of the Department. Students are advised of the faculty recommendations and invited to elect the course Theory of Sets during the Spring semester. This course is designed for the students to study some basic mathematical concepts and to help them develop the ability to work independently, read abstract mathematical literature, and give mathematical proofs which require a high level of creative thinking. Past experience has shown that students who have been successful in this course and who pursue the B.A./M.A. program have been successful in this program. About half of the students invited to elect this course do so.

Thus, students apply for the B.A./M.A. program only upon the invitation of the mathematics faculty. A high cumulative college average, the mathematical maturity of the student and the student's enjoyment of the study of mathematics are three of the most important considerations of the mathematics faculty in making recommendations for a student to be admitted to the program. The faculty is careful to recommend for admission to the program only those students that are most likely to successfully complete the program and to whom the opportunity to study in the program is a pleasure rather than a burden.

Since 1978, Potsdam College has graduated 93 students (an average of more than 6 students a year) in the B.A./M.A. program.

The department does not give placement mathematics examinations in order to assign students to mathematics courses. Nor does it offer any remedial math courses.

Support Systems

A student taking a math course at Potsdam and having difficulties in understanding the course material can seek and find help from three different sources: (1) classmates, (2) the teacher and (3) the math lab. These support systems have been firmly established and have become a tradition on the campus, and so, the students are very comfortable relying on them.

Classmates. Many teachers make it a point to prepare a class directory of the students with their residence address and phone numbers. Many of the teachers organize study groups or ask the students to form study groups so that they may help each other. We will discuss this in group strategies but what we would like to emphasize here is the fact that class directories and study groups bring the students together and create a comfortable support system for the students.

The teachers. The willingness of the teachers to help the students whenever possible provides extra support to the students. The fact that his or her teacher is accessible most of the time makes students very assured of help and success. This aspect is described in office hour strategies.

The Math Lab. The math lab is by far the most striking support system on campus. The math lab is supervised by a faculty member but it is run by juniors and seniors, who are paid by the hour. The lab is open from 9 a.m. to 8 p.m. and is permanently located in a 16' x 20' room sandwiched between math classrooms. It is comfortably furnished and has a large selection of math textbooks and math books of interest on the shelves.

Role models. Clarence Stephens believed that, "A favorable environment for nurturing mathematical talent must be one that minimizes, both in the mathematics classroom and in the college environment, fear of mathematics and mathematics avoidance. Perhaps the only way such a favorable environment can be developed is by producing examples of many students who reach a high level of achievement in mathematics. As a general rule, these examples will be few at the beginning and these few successful examples will make it easier to produce more examples." [29]. He would then use these successful students as role models. Stephens was a master in creating and using role models to inspire and motivate others. He almost perfected the art and the techniques of role modelling in the world of mathematics. He could create role models for people who were not good in math, for women, for students who were not majoring in math as well as for students majoring in math. He would create role models in class, among the math graduates and in the outside world. He would then use them so effectively that in the end every math student finds a role to play in the department and becomes a role model of some kind. Perhaps this can be better narrated by some examples.

(1) "During my first year as a college teacher I was assigned to teach a course in College Algebra. When I gave a diagnostic examination to the class, I learned that one student had mastered the material of the course as a high school student. I told the student that he had already earned a grade of A for the course and that I would give him special assignments which he could do independently. However, I requested that he attend class since I wanted to use him as a teaching assistant for the class although he was a freshman. I wanted to provide for my College Algebra class an example of a student who had mastered the course and who had graduated from the same high school as that from which many other students in the class had graduated. The student who was recognized as indicated later earned the Ph.D. degree in mathematics from the University of Michigan [29]."

(2) "Although the undergraduate students who were admitted to our Double Degrees program were better mathematics students than our regular graduate students, these undergraduate students did not recognize this fact. Then, a few years after the establishment of this program a young woman enrolled in my Theory of Sets course as a freshman and made the highest score on our Master's written comprehensive examination for the Master of Arts degree in Mathematics as a sophomore. We publicized her success. As a result we enroll each year one or two students who make a similar achievement as this young woman [29]."

(3) "As a general rule, my Theory of Sets course now contains a mix of students who are freshmen, sophomores, juniors, seniors, and first year graduate students. One year I decided to use as a textbook for

this course the book "Introduction to Set Theory" by J. Donald Monk. When a senior in the class wanted to complain that the book was too difficult, he made a greater effort to understand the material in the book when he realized that the best student in the class who was achieving very highly in the course was a freshman. This senior later earned the Master of Arts degree in mathematics from Michigan State University [29]."

(4) One reason why Potsdam graduates a very high percentage of female math majors is its ability to show many role models. Then there is the recent role model as described in a news item of the October 29, 1991 issue of GREECE POST, Pittsford, NY:

"What are the odds that someone who had trouble deciding on her major would end up teaching probability theories at Ohio State University at age 25?

Kimberly Kinateder could probably figure it out.

The 1984 Greece Arcadia valedictorian (known by her classmates as Kimberly Johannes) is in a position to know: She's 25 and teaches probability in OSU's statistics department, where she has worked since the Fall of 1990....

She earned both her bachelor's and master's degrees at SUNY Potsdam in a special four-year program that she finished in three. She was able to do that because of all her advanced-placement credits from high school, . . .

At Michigan (Michigan State), Kinateder earned her doctorate in probability in three years; again , it should have taken four."

(5) The Honors Calculus sections are used to recognize the excellent academic achievement of high school students and their math teachers. Entering freshmen with an excellent record in high school mathematics are invited to join the honors sections of Calculus. Each student is sent a personal letter of invitation. With love and respect, the invited students are led to an enjoyment of the study of mathematics, to understand the meaning of a mathematical proof and respect for a mathematical proof, to learn how to learn mathematics, to develop the ability to read a mathematics textbook for pure enjoyment, and to study independently. "These students serve as role models to help us provide an intellectual climate where the mathematical potential

of all students who elect to take mathematics courses in the department can be identified and nurtured. Some of these students tutor in our mathematics lab and provide leadership in our large chapter of Pi Mu Epsilon [31]."

(6) Every year the department hangs on the walls of its narrow corridor the photographs of the students who graduate in mathematics that year. Underneath each photograph the name of the town where the student comes from is given in addition to the student's name. The students with their bright broad smiles give the impression that each one of them is some kind of mathematical ambassador of his/her town. Trivial it may seem to the outsiders, these serve the purpose of role models. On more than one occasion, I have overheard students say things like, "...., guess what? Our pictures are going to be here next year," and on more than one occasion, I have met ex-students who brought their friends or relatives just to show their pictures hanging on the corridors of the math department.

(7) The annual newsletter of the math department is another tool that Clarence Stephens introduced to create and use role models. The newsletter contains, among other things, the successes of the math majors in the professional world. A copy of this newsletter is sent to every high school represented by a mathematics major in a given graduating class.

The Teachers It should be pointed out that by 1975, the humanistic environment for learning math was well established and teaching traditions of Potsdam mathematics had taken deep roots. So much so that when a new member, who had a good reputation as a good teacher and who was confident of his teaching excellence, joined the department in 1980, he found that the teachers here were way above him in teaching techniques and excellence. In any case, hardly any of the new members of the department had known about the teaching traditions here, nor had any of them heard about it before coming here. Most of them came here either because they liked the area or because the jobs suited them well, but all of them here decided to stay on because they like what is going on here and they like to be part of the program here. They have all come from different backgrounds and from different parts of the world, they have all come to possess some common traits, which stand out nice and clear.

(1) First, they all love mathematics and are all overwhelmed by its beauty, power and its interrelationship with other subjects. They all think that the best way to enjoy this beauty is to help the students appreciate and enjoy it the way they are doing.

(2) However, their love for math is superseded by their love for the students. As observed by Poland, "It is even a love that surpasses the love of mathematics. They would select their textbooks for their courses more on the basis of the book being the best possible aid to help them develop all the students in their classes, rather than primarily on the beauty of the mathematical treatment of the topic [22]."

(3) Third, they do not put their students down. Such comments like "Students can't do math," "Students are lazy," "They are all a spoiled bunch," "They don't have it up here," "They don't care - all they want to do is to get a grade and get it over with," "Students are not well prepared," etc., will rarely roll out of the lips of a math teacher at Potsdam. If they do make comments like these about students, they are not made as a terminal, limiting statement about a course of action - but, rather as a challenge. Instead they say things like "we know students are not well prepared, our job is to teach and prepare them," "They have other courses to take".

(4) They all like to establish good rapport with students and try to know their students by name. As one of them put it, "It makes teaching more fun if you get to know the students." They are all committed to see their personal achievement through the achievement of their students.

(5) They all subscribe to the view expressed in the position paper of the department, "Careful and considerate teaching by a well trained and dedicated faculty, continual encouragement, successful role models, enough success to develop self esteem, enough time to develop intellectually, recognition of their achievement, and the belief that the study is a worthwhile endeavor. We are dedicated to providing this supportive environment."

(6) A very striking characteristic of the math teachers at Potsdam is that each one of them voluntarily accepts a role he or she can play

for the well-being of the department. In addition to the committee work that is assigned to them from time to time, almost every member finds for himself or herself something that he or she can or is willing to do better than others. Thus, one member feels he is very good in working with freshmen students, especially in getting them interested in math, and he goes out of his way to reach them. Another member became acquainted with personal computers, and so he took upon the role to bring the department up to the PC's age. Now, every member has or is in the process of getting a Macintosh computer in his or her office and use them extensively. Again, another member has taken the role of keeping others informed and trained in various software. This kind of voluntary role playing adds to the well-being of the department because there are many little things that need to be done for creating a humane environment for learning, and it is not possible nor desirable for the chairman to do or delegate all this work to others. It is healthy and enjoyable if able members do them willingly and voluntarily.

(7) The math teachers in Potsdam always like to keep their office doors open whenever they are in the office or in the building. This, I believe, is a gesture to the students that they can come in any time the teacher is in and not busy with other students. Keeping the door open is somewhat of a tradition in Potsdam. In the beginning, I was not very aware of this tradition, and as I was always used to working with the doors closed, my door was always closed. One day I met a faculty member and his wife somewhere in town and when he introduced me to his wife, the first thing she said was "Oh, you are the one who is never in his office." When her husband corrected that I was in my office quite often, she said with a very surprised look, "Why do you keep your door shut when you are there?" Since then I started keeping my door open whenever I was there and was thrilled to see the ease with which students would walk into my office sometimes for help with math problems and most of the time to use the pencil sharpener. Surprisingly, there were two pencil sharpeners in my office but there are none on the hallway outside the classrooms, which were near my office - If this is by design or not, I don't know.

(8) The Potsdom math gurus regard every class hour as a very sacred hour - None of them would ever be late for class nor would he or she like to miss a class. If somebody has to miss a class for a truly unavoidable reason, he or she takes utmost care to see that the students' time is in no way wasted. Once I volunteered to take a few classes for one of the teachers. Even from her hospital bed, the teacher sent me instructions in meticulous detail about what to do in the classes she was going to miss. The way the teacher and the chairman took trouble to send me written thank you notes afterwards revealed to me the reverence they have for students' class time.

(9) According to a survey conducted by the author, the average teaching load of a Potsdam math teacher is 11 hours per week. A math teacher on an average spends 31 hours (including class hours) a week in his department and he spends another 10 hours a week at home preparing lectures or grading home work. In the beginning of the semester, a teacher spends an average of 4.7 hours a week (about 15 % of his time in the department) talking with students. This is the actual time spent with students and not the assigned office hours. In any case, the average contact time with students outside class room slowly increases to 7 hours a week (more than 25% of his time in the department) towards the end of the semester.

Chapter 3

THE TEAM

The most important component of the humane environment of teaching and learning mathematics is the team of teachers. Without their dedicated efforts, nothing would have been possible. In that team of teachers, I would like to include all the present teachers holding a tenure track position and all the past teachers who served here at least ten years since 1969. This is truly a championship team. The players in this team have contributed differently in the total team effort. Through a variety of teaching styles and personalities they have provided through the years an environment which has served all the students who have wished to study mathematics at Potsdam. There is no mathematics teacher who repels all students and none who attracts all, though many come close to the latter. One of my objectives has been to find the common traits of the teachers here, the common traits that made it a championship team. Before stating my observations in this regard, it would be wise to briefly indicate how the team was formed.

Dunn, Foisy, Kilroy, Magee and Smith formed the core of the team, which existed before Stephens joined them in 1969. These teachers must be commended for their concern for the well-being of the department and for the wisdom they displayed in asking Clarence Stephens to come and take the leadership of the department. Smith retired in 1988 but he continues to teach one or two courses each semester. These teachers have been the role models of good teachers in the department upon whom Clarence Stephens relied heavily.

Soon after Stephens was appointed Chairman, the President of the College asked Stephens to hire some Ph.D.'s for the department, perhaps thinking that persons with the Ph.D. degree will bring prestige to the College. To which Stephens is reported to have replied, "I can get Ph.D.'s but will they be good teachers?" So, he set about looking for people with Ph.D. degree who were likely to be good teachers. It was not an easy task because the job situation in those days was bad and there were many candidates (in one year, there were 500 applicants). Accordingly, Kulkarni, Cheng and Spencer were appointed. In 1973, Cateforis, a former student of Stephens at Morgan State University and the present Chairman of the department, joined the team. Parks,

Mahdavi and Schensted joined the team later while Chapman, Miller, Person and Spellman have been recent additions.

CATEFORIS, Vasily C. (1973 -)
Education: B.S. (1961, Morgan StateUniversity); M.S.(1963) and Ph.D. (1968), University of Wisconsin, Madison.
Professional History: Morgan State College (1963 - 64), University of Kentucky (1968 - 73)
Area of Interest: Algebra

CHAPMAN, Kerrith (1987 -)
Education: A.B. (1972), Assumption College, Worcester); M.S.(1975) and Ph.D. (1980), Kansas State University
Professional History: LeMoyne College, Syracuse (1980 - 83), Naval Underwater Systems Center (1983 - 87)
Area of Interest: Harmonic Analysis

CHENG, Chao-Kun (1970-1984)
Education: B.A. (Taiwan University), M. A. and Ph.D. (University of Notre Dame), Ph.D. in Computer Science (Clarkson University)
Area of Interest: Algebraic Topology, Computer Science

DUNN, Arnold M. (1962-1991)
Education: B. A. (1956), SUNY at Potsdam; M. Sc. (1960), Clarkson College of Technology; M.A. (1961) Harvard University; M.A. (math), (1970) and Ph.D. (1974), Clarkson University
Professional History: High School (1956 - 62)
Area of Interest: Functional Analysis

FOISY, Hector B. (1962 -)
Education: B. A. (1958) St. Michael's College, Vermont; M.A. (1962), University of Illinois, Urbana-Champ; Ph.D.(1971,)Peabody College
Professional History: St. Lawrence Central High School (1958 - 61).
Area of Interest: Mathematics Education

KILROY, Jerre F.(1960 -)
Education: B.S. (1957) and M.S. (1960) SUNY
at Albany; M.A. (1963) University of
Illinois, Champagne-Urbana); ABD, Oregon
State University
Professional History: Hudson Valley
Community College (1958 - 60)
Area of Interest: Algebra

KOCAN, Daniel (1968-1990)
Education: B. A. (1950), Columbia College; M. A. (1951) and
Ph.D. (1965), Columbia University
Professional History: New York University,
University Heights (1956-64), Stevens Inst. of Technology (1965 - 68)
Area of Interest: Functional Analysis

KULKARNI, Ramesh (1970 -)
Education: B.Sc.(1957) and M. Sc (1961)
Bombay University; M.A. (1967) and Ph.D.
(1970), Indiana University
Area of Interest: Functional Analysis

MAGEE, James (1962 -)
Education: B. S. (1958), St. Lawrence
University ; M. A. T. (1959), Harvard
University; M.S. (1966), University of Notre
Dame; Ph.D. (1974), Clarkson University
Professional History: Portsmouth School, R.I.
(1959 - 62)
Area of Interest: Functional Analysis.

MAHDAVI, Kazem (1983 -)
Education: M.E. (1975), Tehran University;
M. A. (1980) and Ph.D. (1983) SUNY
Binghamton
Area of Interest: Algebra

MILLER, Cheryl(1989 -)
Education: B.A. (1984) John Carrol University,
Ohio; Ph.D. (1989), Weslyan University
Area of Interest: Logic

PARKS, James (1980 -)
Education: B. S. (1963) and M. S. 1965,
Wichita State University; Ph.D. (1971)
University of Houston
Professional History: Houston Community
College (1972 - 74), Howard University,
Washington, D.C. (1974 - 80)
Area of Interest: Algebraic Topology

PERSON, Laura (1989 -)
Education: B.S (1981), M. S.(1982) and Ph.D.
(1988), University of California, Santa Barbara
Professional History: University of Santa
Barbara (Spring, 1989)
Area of Interest: Topology

SCHENSTED, Irene (1985 -   )
Education: A.B. (1949) Radcliffe College; M.
S. (1953), University of Minnesota; Ph.D.
(1961), University of Michigan
Professional History: Middlebury College (1983
- 84), Amherst College (1984 - 85)
Area of Interest: Mathematical Physics

SLOAN, William (1959 - 66, 1991-)
Education: M.Ed. (1959), St. Lawrence
Univeristy; M.A.(1965), University of Illinois
Professional History: During the years (1969
1990) held various adminstrative posts in the
college including Vice President for
Adminstration.

SMITH, Charles L. (1958-1988)
Education: B. S. (Engr.) (1946), Rensselaer
Polytechnic Institute; M.S. (1948), Syracuse
University; Ed.D. (1964), Columbia University
Professional History: Public School
Mathematics Teacher (1948 - 49), (1952 - 58);
Acting Chairman of the Department at SUNY
Potsdam (1961 - 64), (1968 - 69); Chairman of
the Department at SUNY Potsdam (1964 - 66)
Area of Interest: Math Education

SPELLMAN, David (1989 -)
Education: B.A. (history, 1977), University of
Texas, Austin; B.S. (Math, 1979) University of
Texas, San Antonio;   Ph.D. (1986), University
of Texas, Austin
Professional History: Santa Barbara City
College
Area of Interest: Topology

SPENCER, Armond E. (1971 -)
Education: B. S. (1958), M.S. (1961) and
Ph.D. (1967), Michigan State University
Professional History: High School (1958 - 60),
Lansing Community College (1962 - 64),
Western Michigan University (1966),
University of Kentucky (1967 - 71).
Area of Interest: Algebra

STEPHENS, Clarence F. (1969 - 1987) [See Chapter 7]
Education: B.S. (1938), Johnson C. Smith University; M.S. (1939)
and Ph.D. (1943), University of Michigan, Ann Arbor
Professional History: Prairie View University, Texas (1940 - 42,
1946 - 47), Teacher Specialist, U.S. Navy (1942 - 45), Morgan State
University, Baltimore (1947 - 62), SUNY at Geneseo (1962 - 69)
Area of Interest: Analysis, Algebra

The following are other teachers who have served the math deparetment at SUNY Potsdam some time since 1969.

Annie Alexander (1969-1972), Mark Armstrong (1991), Joseph Bertorelli (1969-1971), Mitch Billis (1964-1965), Michelle Bloom (1982-1984), Gille Blum (1985-1986), James A. Burns (1963-1967), James Calarco (1967-1973), Bruce Conroe (1967-1991, he was an adminstrator and occasionally taught math courses), Joan A. Mellon French (1963-1967), Maggie Furst (1974 - 75), Pauline Graveline (1976-1979), Elmer E. Haskins (1964-1973), K. Hemmenway (1978), Gerald Hobbs (1973-1976), Harold K. Hughes (1976-1977), Kapil Joshi (1985-1986), Susan Kirkey (1981), Stephen L. Knodle (1977-1980), Dale W. Kreisler (1968-69), Gan S. Ladde (1973-1980), Douglas M. Leigh (1973 - 74), Ellen Magee (1980-1981), Brian Marsh (1981-1983), Eileen McLaughlin (1967 - 68), Catherine McMillan (1978), Wesley Mitchell (1982-1990), Khadid Naeem (1965-1966), Susumu Okada (1985-1986), Shivappa Palled (1980-1986), Mary Lou Potter (1983), Kirby Pressly (1968-1970), Richard Propes (1969-1970), Jim Sasser (1966-1969), Chanchal Singh (1966-1969), Ralph Stinebrickner (1969-1973), Margaret Taft (1973-1976), Chi-Ming Tang (1976-1979), Roman Tarnawsky (1982-1985), Jeffrey Terrillion 1976-1977), Ronald Turbide (1967-1972), Arthur Ullman (1967-1968), Laura Weiss (1973-1976), Parl West(1934-1961), William M. Woodruff (1967-1969), David Wycoff (1985-1989).

In the championship team, we also have to include the departmental secretaries without whose relentless efforts much of the work would have remained undone. They are: Joyce C. Flint (1973-1983), Gail Sheldon (1984), Veronica O'Brien (1985 - 1987), and the present secretary Patricia A. Beaulieu .

BEAULIEU, Patricia A. (1987 -).

Chapter 4

CLASSROOM STRATEGIES

We have already indicated some of the good traits of the math teachers at Potsdam. Now we would like to give an overview of how these traits translate into classroom activities of the teachers.

First day of class

For most of the teachers, the first day of class is like the first act of a Shakespearean play and they use it to strike the keynote of the drama that is to unfold. The teachers immediately show their concern for the students by trying to know and understand them. Then they try to start a personal friendship with the students by telling about themselves. Above all, they start giving them a glimpse of the subject matter that would be taught and how the students will be helped to learn the material. The thought and preparation that the teachers put into planning the first day's activities is simply admirable. Figure 4 gives an example of the plan-sheet of one of the teachers.

At least two of the teachers give a 3" x 5" card to each student asking him or her to give his or her name, major and the name of high school etc. They then carry these cards to every class and use them to call on students for classroom activities. Another asks each student to write something about himself or herself. Another asks them to find a comfortable place where he or she would like to sit and gets the class to make a voluntary seating plan. Figures 5 and 6 give two samples of a questionnaire passed out on the first day and the planned activities for the first day.

The most intriguing question is how much does the teacher tell the students about themselves. The answer is quite a lot. Of course, one or two of them answered by saying "very little" or "not enough". It seems those who do are able to establish closer relationships with the students than those who do not - the sharing of concerns always leads to love and respect for each other.

Course/Section   FIRST DAY   FALL 1989
Time/Days/ Room

PRELIMINARIES
GENERIC
1. Course and instructor identification/Prerequisite announcements
2. Pass out syllabus
3. Pass out yellow pad for name, class, major
4. Call out names
5. Go over syllabus
ADVICE: It will be a good idea to make a folder for the course.

METHOD OF TEACHING: Participatory - Usually I will tell you a few things and let you work with them alone or together - Not much note taking should go on.

SEATING: Find a comfortable place and stay so that I can learn your face and your name.

COURSE BEGINNING
1. Reading Assignment for Thu 9/7, Section 1, pp. 3-7, Exercises on pp.6-7, Orally - Exs. 1-11. Exercise 20, p.7- justify your answer.
2. V/I "warm-up" exercise. Supply little answer sheets.

PUT YOUR NAME ON IT SO I CAN RETURN IT.

Figure 4. Plan sheet of first day activities

One day, I had to take the class of a female teacher. When I entered the classroom, I could not believe the concerns of the students. Only after answering several of their concerned questions, I realized that the teacher was expecting a baby so I changed the subject by saying, "Gee, my eyesight must be getting really bad, I did not even notice she was pregnant." Needless to say the teacher had shared this information with her students.

Another teacher lets his students know that he has ten cats, two dogs, and so on. Another teacher tells the students about his interests in mountain climbing and seizes the opportunity to tell them that learning mathematics is like climbing mountains, always an uphill task but very enjoyable and very rewarding; once you have mastered a difficult topic, there is one more mountain to climb.

STUDENT PROFILE

COURSE_____CLASS   TIME_____

PRINT_____
                  last name   first

When spoken to, I prefer to be called_____

Class standing: Fr_____Soph_____Jr_____Sr_____Other_____

Declared or Prospective major_____

Second Major_____

Academic Advisor_____

Campus Phone_____

Hometown_____

List of all high school mathematics courses completed:

List of all college mathematics courses completed:

List of all courses enrolled in this semester:

Signature_____

Figure 5. First day questionnaire

NAME_____SEAT_____
    Print last, first, initial

COURSE_____SECTION_____SEMESTER_____

CLASS   YEAR_____MAJOR(S)_____

LOCAL PHONE_____

LAST HIGH SCHOOL MATH COURSE TAKEN_____

COLLEGE MATH COURSES TAKEN_____

YOUR PRESENT CONFIDENCE LEVEL CONCERNING

THE OUTCOME OF THIS COURSE ____ (0 to 10)

YOUR PURPOSE IN TAKING THIS COURSE_____

SOMETHING ABOUT YOU:

Figure 6. First day questionnaire

Classroom Styles

In a separate section, we shall discuss various teaching styles that the math teachers of SUNY Potsdam use. Here, we wish to describe how the teachers spend a typical class hour. Every teacher prepares for his class well, makes sure he or she has the homework that is to be returned, and it is graded. No matter what class it is, no matter how often they have taught the same subject, they prepare a plan-sheet for every class.

It seems that almost every one of them spend a few minutes in the beginning of the class to review what was done in the previous meeting. All of them like to introduce something new in each class but look for an opportune moment to do so after making the class comfortable about previous material. No matter what style of teaching they have, they try to get the students involved in what is going on. So each one of them tries to bring students up to the board on some pretext or other. Prof. H. likes to read a name randomly chosen from his class cards. Prof. M. actually marks some of the homework problems as the ones that the students may have to present to class. Others like to call on members of each group, when groups are formed, to come to the board.

Also, every teacher thinks, "I should not be the only one to talk" and makes the students become involved. Thus, one teacher asks the students to read in class and to explain it to the others or asks them to try some problem in class and goes around helping them understand what they are reading or trying to solve.

Another important strategy the teachers adopt is to teach by the way they behave. They always make it a point to show to the students that they love math and that they are having fun teaching it. So, as far as the teachers are concerned, there is never a dull moment in the classroom. This kind of love and enthusiasm is bound to rub onto the students. One of the teachers regards himself as a mentor.

As to the question of how they treat their students, most of the answers were of the type "like adults," "like friends," "like one in the family," like a member of the department," etc.

Most teachers realize that as students they were far bettter than the average, if not brilliant. However, their class is a heterogenous mix of students with abilities that rank from 1 to 10, on a scale of 1 to 10. So teaching the student is very different from their own experiences of learning. Clarence Stephens emphasizes the moment of independence to the teachers - he emphasizes that every math teacher, at some moment in their career, becomes independent as a student and from that moment he or she becomes able to read and learn mathematics on his or her own. The strategy of a teacher should be to help the students achieve that independence, if not in learning math, then at least in learning the material of the course. Making the student independent in learning math is a major goal of most of the teachers at Potsdam.

In this context, it is interesting to note that many of the teachers learned to be independent the hard way. Here are some examples.

"As an undergraduate I had teachers, who literally wrote with their right hands and erased with the left. Soon I realized that I was on my own."

"We had some excellent lecturers, who always lectured and lectured. I could listen to them for hours, but they never taught. So I would read the textbook and try to teach myself."

"Students at other universities that I have seen see the University as an adversary. It has something they want, namely credits and a degree. The students see the teacher as an agent of the University and as trying to stop them from getting it."

"One of the teachers in my college once failed the whole pre-calculus class because he thought that they did not belong there." It is needless to say that math students at that college started learning on their own so that they would not be forced out of college.

"One of my teachers had some ungodly hours like 7 o'clock in the morning and late Friday afternoons as office hours so that it was not convenient for students to go and see him."

"I had a calculus class beginning at 8 o'clock in the morning. The calculus teacher would look at his pocket watch and exactly one minute after eight, he would close the doors to the classroom and would not let anybody come in till the period was over."

The math department tries to make the students able to read math, write math and above all, to prove theorems. To achieve these they do some very clever and effective things. For example, Prof. C. prepares lecture notes for his Concepts of Geometry class. His lecture notes will have theorems without proofs or sketches of proofs, and the students will have to supply or complete the proofs. Prof. K. assigns selected theorems to the students in his advanced calculus course and makes each one of them present the proofs of theorems to the class. Prof. D. will often give an overview or an informal proof of a theorem in class and then ask the students to read the proof in the text.

Hour Tests and Final Examinations

I often think and wonder what purpose is served by hour tests or a final examination given in a course. It is my observation that a teacher gives hour tests to serve one or more of the following purposes:

1) They help the teacher to assess how much a student has learned in the course and thereby assign a grade.
2) They help the teacher to justify the grades he or she gives to the students.
3) The tests help the students to know how they are doing in the course and what grade they may get in the course.
4) They allow the students to know what is to be memorized and what is important in the course.
5) The tests give the students a chance to learn what mistakes they may make so that they would not make the same mistakes again in the final examination.
6) The tests help the students to put together what they have been learning and get their mathematical knowledge organized.
7) The tests provide a good way to determine what the students do not know, a good way to teach them a lesson for not working hard, not coming to class regularly, not paying attention in class, and so on.
8) They help the teacher to assess how well the students have learned to solve problems and to write mathematics.
9) They provide a way to test the understanding, writing skills (mathematical), and the mathematical knowledge of the students.
10) The tests form a part of the learning process - where a student learns to use the resources that he or she has accumulated on solving typical problems in a pressure situation.
11) The tests give every student a chance to put it all together and feel the strength of mathematical knowledge at his or her command.
12) The hour tests and the final examination give every student the opportunity to reinforce what he or she has learned.

It should be mentioned that multiple choice tests serve (1) and (2) well. However, in fulfilling any of the other purposes, the benefits of multiple choice tests are minimal. Of course, multiple choice tests make the teacher's life a lot easier, and in a course with many sections and hundreds of students, it provides for a fair and uniform grading system.   However, multiple choice tests create an environment of cheating and gambling.   Many students do not work out the problems in a multiple choice test but try to figure out which answer seems to be correct.

In a precalculus course, I once told the students that the hour test would be multiple choice - and then on the day of the test handed out a traditional test.   Several students were furious and they bitterly complained that they had not prepared for a traditional test.   I tried to calm them by saying that the purpose of the test was to see what they had learned, and so, it should not matter whether it was multiple choice or traditional one.   Since they did not buy that argument, I told them that I had a multiple choice test as well and offered to give it to anyone who wished to take the multiple-choice instead.   I told them that they could not compare the two tests and I would give the multiple-choice test only if they returned the traditional test - but, if they did so they must take the multiple choice test.   Twelve of the 19 students took the multiple choice without any qualms about it.   I have also known instances where students developed signals to communicate answers for multiple-choice tests, which of course would be a very simple matter. A student, who was very friendly with me, once told me how he put the wrong answer for a problem because his friend, who was giving him the answers, had to scratch his right ear because it was itchy -- unfortunately, scratching the right ear was the signal for an answer. Then there is the famous *stick-shift method* - where driving signals are used to move feet in different directions, indicating multiple-choice responses.

It is true that as far as grading is concerned, it does not matter whether we give a multiple choice test or a traditional test since the grades of students are not likely to be different in the two tests (unless of course they are cheating).   Therefore, if the purpose of a test is simply (1) or (2), then multiple-choice tests may not do any harm.   My own experience is that in a class of less than 30, it is very easy to determine which student deserves which letter grade.   In such classes, tests may be used to give the students some enjoyable learning experiences.   I find that most of the teachers at SUNY Potsdam try to use the hour tests to give the students some enjoyable learning experiences and they have perfected some strategies to achieve this, that is, make them enjoyable for the students.   In particular, they try to administer the tests so that the tests serve purposes (8) - (12) listed above. The strategies commonly used are:

(1) Prepare the students well for the test - by announcing the test well in advance (at least a week), by telling them what would be in the test and by giving sample tests and/or review problems.

(2) Review the material in the class before the test.

(3) Make the test following the golden rule set by Clarence Stephens, "(a) Write tests carefully -- know what your average student can do; and what your best student can do. Give a balanced test. (b) Build students' confidence by giving them problems they can do." [2]

(4) Do not rush the students. See that they get ample time to answer. At least one teacher always tries to give hour tests in the evening so that the students can have more time to answer.

(5) Grade the test carefully and point out where mistakes are and return it possibly by the next class meeting.

(6) Do not give or review the answers to the test in class. As one teacher puts it, "that is a waste of time." Instead, ask the students to correct the mistakes and rewrite the answers and give them some credit for it (at least 50% of the points they lost for the mistake).

(7) In the calculus sequence, nobody should fail an hour test in the sense that a student should get as many chances as necessary to pass each hour test, but to pass the course they must pass a common final.

I am happy to see that the teachers at Potsdam do not in general give multiple choice exams. In the Calculus courses, students have to take a common final exam. Usually, a student's grade in Calculus courses is based on a weighted average of 1/3 for the final and 2/3 for class tests and homework.

Classroom notes

(1) The atmosphere in the classrooms is very cordial. The teachers treat the students with a lot of respect. For example, one teacher will always end every "Let.." sentence with "please", since he regards all such sentences to be addressed to students. Thus, he would say: "Let f be a function, please-"

This kind of attitude of the teacher makes the students respect the teacher, the classmates, and the class in general. Thus, one student, who had asked one or two questions, was asked by the teacher, "Is it clear, now?" The student politely replied, "Not really, but I do not want to waste time, I can ask you after class."

On another occasion, I found a student cleaning the big blackboard in the classroom before the teacher came in.

(2) In almost all the classes I attended, I found the teacher engaging the students into conversations. In a classroom, these conversations are consciously or unconsciously set to help the stduents read, write and think mathematics correctly. Here are some examples:

Teacher: Angela, what are we trying to prove here?
Angela: f to the negative one composed with f...
Teacher: No, that is f inverse...
Teacher: Anybody have any problem?
Student: Will you please show us how to do problem 21?
Teacher: Please tell me what is problem 21.
Student: It is a problem with one of those funny looking "e" things.
Teacher: Can you tell me what that funny looking "e" thing means?
Student: It means summation - but I don't know what it is called.
Teacher: Can someone help him?
Another Student: It is the Greek letter sigma.

After that the teacher clarifies the summation notation and makes the student read the problem correctly.

Student: Will you please do problem 31?
Teacher: Have you tried it?
Student: Yes.
Teacher: How many times?
Student: Several times, but I keep getting the wrong answer.

Teacher: O.K. Read me the problem and tell me what you should
do and I will write. I am at your service.
So, the student reads the problem and tells the teacher what to do and
the teacher writes it on the blackboard. After some time, the correct
answer is arrived. Then-
Student: That's what it is?
Teacher: But, I did not do anything, I just did and wrote what you
told me to do. How come we got the correct answer?
Student: I think better when you are writing.
Teacher: You have a problem then. You must learn to write the
way you are thinking.

(3) Professor Spencer uses the vedic trick of using mantra. The
Sanskrit word "Mantra" means the one that delivers or conquers the
mind. Mantras are an integral part of Hindu society. In old days,
mathematical formulas or steps of solving mathematical forms were put
in the form of a mantra. A mantra is usually written in the form of a
small poem, which must be recited over and over, so that the message
contained in the mantra completely dominates and guides the mind.
Here is Professor Spencer's mantra to create and write proofs, which he
has a student recite anytime a student has trouble proving or writing the
solution of a mathematical problem. His mantra seems to have magic
charm and students use it long after they graduate from Potsdam [see
Figure 7].

(4) While most teachers do not like interrruptions in class and do
not like students to talk in class except in a participatory manner, one
teacher thinks, "Little bit of talking does not bother me." She actually
encourages them to talk to each other and does it quite artfully. If she
finds somebody trying to explain something to another student she
would actually pause to let them finish the conversation. She usually
assigns problems to be done in class and goes around helping the
students. This gives the students good breaks to talk to each other and
to explain things to each other. This helps to create a relaxed
atmosphere in the classroom. Even though she hopes that students talk
math most of the time, students do include their bit about boyfriend-
girlfriend stuff or the snowstorms, of which Potsdam has a good share.

DR. SPENCER'S MANTRA FOR THE RELIEF OF ANXIETY THAT
ACCOMPANIES ATTEMPTS TO CREATE AND WRITE PROOFS

The MANTRA consists of three parts:

The LINES , the REFRAIN,and the COMMAND.

THE LINES: To be chanted slowly as the situation demands. It is
suggested that if a line contains k words, then it should be chanted k
times, shifting the emphasis from word to word.

1. What exactly am I trying to prove?
2. What are the hypotheses? (What may I assume?)
3. What is the conclusion I seek?
4. What do some of the elements look like?
5. Why do I believe it? (What do the examples show?)
6. What if it wasn't so?

THE REFRAIN: To be chanted between the lines, slowly and with feeling.

WHAT DOES THAT MEAN ?

Of course, the mood should be changed as necessary. i.e. sometimes the

REFRAIN should read WHAT WOULD THAT MEAN?

THE COMMAND: To be followed regularly, after chants.

**Write it down.   Write it down carefully.   Write it down
completely.**

If symptoms persist see your local professor

Figure 7. Dr. Spencer's Mantra

Chapter 5

SUPPORT SYSTEM STRATEGIES

Office Hour Strategies

The math teachers at SUNY Potsdam take their office hours very seriously. They put at least 3 hours a week as office hours, when the students will definitely find them. They usually select these hours by taking the convenience of the students and normally select hours before or after class. However, in addition to these assigned office hours, most teachers are available in their offices for good many hours and the students are welcome to see them whenever they are not otherwise busy with some other students. Most teachers are ready to put aside their own work if a student comes in for help. During the advanced registration week and before the hour tests, some of the teachers hang outside their offices appointment sheets indicating every quarter of the office hours so that students may sign up to make sure he or she will not be disappointed.

In any case, most of the teachers look forward to office visits of their students. As a matter of fact, two of the teachers regretted that not many students take advantage of visiting them in their offices. According to the teachers, they use the office hours not merely to help the students with what is going on in class but also to achieve the following:

(1) To show the students that they care about them and to establish a one-to-one relationship.
(2) To get feedback about how the class is doing and how much each student is being able to learn individually.
(3) To help the students get interested in mathematics and feel good about mathematics.
(4) To help the students take charge of their own learning.

To clarify the last point, let me state the view expressed by one of the teachers, "I try to find out how they think and how they make connections between ideas. I wish to get back to what they really understand and what they really believe, and start from there. Then only students start to take control of what they are learning." In other words, it is only through the one-to-one contact in office visits that he is able to put a student in control of what he or she is learning. The teachers make it a point not to do homework problems during office visits, instead they try to put the students on the right track. Therefore, it is not uncommon to see students working on the blackboard in a teacher's office. It is also not uncommon to see groups of students talking and working together while waiting for their turn with a professor. The math department reading room in the math office is often used as a waiting room by students. What do the teachers think about such long lines -- "Usually the students leave happier than before - I like it," "It is important because the students are able to ask me questions which they are afraid to ask in class."

Another professor told the story of a student who was having a hard time keeping up with what was going on in class and she was doing poorly in the tests. But after spending some time in his office and after he straightened out her difficulties, she felt good - good about the course and good about math. The teacher came to know of her feelings when her roommate showed up in his office the next day. The roommate was also in the same class and was doing very well but she told the teacher something like, "I am doing well in your course and I am coming to see you because I want to feel as good about it as my roommate, her outlook has completely changed after talking to you yesterday."

The Math Lab Strategies

The math lab is a program and a place designed to give the students help when and where they need it. It is situated in between classrooms and is usually open from 9 a.m. in the morning to 8 p.m. Students can drop in before or after a math class. Also, since it is open in the evenings, they can come and seek help when they are having difficulties with their homework. The lab contains tables with chairs, blackboards on the walls, and a small library of textbooks donated by members of the department.

The math lab is designed for students taking any lower-level math courses, and it is staffed by students majoring in mathematics who have completed much of the major. This serves the dual purpose of showing role models to the students in lower-level math courses and of rewarding the bright students of senior classes. In the opinion of Steve, bright students encounter violent opposition in some academic communities. According to him, often the opposition comes from students who believe that bright students threaten them with low or failing grades. The math lab in some ways alleviates this problem because students pursuing mathematics courses and getting help in the math lab start to consider the bright students as helpers, and the bright students begin to feel their worth by making a significant contribution to the math program. In addition, the students working as tutors in the lab receive remuneration for their services, which they view as rewards for their good performances in math courses. The cost of all these is about $2,500.00 a semester.

The tutors are selected by a member of the math faculty, who acts as a supervisor of the lab. The supervisor usually selects some good students to run the math lab and prepares a detailed announcement about the math lab showing what time it is open and who is in charge when. The student in charge usually makes a list of the areas for which students come for help. The announcement for math lab is widely distributed in the beginning of every semester and posted all over the campus.

In addition to the above, there are also other support services by students and other tutors.

Here is an example of how a teacher at Potsdam uses all the available (?) resources at his disposal to help the students. When a student in his class has great difficulties understanding what is going on in his class and if the math lab is no help, he then tells the student to contact a certain math tutor, who would probably help the student, free of charge. So saying, he gives the student the phone number of a lady - the lady is no other than his wife, who is also a math teacher.

Pi Mu Epsilon

The large and active chapter of Pi Mu Epsilon provides special support to the math students and promotes the mathematics program. I am told that most of the tutors of the math lab are members of the chapter. The chapter makes an award each year to a graduating senior. The chapter holds two open house meetings during the year, one in the fall and one in spring. The chapter also organizes an annual picnic. All students interested in the study of mathematics are invited to attend the open house meetings and the picnic. These provide opportunities for the students and faculty to meet informally and to get to know one another. In addition, the chapter sponsors one induction ceremony each semester with guest speakers. Often the guest speakers are members of the mathematics alumni. In addition, members of the alumni frequently return to attend induction ceremonies as guests. These alumni discuss some of their experiences in the world of work, or as graduate students.

The Pi Mu Epsilon and the department newsletter play very important roles in giving much needed moral support to the math students and in helping them find directions in life. Above all they keep the students, the faculty and the alumni together, which is very important to create a sense of belonging to a family.

The Newsletter

The Department publishes a student-alumni newsletter each year. This is sent to all mathematics alumni, the mathematics majors and to the high schools, whose students have graduated as math majors from Potsdam College. Copies may also be sent to students who may seek admission to the college. This newsletter contains a list of math majors who graduated during the academic year, indicating the academic honors and job offers received. It also gives the names of math majors on the President's list, students who received awards given by the department or Pi Mu Epsilon or the University. The newsletter also contains a lively amount of news about the faculty, the department and the alumni. In addition, the newsletter publishes important statistics about the math majors, double majors and math minors. The most popular item of the newsletter is perhaps the communications from the alumni.

Chapter 6

METHODS
OF TEACHING

There is no unique teaching method used by the math teachers at Potsdam College. "The 15 faculty members use a diverse collection of methods. Some use the basic lecture-examination method as found in most departments, some do not lecture at all, but have their students present the material, some conduct tutorials in which students meet privately to discuss material, some have their students form problem solving groups, some are strict and demanding, some are lenient and easygoing, some emphasize the skill of reading a mathematics text, some use a modified "Moore method" in which students work without a text. But given the diversity there are some things that are shared"[22]. The source of the common elements may be found in the guiding principles laid by Stephens in his circular [23]. These guiding principles have now become traditional and are described in the department handout "Academic Advising for Mathematics Majors." We reproduce here the section on methods of teaching from the said handout.

Methods of Teaching

You will learn that members of the mathematics faculty will use many different methods of teaching. A given teacher may use several methods in a given class or different methods in different classes. The members of the mathematics faculty continue their efforts to remain effective teachers by learning through experience and studying educational materials such as "College Mathematics: Suggestions on How to Teach It." prepared by the Committee on Teaching of Undergraduate Mathematics, Mathematical Association of America, March, 1979.

Some of the aims of the faculty are to help you

    (a)   learn the basic materials of the course and its applications

(b) give correct mathematical proofs
(c) write correct proofs in clear and neat form
(d) read mathematical literature with understanding and enjoyment
(e) develop the ability to work independently (to free you from the need of a teacher) so that you will enjoy that life of the mind in which the pursuit of knowledge and understanding is its own justification and its own reward as a life-long goal, and
(f) progress through the different levels of mathematical maturity and recognize the different levels of abstractions in mathematics as are explained below.

Four   Levels   of   Mathematical   Maturity   and Understanding

Level I.

(a) The learner can develop the ability to solve moderately difficult "find" problems. An example of this type of problem is:
    Find the indefinite integral of a given function.
(b) The learner can obtain some understanding of abstract mathematical concepts provided he or she is given an opportunity to study these concepts through simple concrete examples.   The learner should work independently through the details of these examples. This method of learning differs from that in which examples are used to help the learner understand required abstract mathematical proofs.
    The learner who remains at this level has almost no understanding of an abstract mathematical proof.

Level II.

(a) The learner has advanced above Level I and can solve moderately difficult mathematical problems.
(b) The learner can understand some moderately difficult mathematical proofs provided they are explained clearly

and written in complete uncrowded sentence form where each sentence begins with a capital letter and ends with a period.

(c) The learner can construct correct proofs and provide counterexamples of mathematical propositions dealing with concrete mathematical objects. Such propositions may, for example, deal with linear independence in R^n or subgroups of $<Z, +>$ or convergence of sequences in R^n.

The learner who remains at this level will often write inadequate proofs or incorrect solutions when requested to give difficult proofs of theorems or solutions of problems if the proofs or solutions have not been explained previously to the learner.

Level III.

(a) The learner can solve some difficult mathematical problems.

(b) The learner has a good understanding of a mathematical proof.

(c) The learner can construct correct proofs and provide counterexamples to mathematical propositions dealing with abstract mathematical objects such as abstract groups, rings, vector spaces, topological spaces, metric spaces and abstract notions of continuity and convergence.

(d) The learner can read independently advanced mathematical literature with understanding and enjoyment.

The learner who remains at this level can pass most required mathematical examinations but may not be able to advance to Level IV.

Level IV.

(a) The learner can propose significant mathematical problems and can solve many of them.

(b) The learner can give proofs of difficult mathematical propositions.

There does not seem to be a well defined teaching

method which will maximize the development of the learner at this level. Independent study and seminar courses can help. A favorable learning environment is very important.

Based on the above guiding principles, the department has some teaching goals, set code of attitude and expectations for rewards.

"Teaching goal: To help each student reach his or her highest possible level of mathematical achievement. To encourage and inspire each student to maximize his or her ability to work independently.

Code of attitude: (a) We believe in our students and care about them. (b) We teach and test learning in all mathematics courses at levels I, II, and III, and whenever possible at level IV. (c) We put forth our best efforts to help each student advance from the level of mathematical maturity and understanding where we find him or her to the next higher level, unless we recognize that a student has reached what is for him or her the highest possible level. (d) We can develop a favorable environment which will nurture mathematical learning.

Expected Rewards: For a teacher seeing the joy and gain in self-respect of students which result when a good understanding of mathematics is achieved is a reward in itself. The success in helping the students learn the beauty of mathematics is a worthwhile experience."

Even though every teacher follows one or the other method of teaching he or she adopts changes to achieve the goals set in the guiding principles of the department. We shall now discuss the pros and cons of each of the teaching methods seen at Potsdam and point out how individual teachers have modified them to suit the purpose of the department.

The Lecture Method

Two of the teachers said that they usually adopt the lecture method of teaching and at least two others said that they use this method once in a while. According to them, the advantages of this method are:

(1) "It is the method I am more comfortable with." The teacher is able to organize what is to be taught in a definite order, select examples and relevant materials for better effects.

(2) With the lecture method, it is possible to cover the prescribed curriculum.

(3) Students find it easy to write notes in a class when the teacher is lecturing and are able to read back. This way, what they do not understand today, they may understand tomorrow or some time later. This is especially helpful if the student had to miss a class or two because of unavoidable circumstances. Because the student can easily borrow the notes from a classmate and catch up.

(4) The lecture method helps the teacher to free the students from the tyranny or the limitations of a textbook. Math texts have to be written in a definite order and materials are often presented in compact and crowded manner. The style of writing is usually precise to the point and often dull. A good lecturer can present material in a more pleasant manner than a text. Also, since a teacher can go back and forth, which a text writer cannot do, the teacher is in a better position to clarify difficult points in his lecture by using all kinds of techniques like making short cuts, ignoring details, avoiding tedious computations, etc.

It is interesting to note that the two teachers who claimed to use the lecture method also put emphasis on covering a definite amount of material as prescribed and feel unhappy, "if somebody else does not cover the course material."

According to Halmos, "the worst way to teach mathematics is to lecture." So, the lecture method has many opponents. The main drawbacks of the lecture method are:

(1)   Using the lecture method is like pressing a clutch of a car - it disengages the engine (the teacher) from the body (the students). The engine keeps running at its own pace, but the body does not move. A teacher who follows this method will usually lecture for some time, do a few examples, and then assign some homework. He would then collect the homework, have them graded by a grader and give a quiz at

some regular intervals. Often, he would not ask questions in class because that would mean getting slowed down.

(2)   Students often find it difficult to concentrate on a lecture for the whole hour and often get bored or lose interest.

(3)   The lecture method is dehumanizing because it drives a wedge between the teacher and the students. In the classroom, the two stand on different platforms. The teacher holds all the power and the students are helpless prisoners who can't talk, can't move or can't do anything except listen and obey. It does not involve the students in the journey.

To offset the drawbacks of the lecture method, the math teachers at Potsdam adopt the following strategies:

(1)   Spend about 10 minutes in the beginning of each lecture to answer questions and/or do homework problems.

(2)   Grade all homework himself or herself.

(3)   One of the teacher calls his method an "interaction lecture style" because he constantly tries to feel the pulse of the class by asking questions and extracting answers.

(4)   They try to lecture at the level of students' understanding.

(5)   By encouraging the students to come and see them in office, they try to get feedbacks.

The Moore Method

The Moore Method has been beautifully explained by Professor Halmos in *The Teaching of Problem Solving* [11]. We reproduce his description by courtesy of the *American Mathematical Monthly*.

"What then is the secret — what is the best way to learn to solve problems? The answer is implied by the sentence I started with: solve problems. The method I advocate is sometimes known as the "Moore method," because R. L. Moore developed and used it at the University of Texas. It is a method of teaching, a method of creating the problem-solving attitude in a student, that is a mixture of what Socrates taught us and the fiercely competititive spirit of the Olympic games.

"The way a bad lecturer can be a good teacher, in the sense of producing good students, is the way a grain of sand can produce pearl-manufacturing oysters. A smooth lecture and a book entitled "Freshman algebra for girls" may be pleasant; a good teacher challenges, asks, annoys, irritates, and maintains high standards — all that is generally not pleasant. A good teacher may not be a popular teacher (except perhaps with his ex-students), because some students don't like to be challenged, asked, annoyed, and irritated — but he produces pearls (instead of casting them in the proverbial manner).

Let me tell you about the time I taught a course in linear algebra to juniors. The first hour I handed to each student a few sheets of paper on which were dittoed the precise statements of fifty theorems. That's all -- just the statements of the theorems. There was no introduction, there were no definitions, there were no explanations, and, certainly, there were no proofs.

The rest of the first hour I told the class a little about the Moore method. I told them to give up reading linear algebra (for that semester only!), and to give up consulting with each other (for that semester only). I told them that the course was in their hands. The course was those fifty theorems; when they understood them, when they could explain them, when they could buttress them with the necessary examples and counterexamples, and, of course, when they could prove them, then they would have finished the course.

They stared at me. They didn't believe me. They thought I was just lazy and trying to get out of work. They were sure that they'd never learn anything that way.

All this didn't take as much as a half hour. I finished the hour by giving them the basic definitions that they needed to understand the first half dozen or so theorems, and, wishing them well, I left them to their own devices.

The second hour, and each succeeding hour, I called on Smith to prove Theorem 1, Kovacs to prove Theorem 2, and so on. I encouraged Kovacs and Herrero and all to watch Smith like hawks, and to pounce on him if he went wrong. I myself listened as carefully as I could, and while I tried not to be sadistic, I too pounced when I felt I needed to. I pointed out gaps, I kept saying that I didn't understand, I asked questions about side issues, I asked for, and sometimes supplied, counterexamples, I told about the history of the subject when I had a chance, and I pointed out connections with other parts of mathematics. In addition, I took five minutes or so of most hours to introduce the new definitions needed. Altogether I probably talked 20 minutes out of each of the 50-minute academic hours that we were together. That's a lot - but it's a lot less than 50 (or 55) out of 50. It worked like a charm. By the second week they were proving theorems and finding errors in the proofs of others, and obviously taking pleasure in the process. Several of them had the grace to come to me and confess that they were skeptical at first, but they had been converted. Most of them said that they spent more time on that course than on their other courses that semester,and learned more from it.

What I just now described is like the "Moore method" as R. L. Moore used it, but it's a much modified Moore method. I am sure that hundreds of modifications could be devised, to suit the temperaments of different teachers and the needs of different subjects. The details don't matter. What matters is to make students ask and answer questions.

Many times when I've used the Moore method, my colleagues commented to me, perhaps a semester or two later, that they could often recognize those students in their classes who had been exposed to a "Moore class" by those students' attitude and behavior. The distinguishing characteristics were greater mathematical maturity than that of the others (the research attitude), and greater inclination and ability to ask penetrating questions."

Here is how a modified Moore method is used by a Potsdam teacher. Instead of giving them a set of problems for the course, the teacher selects a suitable textbook, which treats a good range of topics in clearly defined sections and which is written in a style that the students may find readable. Thus for Advanced Calculus I, he selects "Analysis, An Introduction to Proof" by Steven R. Lay and for Advanced Calculus II, he selects "A Primer of Real Functions" by Ralph P. Boas. Both of these texts are well suited for this method of teaching.

He then assigns to each student a selected section of the text to present in class. The Boas text has a good sprinkle of phrases like "it is clear", "plainly", "it is trivial", which, according to the author are abbreviations for a statement something like "it should seem reasonable, the reader should be able to supply the proof, and he is invited to do so." The Potsdam teacher requires each student to do exactly that — supply the proof and explain the phrases "it is clear", "it is trivial" etc. by supplying the necessary information.

Other students are expected to grill the student presenting the material with questions, pointing his or her mistakes and demanding explanations. After all, they all will have to take tests on all the material.

The teacher helps the student before his or her presentation by general guidance. In the class he restricts his role to simple questions and conversations about what is being done, what is missing, etc. This method is specially effective in making students independent.

The Group Method

In recent years, more and more teachers are dividing the students into smaller groups to work in class together, to do homework together or to work on specific projects. The benefits of a group method are:

(1) It takes away the boredom of listening to the teacher for the whole class.

(2) It allows the students to use the resources of each other in the learning process.

(3) It brings down the material to the level of students' understanding instead of being presented at the level of the teacher's understanding.

(4) The group learning introduces students to experiences they are likely to encounter in the world of work, "where problems are solved or decisions are made in groups rather than as individuals."

(5) It makes grading also easier for the teacher because the teacher may grade the answer of one member and give the same score to everybody in the group.

The drawbacks of this method are:

(1) If the group is small or if every member of the group is relatively poor, the group lacks resources and is no help to the individual members.

(2) If the group is large or if they live far apart, then the group has hard time getting together.

(3) Often one or two members of the group do all the work and others simply copy it or sit passively.

(4) Personality clashes can also harm the learning experience of groups.

Some studies of this method are contained in [6, 7, 35]. The term cooperative learning is also used to describe this method [35]. Some of the strategies teachers can adopt to make group work more beneficial and pleasurable, and suggested in those articles are:

(1)   Make at least some class time available for group meetings and include a substantial group performance component in the grading system.
(2)   Explain why group work is relevant to them.
(3)   Create diverse groups.
(4)   Give multiple opportunities to make decisions.
(5)   Listen in on group discussion and offer advice.
(6)   Provide immediate feedback.
(7)   Let them sit in their groups during regular class time.
(8)   Help them set realistic expectations.

Most of the teachers in Potsdam encourage the students to form groups and study together. The consensus is that the group method does work very well in lower-level courses as well as in honors section of Calculus I and any middle- or upper-level courses. However, one should take a slightly different approach in the lower-level courses. In the lower-level courses, the teachers are usually trying to know the potential of each student individually, and students also usually try to feel themselves as to how much math they each can handle on his or her own. Therefore, the group method is perhaps not in the best interest of average students in an elementary course.

However, as one teacher put it, "I would be very uncomfortable teaching an honors section of Calculus I or any higher-level course without forming study groups." Since he has an interesting way of dividing the class into groups, let us describe his strategy in a nutshell.

On the second or third day of class, he asks the students if they were good in math in high school (of course, most of them say "yes"), and if they all had good grades in math (again, the answer is usually overwhelmingly "yes"). Then he asks if any of them had to struggle in math, again the answer would be "not really." Then he drops the bombshell saying, "I see things have been easy in the past. But, now it is not going to be so in College math. Here you will have to do proofs and really understand what you are doing. At times, it is going to be difficult and often you will have to struggle. You must learn to persist through these difficulties. You will need support that I could not give entirely. You will have to learn to study together. Therefore, I will help you form groups. It is not mandatory. But students in the past have always benefitted by this approach." After telling them about the benefits of study groups, he asks them for some volunteers, who would like to be the convenors of groups. The job of a convenor is simply to convene the group and to relay the teacher's messages, instructions, etc., to his group. The convenors need not be the best students but the job demands some time since the convenor will have to arrange for time and place to meet and contact the group members. After getting a sufficient number of volunteers, the teacher puts their names and the names of dorms where they reside on the blackboard. Then he tells the class, "Now, I am going to go outside for a few minutes and I would like each of you to put your name underneath the name of the convenor who would be the most convenient for you. Please see that the groups do not get very big, at least not more than five. Again, it is purely voluntary, I will no way hold it against you if you don't join any group." Saying this, he leaves the classroom. That allows every student the opportunity to talk things over with one other and sort things out after which one by one every student gets up and writes his or her name in the group of his or her choice. The teacher then comes back and asks one of the students to make a list of the groups, which he later gets typed along with phone numbers and addresses of each student, copies and gives one copy to each student.

After the groups are so formed, the teacher hands out some problems and asks them to do in class by working together in their respective groups. The idea is to get the groups together and help them to learn how to work together. He continues this kind of class activities in groups for two or three weeks and then gives homework problems, and encourages them to answer them by working with their groups. He requires that every student hand in the homework, but with each homework, he asks the student to give a consultation statement indicating if he or she did this by consulting with the group or individually. He tells them the grade they receive in homeworks, tests or the course is no way dependent on their participation or otherwise of the study groups. According to him, it helps him to grade homework or tests when the students studied in groups and he usually grades by putting together the answers of each group. Occasionally he gives homework and tells them that he would grade only the answers of only one member of each group and give everybody in the group the same grade. This way he is able to point out mistakes or write comments on one paper, which gets relayed to the group.

On occasions, whenever the whole class is having difficulties, he would invite the convenors to his office and make them understand the material first and request them to transmit it to the members of the respective group. He constantly monitors the workings of each group and tells every student to report to him if he or she is not happy with his or her group or if the group is not functioning properly. In that case, he may request another group to accept the agrieved member or rearrange the groups. He says such requests are not very frequent.

Another teacher feels that study groups work for all levels of courses and he encourages students to form voluntary study groups. As a matter of fact, he gives a set of written guidelines for homework one of which reads "It is desirable to indicate on your handin whether you received help or not in doing the particular assignment." These guidelines have been developed in consultation with another teacher, who also uses them.

He thinks that in study groups both the good students and the timid students learn something directly — the good students by teaching and the timid students by asking. Once he finds that they have got organized into groups, he encourages them to sit together in class and he gives them assignments to do as group projects both inside classroom and as homework. He finds that most of the times the groups would be buzzing with activities. But occasionally there are problems like some people do not get into a group or that some passive members just copy other's work or that certain groups lack talent. Therefore, he actively monitors the groups and tries to make suitable adjustments.

Thus if a group is lacking resources, he would join the group and volunteer to be its leader or organize a different set of groups. For example, he would give each student a number and ask them to form groups according to congruence mod 4 or congruence mod 5. He makes sure that the groups become balanced and also seizes the opportunity to introduce the theory of congruent numbers.

Then if he finds that some member of a group is becoming passive, he gives assignments such that solutions to different problems be written by different members of the group, and signed by the author. To discourage students from copying without active participation, he has the word of caution: "Know your solution. Understand what you hand in, especially if you received help with your solution. Short quizzes on or after the due date, based on the handin, are possible."

The groups are always voluntary and if an individual does not choose to get into a group, he or she is not penalized. The teacher is always available as a "group member" for any individual or group.

Here is another example of how group strategy was used by a Potsdam teacher: "I began to teach students in this class how to read the textbook by selecting a statement in the proof of a theorem which is not clear. The homework assignment was to write the given statement in one color pencil and the student's explanation of how that particular statement followed from previous statements in the proof of the theorem in another color pencil. I collected the homework assignments and read the papers, made a note of the progress of students in my record book, and returned the papers without grading them. I had expected about 25 students for the class, but 59 students enrolled in the course. Hence, I had them working in groups of 7 or 8. When I returned the first homework assignment, I told the members of the class that they did not agree on the explanation for that statement. They were to work in their groups in class and convince the members of their group that they had a good explanation how the given statement followed from the previous statements in the proof of the theorem. When students observed that they did not agree with each other and had difficulty reaching a common agreement, they realized that they did not know how to read a mathematics textbook. I continued this process gradually throughout the course."

The Coach-Trainee Method

This is an interesting approach to teaching which has earlier been observed and described by Pat Rogers [24]. The coach and the power wielded by a coach are familiar with most American students. Whether in little league, youth soccer league or a high school basketball team, the coach is the supreme authority of the skills, knowledge and strategies of the game. The team or the players are the hard working ever obedient trainees who try to do everything the way the coach tells. There is no room for argument with the coach because like an English monarch "the coach can do no wrong." The players' duty is to listen, learn and execute.

According to this method the teacher is the coach who knows all the skills of math and the students are the mathematicians-in-training. It is the duty of the students to listen, learn and work hard, the way the coach tells them to do. But the coach and the players are one team whose common aim is to win every game — learn every trick in the book. The atmosphere in the classroom is like practice game of a team. The teacher gives a set of problems to be solved, some theorems to be proved or some concepts to be mastered and they work hard at it. The coach walks around, looking over shoulders, helping them, showing finer details or correcting mistakes. "From time to time he sends a student to the board to write up her solution. Then there is some discussion with the student-teacher taking a leading role. The class may end with a brief lecture on some new material or an assignment of new problems to be taken up at the next meeting"[24].

Like a coach the teacher is quite intimidating to the students striking fear in their hearts and puts up with no nonsense. You cannot be late or miss practice without receiving some form of punishment. One of the teachers once refused to let a student take a test because he was absent in seven out of ten classes. Another time he told a student who was not behaving properly in class "to get out and never come back." The teacher picks on the students, yells at them, jokes with them but always gets the work done. In return, the students regards the teacher as the meanest S.O.B., a teddy bear, or a loving father and come back to take a course with him again. The teacher will refuse to help a student who missed practice (class) and have not tried to catch up with what went on in class before coming to see him. Once I saw a female student very sarcastically annoy the teacher, "Gee, thanks for the help" when he refused to show her how to do a problem because he alleged that she had not learned the necessary material to do the problem.

The coach is tough to the bones. He would not even accept more than 20 students in his team. He would much rather have two teams (classes) of 20 each rather than one of 40. The response to this method has been captured beautifully by Pat Rogers through the words of a student, "As one female explained to me: Sure you hate him while you 're going through it, but, in retrospect you look back and 'Wow! What a great teacher. I learned so much. I want to get him again!'" [24].

This approach has proved very effective in mid-level courses like Set Theory and Logic, and Linear Algebra I. This approach is more effective in a class of about 20 or less. It goes well with the theme of making the students independent. Because the teacher keeps reminding the students that the aim is to be independent and keeps telling them, "I am not trying to be rude to you, I am trying to make sure that you understand what you are doing, the way you are doing it and why you are doing it. Because when you go out there in the field you are on your own."

Two other teachers employ the coach-trainee method but instead of using power pedagogy, they use a gentler and kinder approach. They are sort of kind and gentle coaches, who never want to be rough on the trainees. They usually adopt the winning strategy of "I don't want you to take this course again" or that "we want to make sure that you are well prepared to take Calc II". They lecture very little, spend a good deal of time explaining how the problems are to be solved and then give a lot of problems to do in class. After which it becomes a team effort. They go around looking over shoulders, pointing out mistakes and asking them to help each other. Often they send a student to the board and show the class how he or she did a certain problem. These two teachers do not yell at the students but they always treat them with kind encouraging words like, "That looks good," "I knew you could do it," "that's wonderful," "how clever," "you almost had it," "What a good job," etc. Their gentleness and kind attitude draws the students to them and I have seen them being inundated with students in their offices.

NOTE: Clarence Stephens is known to have been a very gentle and kind person and he was able to infuse a spirit of gentleness and kindness long before President Bush adopted the theme of a "gentler and kinder America." Therefore, the math teachers of SUNY Potsdam are in general gentle and kind to the students. As one of the new members of the department says, "I have really learned to be gentle and kind after coming here. You can achieve a lot more by being gentle and kind to the students." In this context, one of the older members of the department tells the story of a conversation he had with a student of Steve. He asked the student, "You have studied with this man before. He makes no demands on you. You know you will get a good grade in this course. What causes you to work so hard in his course?" The student's reply was, "Oh, Professor Stephens will feel so bad if I didn't. You see, he is such a kind person that he will be terribly disappointed if I do not do my best in his course." The only appeal was that Steve was kind and was so concerned about the student that the student did not want to make him feel bad.

Chapter 7

THE MAN
WITH THE VISION

Clarence F. Stephens was born in Gaffney, South Carolina in 1917. His mother died when he was two years old and his father brought him up with his five brothers and sisters. He became a helpless orphan when he was eight years old. Then he moved to North Carolina to live with his grandmother. But Steve's misfortunes did not end. Two years later his grandmother died and he moved in with his grandmother's sister.

It seems that Nature equipped Steve with a special gift to cope with his early misfortunes, namely, the ability to learn mathematics. As early as elementary school, he realized that he could learn mathematics with very little help from his teacher. "As an elementary grade student, I recognized that I could read mathematics literature with understanding with very little help from my teacher. This ability was very helpful to me as a high school, or college or graduate student. Early in my teaching career I learned how to develop this ability in many of my students and to help them become independent learners." From elementary school on, he was always interested in mathematics, and that kept him going. When he was twelve years old, his eldest sister helped him to enroll in the Harbison Institute of South Carolina, a private school supported by the Presbyterian Church. [Harbison Institute is now a two-year technical college supported by the state of South Carolina.] At Harbison, he earned a name as a good football player and one who was always willing to tutor (free of charge) others in math. For some curious reasons, they all thought that since he was good in math he would make a good quarterback. This theory proved to be correct and he, as quarterback, led the high school team to such a successful season that Steve received an offer for a football scholarship.

However, he did not accept the football scholarship and after graduating from Harbison Institute, Steve, like many other graduates of his school, went to Johnson C. Smith University to study mathematics under Professor Robert Douglas. For the students from Harbison Institute knew about Professor Douglas long before they reached

Johnson C. Smith University. "As soon as you walked on campus and someone knew you were interested in mathematics, they would say you must take classes under him." At Johnson C. Smith University, Steve was preparing for a career as a high school teacher, but that suddenly changed and he realized that he had the potential for higher studies in mathematics because of a simple incidence.

Clarence B. Stephens as a first year graduate student, University of Michigan, Ann Arbor (1939)

The Dean of the College of liberal studies at Johnson C. Smith, T. E. McKinney, was on sabbatical leave at the University of Michigan during Steve's senior year. When he saw Steve after his return, he very enthusiastically said, "The University of Michigan is the place for you!" So after graduating from Johnson C. Smith in 1938, Steve went to the graduate school of University of Michigan at Ann Arbor.

At Michigan, Steve was just trying to get a master's degree, but for a while he thought of becoming a lawyer because he felt that the poor people were always being cheated, and by becoming a lawyer he could help the poor. However, he could not get interested in law, so he reconciled himself to becoming a math teacher. He would have been happy with a master's degree in math but one day a professor named George Rainich opened Steve's eye to his potential. While talking to Steve, Rainich said, "When you return next year to begin studying for your doctorate degree, this is what you should do....." Professor Rainich's words ignited new zeal in Steve's mind. For the first time it occurred to him that a math professor thought he could earn a doctorate degree in mathematics. Professor Rainich's comments inspired Steve to set new goals for himself and after completing his M.S. in 1939, he went back to the University of Michigan and completed his Ph.D. in 1943. The topic of his dissertation was Nonlinear Difference Equations Analytic in a Parameter.

Clarence F. and Harriette J. Stephens with some members and family members of the National Science Foundation Summer Institute for College teachers, Williams College, Williamstown, Mass (1956).

While working for his doctorate, Steve worked as an Instructor at Prairie View A. and M. College during the years, 1940-1942 and then he served as a Teacher Specialist of the U.S. Navy for the years 1942-1945. He joined the Prairie View A. and M. College as a professor of mathematics in 1946. However, he did not stay there very long since he was invited to become the chairman of the department of mathematics of Morgan State College. He held that position for 15 years from 1947 to 1962. In 1962, he moved to SUNY at Geneseo as a professor of mathematics, where he served for 7 years before coming to SUNY at Potsdam in 1969. The question may be asked why did Steve leave Morgan State University. According to Steve, he was simply trying to run away from the chairmanship and his wife was getting tired of the city life. They both longed to be in a small town. They were both quite happy in Geneseo, but the offer from Potsdam was both challenging and inviting and to which they got pulled in slowly, if not reluctantly. As a matter of fact, when the President of SUNY Potsdam met Steve to discuss the possibility of his appointment, Steve made so many demands that he thought he would be turned down. But surprisingly, the young President agreed to give Steve everything he was asking for, and offered to do everything he wanted to do to establish a good math department. Then all of a sudden, Steve felt that it would be really great to work with such a young and enthusiastic President. Earlier, everywhere Steve worked the Presidents were older persons, who left the institutions in two or three years. So, Steve counted on working with a young and cooperative President for many years to come. However, for once, Steve's calculations proved wrong - the young President died a year later.

In any case, from the experiences of his own life as a student, knowing how the comment of Dean McKinney made him realize that he had the potential to pursue graduate studies in mathematics, and knowing how he was inspired by the comments of Professor Rainich to go for a doctorate in mathematics, Professor Stephens came to believe that, "College and University professors, with adequate support from administrations, can inspire many college students to reach a high level of achievement in mathematics if professors would use their creative abilities and time to do so."

His goals, experiences and experiments with math teaching at these institutions are described in personal communications to the author and others. In addition, Steve's views on various topics of pedagogical interest are captured well in the article, "An Interview with Clarence Stephens" by Gloria F. Gilmer and Scott Williams published in the UME TRENDS Vol. 2, Number 1, March 1990. In the following, we are reproducing excerpts of Steve's views and comments from these sources. The words are those of Steve; we have simply added subheadings to assist the readers.

Clarence F. Stephens as a faculty member, SUNY at Geneseo (1969)

Primary Goal as Chairman of the Mathematics Department

"My primary goal as Chair was to help establish the most favorable conditions I could for students to learn and teachers to teach. I adopted a method for developing the mathematics potential of students at Potsdam which had worked very well at Morgan State College, Baltimore, Maryland and in National Science Foundation Summer Institutes for secondary teachers of mathematics. A team of mathematics faculty members with me as a member was formed to teach students in their early (freshman and sophomore years for undergraduates - first year for graduate students) study of mathematics, "How to Read Mathematics Literature with Understanding and to Become Independent Learners." A person selected for the team was a person who, in my opinion, had a warm relation with beginning students, strong loyalty to the department and college. The team was informally formed by the way courses were assigned without informing faculty members that they were members of the team. Since each member of the mathematics faculty was given an opportunity to teach across the mathematics curriculum, every effort was made to add as many members to the team as possible.

Sometimes I would teach a section of the same course with team members, and often I would teach a following required course for the mathematics major. From my earlier experiences at Morgan State College and in National Science Foundation Summer Institutes, if team members were successful in reaching their goal, then I had confidence that any caring mathematics faculty member could effectively teach the students developed by the team. Also, the students who were developed by the team would help us teach other students How to Learn Mathematics as participants in class study groups and as tutors. The indicated method for developing the mathematics potential of students was as effective at SUNY Potsdam as it had been at Morgan State College."

Lack of Tradition at Potsdam

"When I joined the SUNY at Potsdam Mathematics faculty in the fall of 1969, perhaps no graduate of SUNY at Potsdam had earned the Ph.D. in mathematics, although the college was founded in 1816. To the best of my knowledge, Dr. Arnold M. Dunn is the only graduate of SUNY Potsdam before 1970 who later earned the Ph.D. in mathematics. He was a tenured member of the SUNY at Potsdam Mathematics Department when I joined the faculty in 1969 and he earned the Ph.D. degree several years after 1969 at Clarkson College of Technology in Potsdam, NY. If any graduate of SUNY at Potsdam before 1970 earned the Ph.D. in Mathematics, other than Dr. Dunn, this knowledge seems to be unknown to the faculty and administration of the College. Hence, the achievement of such a possible graduate could not be used as a role model to help inspire a high level of achievement in mathematics at SUNY Potsdam.

SUNY at Potsdam was offering the Master of Science in Secondary Mathematics when I joined the faculty in 1969. This degree required only 9 semester hours credits in mathematics and the courses in mathematics were at the level of upper level undergraduate mathematics courses. We did obtain approval of a Master of Arts degree in Mathematics during 1969-70, my first year on SUNY at Potsdam Faculty. However, we did not have funds for graduate assistantships in order to attract able graduate students to enroll in the Master of Arts Degree Program and undergraduates were required to be within 9 semester hours of completing their bachelor's degree before they could enroll in graduate courses in any subject at SUNY Potsdam.

Thus, by the academic year 1969-70 there had not been established at SUNY Potsdam a tradition for sophomores and juniors studying graduate mathematics courses. In fact, sophomores and juniors were not permitted to enroll in graduate coruses. When I joined the faculty at SUNY Potsdam, I found 6 tenured members of the mathematics faculty and only 2 of them had been awarded doctoral degrees, one in mathematics education and one in physics. The 2 tenured members with doctoral degrees had completed their undergraduate studies in engineering programs. Three of the four tenured members were awarded doctoral degrees after 1970 and the other completed all requirements for the Ph.D. in mathematics, except the dissertation. When I visited with his former major adviser, he stated that he gave this tenured faculty member a problem which was too difficult and the problem had not been solved when he discussed this matter with me last year. One member of the mathematics faculty with a Ph.D. in mathematics joined the faculty one year before I did and two members with Ph.D.'s in mathematics joined the faculty the same year I did. Hence, less than half (6 members) of the 13 members mathematics faculty held the doctoral degree during the academic year 1969-70. When I proposed our B.A./M.A. or M.S. programs, some members of the mathematics faculty had great doubts about the ability of any of our students being successful in such a demanding program. Since I was serving as chair of our Mathematics Department, I was able to persuade a majority of the members of mathematics faculty to approve our B.A./M.A. or M.S. programs.

Once the M.A. and M.S. mathematics programs had been approved, the establishment of the B.A./M.A. or M.S. programs required no new courses or additions to our faculty. All that was needed was a rule which would permit students below the senior level to enroll in graduate courses."

Four-Year Bachelor's - Master's Degrees Program in Mathematics (The B.A./M.A. Program)

"Nevertheless, I had considerable difficulty obtaining the approval of the college faculty for our B.A./M.A. or M.S. programs. Many members of the college faculty believed that we did not enroll any students who could be successful in such a demanding program. In order to help persuade the college faculty to approve our B.A./M.A. or M.S. programs, I prepared the pamphlet: *Undergraduates in Graduate Mathematics Courses?*

The Mathematics Department was the only department at the college for a period of more than 10 years that offered the B.A./M.A. or M.S. programs. I believe that this is one of the reasons we attracted some very able students to SUNY Potsdam and many of them majored in mathematics; we had a very demanding program (B.A./M.A.) in which students succeeded.

My experiences at Morgan State College gave me confidence that we regularly admitted students who could be successful in our B.A./M.A. or M.S. programs. When I made the proposal for our B.A./M.A. or M.S. program, I knew that I had developed three young women in my Calculus III class during 1969-70 who could succeed in this program. The textbook for my Calculus III course was *Calculus of Vector Functions* by Richard E. Williamson, Richard H. Crowell and Hale F. Trotter, Second Edition, Prentice-Hall, Inc. 1962, 1968.

These three students demonstrated that they could read sections of this book independently and they were the first students who completed our B.A./M.A. or M.S. programs in 1972.

At everywhere I taught before joining the mathematics faculty at SUNY Potsdam, the college enrolled many students with the ability and high school mathematics preparation to reach a high level of achievement in mathematics. By teaming with some members of the mathematics faculty, we inspired many of these students to develop their potential. When I joined the faculty at SUNY Potsdam, I found one major problem. I knew that we could develop freshmen and sophomores who could be successful in studying mathematics courses at a higher level than the level studied by most of the students in the Master of Science in Secondary Mathematics program at SUNY Potsdam in 1969. I did not face this problem at Morgan State College, since no graduate programs were offered at Morgan State College during the 15 years I served on the faculty. How could we inspire our capable undergraduates to achieve at their maximum level in mathematics? In order to overcome this problem, I proposed our B.A./M.A. or M.S. programs during 1969-1970. I acknowledge that better high school preparation in mathematics of entering college students would be desirable. However, in my opinion, college and university professors, with adequate support from administrations, can inspire many college students to reach a high level of achievement in mathematics if professors would use their creative abilities and time to do so. If they would do this, I conjecture that over time the high school preparation of entering college students would improve."

The Newsletter

"We considered high school mathematics teachers as members of our team by making maximum efforts to continue the development of the mathematics potential of students these high school teachers prepared for our college. I believe that these high school teachers appreciated our caring for their former students. For example, you may note that the bachelor's in mathematics in the classes of 1985, 1986 and 1987 at SUNY Potsdam (as shown in the Mathematics Newsletters for these years) graduated from about 250 different high schools, over 100 high schools had more than one graduate, and one high school had 14 graduates. Each year, the Mathematics Newsletter was sent to a high school if a bachelor's in mathematics at SUNY Potsdam for a given year was also a former graduate of the high school."

The Liberal Arts Nature of Mathematics

"We emphasized the liberal arts nature of a mathematics education. Over one three year period (1984, 1985, 1986), our bachelor's in mathematics completed second majors (only some completed second majors) in the following Liberal Arts Departments: Anthropology, Art, Biology, Chemistry, Computer Science, Dance, Drama, Economics, English, History, Philosophy, Physics and Spanish.

My conclusion is that many college students can be attracted to elect college-level mathematics courses and they have the high school mathematics preparation to be successful in these elective courses."

How To Make Students Independent in Learning Mathematics

The key to make students independent in learning mathematics is to teach them to read mathematics. This he describes in a letter to Professor Roberts as follows:

"Early in my teaching career and many years before I joined the mathematics faculty at SUNY, I concluded that the best way I could help students to write correct proofs was to teach them to read mathematics textbooks with understanding; perhaps one of the best things a teacher can do for students. This task is not easy, but requires time, patience and encouragement of students. I observed that proofs are written in textbooks and teachers explain proofs in their lectures. However, both students and teachers are often disappointed with the proofs given by students of theorems when they have not seen a proof of the theorems before. I conjectured that most students accept proofs given in textbooks and by teachers in their lectures on authority (they memorize the proofs) and not on understanding. Hence, these students have difficulty giving proofs on their own. Any student who demonstrated that he or she could read with understanding the textbook for my course always earned a good grade in my course, since I knew the student would be successful in future mathematics courses the student studied, regardless of how good or bad his or her future teachers would be.

I had some interesting experiences about the task of reading a mathematics textbook with some of my colleagues at two different colleges where I taught before I joined the mathematics faculty at SUNY Potsdam. There was a total of four persons involved on different occasions. Each of these colleagues had earned a master's degree in mathematics at universities with strong research mathematics departments, after two years of graduate studies. Each was considering plans to continue his or her studies for the Ph.D. degree in mathematics.

I wanted to read the following books:

(1) *General Topology* by John L. Kelley, D. Van Nostrand and Company, Inc., 1955.

(2) *Lectures in Abstract Algebra* by Nathan Jacobson, Volume 1, D. Van Nostrand and Company, Inc. 1951.

(3) *Fundamental Concepts of Algebra* by Claude Chevalley, Academic Press, Inc. 1956.

(4) *Topological Vector Spaces* by John Horvath, Lecture Notes, Number 2, 1963, Department of Mathematics, University of Maryland.

On each occasion, I agreed to lead the discussion at the beginning and that we would alternate as leaders. I soon learned that my colleagues could not lead the discussion since they could not read the textbook, although they had completed graduate courses in Algebra and Topology. Hence, I led the discussions and we completed about half of each book. Each of these colleagues told me after our study that this was the first time they had learned how to read a mathematics textbook. Each returned to graduate school, earned A's in his or her graduate courses, was awarded the Ph.D. in mathemtics, although almost all of their grades were B's when they studied for the Master's degree.

We taught Dr. Cateforis, now chair of SUNY at Potsdam Mathematics Department, how to read a mathematics textbook with understanding and the meaning of a mathematics proof, when he was an undergraduate student at Morgan State College. Hence, he was successful in his studies for the Ph.D. in mathematics at the University of Wisconsin, at Madison. For example, he was a member of my Modern Algebra class when I was teaching at Morgan State College. The textbook for the course was *Lectures in Abstract Algebra* by Nathan Jacobson, Volume 1, D. Van Nostrand and Company, Inc., 1951, although no department offered a graduate program during the time I served on the mathematics faculty at Morgan State College (now Morgan State University). Dr. Cateforis demonstrated in my course that he had achieved at a high level the goals of my course.

Also, Dr. Cateforis was one of my assistants when I directed an Undergraduate Science Education Program, sponsored by the National Science Foundation, Morgan State College, Baltimore, Maryland, Summer 1962. Eight students were in the program, four men and four women. Six of the students had completed their sophomore year at Morgan State College during the Spring of 1962. All of the men were sophomores during the academic year 1961-62 and two of the women were seniors, one of them being a graduating senior. Sophomores in the summer project were each given assignments to read independently one of the following books:

(1) *Real Analysis* by Edward James McShane and Truman Botts, D. Van Nostrand Inc., 1959, Chapters I, II, III, pages 1-97.

(2) *Complex Analysis* by Lars U. Ahlfors, McGraw-Hill Book Co., Inc. 1953, Chapters I and II, pages 1-81.

(3) *Mathematical Analysis* by Tom Apostol, Addison-Wesley Publishing Co., 1957, Chapters 1-6, Pages 1-126.

(4) *Analytic Functions* by Elnar Hille.

(5) *An Introduction to Algebraic Topology* by Andrew H. Wallace, pages 1-89, Pergamon Press, 1957

(6) *Theory of Functions of a Real Variable* by Edwin Hewitt, Chapters I and II, Pages 1-98.

All of the women in the summer program later earned master's degrees and each of the men earned the Ph.D. degree, three in mathematics and the other in the mathematical sciences, with emphasis on computer science. Dr. Scott Williams, Professor of Mathematics at SUNY Buffalo, was a student in the indicated summer program, and he is one of the co-authors of *An Interview with Clarence Stephens,* UME Trends, Volume 2, Number 1, March 1990."

The Case of a Photographic Memory. "You may be interested in the fact that I was not successful in preparing a fourth woman in my Calculus III class for our B.A./M.A. program. At the beginning of my course when I gave some explanation of concepts and students gave presentations in class, she competed very well with the other three students. Then I gave each of the four students individual sections of the textbook to read which the class had not reached. I held conferences with each student to determine the progress the student was making in carrying out the assignment. At the time of the first conference with each student, three of the students were making good progress in completing their individual assignments, but this fourth student had made no progress. Her excuse was that she could not study this assignment since she had unusually heavy workloads in her other courses.

When I heard her excuse, I concluded that perhaps she was an overachiever in the first part of my course and I had given her a too difficult assignment. I decided to examine her high school achievement and SAT scores and compare these measures of academic promise with the other three students' measures of academic promise. Usually, I do not seek these measures of academic promise of my students, since I believe that all of my students can reach a high level of achievement. To my surprise, I learned that this fourth student had more academic promise than the other three students according to the above indicated measures. In fact, she was one of the most promising students at the college. I was completely puzzled. At our second conference, this fourth student enlightened me. She explained that she has a photographic memory. Her high school and almost all of her college teachers lectured and explained concepts. Hence, she never had to study in high school or in college in order to pass her courses. She told me that in order to complete the individual assignment I gave her she would be required to study and to think, two activities she had not practiced. Then she said that she enjoyed going to school without studying, and since most of her teachers would lecture, she was confident that she could graduate from college without studying. I relieved her from the individual assignment I had given her. She was an intelligent student, but graduated from college with a little less than 3.0 college cumulative average.

Perhaps you may be interested in one of my students who is almost the opposite in learning habits from the fourth student described above. I taught this student the last two years before my retirement. He was a transfer student from a community college. When he came to Potsdam, he elected Physics as his major. His grades from the community college were above average, but not outstanding. He did not achieve well in his Physics courses at SUNY Potsdam; but his achievement in his mathematics courses was better than his achievement in Physics courses, but not outstanding.

I first taught him in my Linear Algebra II class. I began to teach students in this class how to read the textbook by selecting a statement in the proof of a theorem which is not clear. The homework assignment was to write the given statement in one color pencil and the student's explanation of how that particular statement followed from previous statements in the proof of the theorem in another color pencil. I collected the homework assignments and read the papers, made a note of the progress of students in my record book, and returned the papers without grading them. I had expected about 25 students for the class, but 59 students enrolled in the course. Hence, I had them working in groups of 7 or 8. When I returned the first home work assignment, I told the members of the class that they did not agree on the explanation for that statement. They were to work in their groups in class and convince the members of their group that they had a good explanation how the given statement followed from the previous statements in the proof of the theorem. When students observed that they did not agree with each other and had difficulty reaching a common agreement, they realized that they did not know how to read a mathematics textbook. I continued this process gradually throughout the course.

This transfer student had no idea of how to read his textbook at the beginning of the course, but he became very good at reading the textbook before the course was over. Hence, I invited him to enroll in my Theory of Sets course. The textbook for the course was Set Theory by Charles C. Pinter, Addison-Wesley Publishing Co. (I used many different textbooks for this course, but I was not satisfied with any of them for my class. I should have written a textbook for my course.) I gave the class the homework assignment to explain in detail the theorem

8.11 Theorem (page 159) *If B is an infinite cardinal number, then*
$$BB = B$$
(We may note that this class enrolled freshmen, sophomores, juniors, seniors and graduate students.) In particular, they were to pay special attention to the statement:

Now it is easy to verify that A satisfies the hypotheses of Zorn's Lemma (The details are left as an exercise for the reader.)

This particular transfer student did an excellent job of writing the details of this proof and I knew that he understood this proof. Also, I knew that he had reached that level of mathematical maturity so that he would be successful in any future mathematics course he studied regardless of how good or bad his future teachers would be. Although he did not have a college cumulative average of at least 3.0, I invited him to enroll in our B.A./M.A. program.

In the fall of the year after he completed my Theory of Sets course, he was enrolled in our courses:

(1) Abstract Algebra, Textbook: ALGEBRA by Thomas W. Hungerford, Holt, Rinehart and Winston, Inc. 1974.

(2) Real Variables, Textbook: REAL ANALYSIS by H. L. Royden, The MacMillan Company, 1968. These classes met twice a week and he would attend class about once every two weeks. My colleague who was teaching the Real Variables course informed me of this situation, and said that we had made a mistake by permitting him to enroll in his class, since he believed the course was too difficult for this transfer student. I told my colleague that I believed that this transfer student could read Real Analysis by Royden on his own. My colleague was of the opinion that I was joking. About two months later, he told me that this student had solved so many exercises out of Royden's book that he did not have time to read all of them. I told him that if he read one of his proofs which he believed to be incorrect, he should look at the proof carefully, since this transfer student almost never wrote an incorrect proof.

My colleague who was teaching our Abstract Algebra course was a new teacher and he lectured in his class. On one of the occasions when this student attended his class, he inquired of this student after class if he understood his lecture. The student responded that when a teacher lectures all the time, he tries not to hear what the teacher is saying since the teacher interferes with his thinking. He received grades of A (4.0) in these two courses.

After his success in our B.A./M.A. program, which he completed in the fall semester, he expressed a desire to study for the Ph.D. in Mathematics. His college cumulative average was now a little above 3.0, but we were able to persuade the Chair of the Mathematics Department at SUNY Binghamton to award him an assistantship, when the chair came to SUNY Potsdam to lecture and recruit graduate students. When the chair visited our college the following year, he told us that this transfer student was the best student in his class. The last information I have on this student is that he is doing research for his Ph.D. in Mathematics.

Students respond to teachers in different ways. One of the students discussed above wanted her teachers to lecture and the other did not.

In one of my Theory of Sets classes, I used Set Theory by Pinter as a textbook. I taught my students how to read Chapter I of the textbook. My students read Chapter II without my help and solved almost all the exercises in Chapter II. My job was to point out some

corrections in the textbook chapter and to act as moderator when
students put proofs of exercises on the blackboard."

Placement Tests

"I began my college teaching career in 1940 at Prairie View A & M
College (now Prairie View University), Prairie View, Texas. As is
true today, college and university mathematics professors were
complaining about the poor mathematics preparation of entering
college students. Placement tests were given in order to assign students
to college mathematics classes. During my first year as a college
teacher, I developed the student in my college Algebra class who later
earned his Ph.D. degree in mathematics at the University of Michigan,
as you report in your paper. He was the first graduate of Prairie View
A & M College who later earned the Ph.D. in mathematics. Placement
tests scores were the reason he was assigned to the wrong class. I have
never had confidence in placement test scores for the purpose of
assigning students to college mathematics classes, unless college and
university professors do not wish to use their creative abilities and time
to develop to a high level the mathematics potential of students
admitted to their college or university.

In 1947, I joined the mathematics faculty at Morgan State College
(now Morgan State University), Baltimore, Maryland. During the 15
years I served on the faculty at Morgan State College, I chaired the
Mathematics Department. During my first year on the faculty, I
learned that mathematics majors were completing Elementary Calculus
in their junior and senior years. Placement tests had indicated that
mathematics preparation of entering students was so poor that students
were spending most of their college years being prepared to study
college level mathematics courses, even for most mathematics majors.
Two years after I joined the faculty we produced examples of students at
Morgan State College who successfully completed Elementary
Calculus as freshmen. When I left Morgan State College in 1962,
some of Morgan's students were studying graduate mathematics courses
after their sophomore year, as indicated in the enclosed materials. Also,
at Morgan State College during my last 10 years on the faculty, the
Mathematics Department often had the largest number of majors on the
Dean's list, and many of the best students at the college majored in
mathematics."

About SAT Scores

To the question, "Over your forty-seven year teaching career, did you find SAT scores useful for predicting freshmen's success?" Steve had the following answer:
"I learned early in my career that SAT scores discriminate against blacks. Later it was found that they also discriminate against women. Examination of high school averages and SAT scores over many years showed me that students who reached a high level of maturity in mathematics ranged from those with the highest to the lowest SAT scores and high school grade point averages.
I'll give you one example. When I was teaching at Morgan, we were trying to convince a group of 50 beginning freshmen that they could be successful in a very demanding program during the first semester of their freshman year. I taught these students in my set theory and logic class. There was one student in the class who started slowly and developed very well. In a conference with her, I told her how pleased I was that she had reached a high level of excellence in the class and expressed my opinion that she could do well in advanced mathematics courses. She told me that when she came to Morgan she elected to major in sociology, since she always feared mathematics and wanted to take a major that required no mathematics at all. She said she had never studied high school mathematics (no algebra, high school geometry, or trigonometry). I showed her an elementary algebra book from my bookshelf and discovered that she did not even know the notation for multiplication in algebra. I knew she had reached a high level of mathematical maturity in my set theory and logic class. Therefore, I explained to her how multiplication in algebra is indicated. Then, I asked her to read a law of exponents for multiplication in algebra and to study the examples explaining this law. She did so and acknowledged that she understood the examples. I then assigned her exercises of increasing difficulty using this law. She was able to give me answers to the exercises almost as quickly as I could assign them. I repeated this process using other material in algebra and she was very good. Then I recognized that this student who feared mathematics all of her life could now learn elementary algebra on her own.
"From my bookshelf I gave her books on high school algebra, plane geometry, trigonometry and precalculus. I advised her to study the precalculus book during the Christmas holidays - using the other books for references. Further, I advised her to enroll in the college's

Pre-Calculus course during the second semester which I was not teaching. I told her it would be best for us not to tell her precalculus teacher that she had no credits in high school mathematics; but after she achieved at a very high level in his class, we could tell him what an excellent teacher he is to be able to teach precalculus to a student with no credits in high school mathematics. I also said I would be willing to help her with difficulties she could not overcome by reading her textbook, discussions with other students, and explanations of her precalculus teacher.

She achieved well in her precalculus class with almost no help from me. She followed this course with a year of calculus, changed her major to chemistry and I was informed that she became a medical doctor" [10].

Starting Graduate Material Early

"The summer before I joined the mathematics faculty at SUNY Geneseo during the Fall of 1962, I taught summer school at Reed College, Portland, Oregon. As you perhaps know, Reed College is a highly selective private liberal arts college. I learned that some students at Reed College enrolled in a course as freshmen which developed the Real Number System. The textbook for the course was written by one of their mathematics faculty members.

During the fall semester of 1962, I was assigned to teach a section of Pre-Calculus and the textbook for the course was *Principles of Mathematics* by C. B. Allendoerfer and C. O. Oakley, McGraw-Hill Book Company, Inc. The textbook used by the Reed College students was a paperback book and did not cost very much money in 1962. My students in Pre-Calculus were willing to buy the book on *The Real Number System* by Roberts as a complement to the regular text. I taught them how to read the book on The Real Number System with understanding. Then, they could read the regular textbook without my help and solve assigned exercises out of their regular textbook.

My Pre-Calculus students and my colleagues at SUNY Geneseo were unaware that my Pre-Calculus students were learning mathematics at a higher level than most students in SUNY Geneseo Master of Science in Secondary Mathematics Program in 1962, where Calculus III and Elementary Probability and Statistics (without Calculus as a prerequisite) were graduate courses in the program.

One student who achieved well in the indicated Pre-Calculus course had been told by his high school teacher that he could not learn mathematics. He was so inspired by his success in this course that he later earned a Ph.D. degree in mathematics education with emphasis on special education. He is now on the faculty of SUNY Geneseo."

Lecture Method is the Least Effective

"Effective teaching is not independent of time and place. I believe that teachers should be free to choose their teaching methods and be held responsible for the results achieved by those methods. I used many different methods of teaching including the lecture method and the active learning method. I did not, however, use the lecture method as my primary teaching method, as I believe it is the least effective method for teaching mathematics to the general college population.

I concluded early in my teaching career that I could teach mathematics effectively to most of my students only if I were successful in protecting and strengthening their self-esteem"[10].

What Retards the Development of a Strong Mathematics Program?

In the opinion of Steve, "four major problems retard the development of strong mathematics programs:
  (1) opposition to bright students;
  (2) excessive faculty concern about the subject matter to be covered;
  (3) excessive faculty concern about academic standards; and
  (4) inadequate support for teaching undergraduate mathematics by institutions of higher education - as described in the publication *Everybody Counts* ."

"Opposition to bright students comes from other students who believe bright students threaten them with low or falling grades. Opposition may even come from administrators who fail to provide favorable conditions for bright students for fear of creating an elitist group in the student body.

Excessive faculty concern about subject matter covered may be manifested by a more rapidly paced class than students can follow, and the selection of textbooks for the beauty of the mathematical treatment rather than students' ability to understand it.

Excessive concern for academic standards may be observed in faculty members who believe that a high level of achievement by most members of the class implies a lowering of academic standards. Such concern may also reflect a general lack of faith in the intellectual potential of the students in their classes."

When he was asked, "How were these problems treated at Potsdam?" Steve pointed out, "In 1970, we established a dual-degree program - baccalaureate and master's degrees - in which a student could obtain both degrees in four years without attending summer school. In this program, we were able to motivate some freshmen to be successful in first year graduate mathematics courses. Some of the high achievers in these courses tutored in our mathematics lab. Other students looked upon the high achieving students as their friends who wished to help them succeed. In this way, they were inspiring role models for students and faculty alike.

Most efforts to improve undergraduate mathematics programs focus on curriculum and technology. While we recognize the importance of these two factors in the improvement of mathematics education, we focus on the human factor of changing the opinions of students, faculty, and academic administrators that mathematics is a subject which is impossible for most students to learn, and only the rare genius can learn the subject with any high degree of success. Once the faculty discovered that some of these courses were teaching students how to reason about mathematical ideas, then the faculty became interested in teaching students to reason (rather than covering a lot of content which students can cover on their own if they know how to reason in this field.)

We never used a placement examination for selecting students for courses in mathematics. We found out that what we could do was (learn how) to develop the students who were coming to our college. In fact, the faculty became very proud of the fact that they could take students at the lower level and raise them to a higher level. In other words, we did not lower the students' self-esteem by giving them a placement examination, failing them on the examination, and then placing them in remedial courses. We never did this!"[10].

An Assessment of Steve as a Teacher and as a Chairman

There is no doubt that Clarence Stephens is a truly great teacher. His approach to teaching mathematics is unique in many ways. The belief that everybody has the potential to learn mathematics, the theory that to teach mathematics effectively to most students - the teacher must be successful in protecting and strengthening their self-esteem, the goal of helping students become independent in learning are perhaps known ideas, but Professor Stephens has demonstrated them so convincingly that there is no room to doubt about the validity of these assertions. As a Chairman, he has shown how a successful math program may be shaped. In doing so, Steve has touched the hearts of students, colleagues and adminstrator alike and have left deep impressions in their mind. We give below a few of these impressions.

"Since my experience with the Fourth NSF Summer Institute at Morgan State College, I have intended to write to you to express my gratitude for the privilege of such a rewarding opportunity.

Morgan State College is truly blessed with the presence of Dr. C.F. Stephens as an instructor. In all my training experience, I have never witnessed a more competent mathematics teacher than Dr. Stephens. Fortunate are the students who share his knowledge."
[Nena Mae Faulcon of Newton Center in a letter dated February 14, 1961 to the Director of NSF Institute, Morgan State College]

"It is with a great deal of regret that I must accept your resignation as Professor and Head of the Department of Mathematics effective August 31, 1962. During your 15 years of service here, you have made a contribution to the developing program of the College. Under your leadership, the Department of Mathematics has become one of our strongest departments. We will miss you. In the event you find your new situation at Geneseo State College to be not all you had hoped, I shall be glad to have you return to Morgan State College."
[Martin D. Jenkins, President of Morgan State College, May 23, 1962].

"Having profited a great deal from your class both in the understanding of mathematics and in the realization of what a teacher should be, I was asked back at Reed last summer. I wrote my paper on Transfinite Numbers and received my degree. Since I do not believe that this could have been possible if I had not had your class that summer, I wish to send you my sincere thanks and my deepest expression of gratitude."

[Hugette L. Bach of Davis, California in a letter dated February 9, 1964 to Steve]

"My principal reason for writing is to renew an earlier offer made by Lloyd Williams, I think. In the opinion of my colleagues you are the most successful "outsider" we have had, and we would like to have you back next summer."

[Professor Burrowes Hunt of Reed College in a letter dated September 23, 1963 to Steve]

"I have just learned of your being honored by the Potsdam Chapter of Pi Mu Epsilon. May I offer you a heartfelt "Congratulations" and add my praise to that already bestowed upon you. Of all the teachers I have had as an undergraduate, you stand out as the one who has had the biggest effect upon my directions. This was not so much by way of the material you taught me (although I did make use of Zorn's lemma in my dissertation) but more of your outstanding ability to make your students think on their own. Quite often we confront problems (in all disciplines) upon which we try to force some known solution or principle rather than think of new solutions. As you would sometimes say, "The real problem is that you know too much."

Having been one of the first graduates of the BA-MA program, I am happy to see its success. I agree with your pursuit of excellence as the principal goal of the department. While many departments seem to be satisfied with their achievements, you never are."

[Harris Schlesinger, Assistant Professor of Economics,Vanderbilt University, Nashville, Tennessee 37235, in a letter dated June 18, 1980]

"Clarence didn't say very much, indeed, at many meetings he spoke not at all. But when he did, I can remember being struck by what he said and I frequently thought, "My God, that all sounds wonderful, but no one can really care that much about students, about the future they face. It's surely all sort of an advertisement for the Math Department." . . When in January of 1984, I became Acting Dean, my relationship with Clarence changed and I had a number of opportunities to work with him and to get to know him. I discovered, first of all, that all he had said about how important students are, the expressions of what can only be called love for those who studied with him and for his colleagues, that all of that was not mere flag waving but instead reflected the very creed by which this man practiced his art."

[Richard Del Guidice, Dean of the School o Liberal Studies, Potsdam College, in a speech to the Potsdam chapter of Pi Mu Epsilon on May 2, 1987]

"I believe he (Clarence Stephens) is the most extraordinary educator I have met."

[Rick Luttman on Teaching &, Sonoma State University, February, 1988]

Steve is a rare visionary, who can see the practicality of his visions. The math program at SUNY Potsdam is truly a vision come true. Even when he appears to be a complete visionary, he is able to convince one about the reality of his vision. Thus in a letter to mathematics majors, written on February 26, 1981, he talks only about the Institute for Advanced Study, Princeton, Field Medal and the like as if some of his students would some day reach those heights. If this suggests that he was a visionary living in world of dreams, then we should listen to the reaction of this vision among the students. This letter was brought to my attention by a former student, who said, "Even though none of us was thinking or dreaming of ever going to Princeton, the letter made us feel very good, kind of noble in some ways that he believed in us that we had the potential to do it."

Clarence Stephens is one of the few individuals to be honored by the governors of two different states. In 1962, he was honored by Governor J. Millard Tawes of Maryland for distinguished service to education and in 1991, he was honored by a distinguished service award by Governor Cuomo of New York. At SUNY Potsdam he was also awarded SUNY Chancellor's award for excellence in Teaching for the academic year 1976 - 77.

A Good Mathematics Teacher

It is good that the math program at SUNY Potsdam and the part played by Steve in building it are now receiving attention of the math community. For the innovative principles that Steve has introduced into the realm of math education are truly remarkable. The present and future math teachers, whether he or she be in college or high school, and who wishes to be successful in imparting mathematical knowledge will have to learn from the experiments and experiences of this great teacher. It is in the interest of the mathematical community that they keep alive the legacy of Steve in their classrooms, in their offices and in their departments — the legacy that to teach math we need to create a humanistic environment for learning, the most important ingredient of which are the teachers.

As a math teacher, Steve took to heart the definition of a good math teacher as given by John C. Egsgard, a former president of the National Council of Teachers of Mathematics. "A good mathematics teacher is one who uses his knowledge of mathematics, as well as his love and respect for his students to lead them to an enjoyment of the study of mathematics"[10]. During his long career as a math teacher, Steve demonstrated how one can create a model for this definition. Lest we forget, we give below some of the guiding principles that Steve suggested about how to become a good math teacher.

- Regardless of time and place, you can teach mathematics effectively to most students only if you are successful in protecting and strengthening the self-esteem of the students.
- Believe in your students - everyone can do mathematics.
- You can best achieve your goal as a teacher by helping the students to learn to think for themselves, to read mathematical literature independently with understanding and enjoyment, and to become free from the need of a teacher.
- If a student learns well the basic concepts of the course and learns to work independently, the student can learn additional subject matter rapidly.
- It is not the responsibility of the students to learn in the style that the professor wishes to teach; it is the professor's responsibility to teach the students in the style in which they can learn.

- You cannot push the students from the bottom; you must also raise them up from above.
- Be more concerned about promoting a favorable environment in which students can learn than about protecting academic standards.
- Go fast slowly.

Since his retirement in 1987, Clarence Stephens and his wife Harriette have been living on a farm in Conesus, New York. Harriette's maiden name is Harriette Josephine Briscoe. Harriette is herself an accomplished math teacher. She graduated top of both her high school and college (Lincoln University, Jefferson City, Missouri) classes. The two met in the summer of 1942 at the University of Michigan where she was beginning her study for the master's degre in mathematics. They married in Ann Arbor, Michigan on December 21, 1942. Harriette later earned her master's degree in mathematics at the University of New Hampshire, Durham and retired from teaching as Professor of Mathematics, Emeritus, SUNY College of Technology, Canton, New York. It is not surprising that the two prodigals of math education will have mathematics children. Their daughter Harriette Jeannette Stephens and son Clarence Francis Stephens, Jr., graduated from SUNY College at Geneseo with high honors and with majors in mathematics. Harriette J. Stephens later earned her Ph.D. degree in mathematics education at the University of Iowa, Iowa City. She is now teaching mathematics in Bellingham, Washington. Clarence Stephens, Jr., earned his master's degree in mathematics at the University of Wisconsin, Madison, while studying as a Woodrow Wilson Fellow. He is now working with a comuter company in Boston.

In 1987, SUNY Potsdam instituted the Clarence F. Stephens Mathematics Award. This award is given annually by the School of Liberal Studies and the Mathematics Department to the non-graduating math major who, by his or her achievement in mathematics, best personifies Steve's vision of the Mathematics student of becoming all he or she is capable of being. The Mathematical Association of America and the Association of Mathematics Teachers of America have both honored Steve by appointing him to various committees and by utilizing his expertise as a math teacher in different ways. However, the best way the present day and future math teachers can honor this great educator is by continuing his legacy in and outside their math classrooms.

Clarence F. Stephens as the Chairman, Math Dept of SUNY at Potsdam (1980)

Chapter 8

PRESENT REALITIES

From the table in Figure 8, it is clear that the number of math majors produced by SUNY Potsdam has been declining since 1986. Even though the percentage of math graduates produced by SUNY Potsdam is still much higher than the national percentage, it is causing some concern that something is wrong and that something may be done to stop this trend. Therefore, we would like to analyze the possible causes of this decline.

year	All	Math	%	Female	%	B.A./M.A.	%
1978	890	58	• 7	37	64	6	10
1979	760	60	8	34	57	10	17
1980	655	73	11	43	59	11	15
1981	712	81	11	52	64	6	7
1982	780	69	9	34	49	4	6
1983	770	96	12	58	60	7	7
1984	738	124	17	61	49	11	9
1985	821	184	22	97	53	5	3
1986	845	213	25	115	54	5	2
1987	745	182	24	107	59	5	3
1988	658	131	20	69	53.4	4	3
1989	640	119	18.7	61	51	6	5
1990	585	83	13.9	40	48	3	4
1991	659	64	9.5	35	54.6	5	8

Figure 8. Percentage of male and female math bachelors

It should be noted that the decline in the number of B.A./M.A. graduates is not as significant as the decline in the number of students in the B.A. program. Also, the percentage of female math major continues to be more than the number of male math majors. In any case, the following are perhaps the major causes of this decline:

(1) The national trend caused by changes in life goals of present day students and changing cultural values.
(2) Personalities of present day students.
(3) Changes in the course requirements for graduation by the college.
(4) Changes in the math program.
(5) Decline in the enrollment of students majoring in computer science.
(6) A changing faculty.
(7) Unhappiness in the department caused by the unfair treatment of the department by the Administration.
(8) Rumour that Potsdam College may be shut down.

The National Trend. The Board on Mathematical Sciences of the National Research Council in its report *Moving Beyond Myths* [19] reports that "Interest in majoring in mathematics is at an all-time low among entering freshmen" and that "Too few students study advanced mathematics." In its earlier report, *Everybody Counts* [18], the board had reported that "Since 1975, the percentage of top high school seniors who expressed an interest in majoring in mathematics or statistics has declined by over 50 percent, even as the corresponding percentage for science and engineering remained relatively constant." (See Figure 9) The decline in the number of math majors produced by Potsdam perhaps reflects these national trends. However, Prof. Cateforis, the present Chairman of the Mathematics Department, is of the opinion that "national trends" are not necessarily valid for Potsdam since Potsdam has bucked such trends in the past and continues to do so now.

Some reasons for this declining trend suggested by the Council are changing pattern of life goals of college freshmen and the changing cultural values. For the report *Everybody Counts* also gives data about life goals of college freshmen for the past quarter century, which "show a consistent trend away from philosophical and scientific pursuits toward those that offer a promise of financial security" (Figure 10). It also notes that "Young Americans' avoidance of mathematics courses and careers arises from immersion in a culture that provides more alternatives than stimulants to the study of mathematics."

Personalities of Present day Students. According to several of the math teachers at Potsdam, many students nowadays do not seem to take pride in working hard, they do not seek satisfaction in learning or doing things well. Many of them either lack self-respect or do not try to build self-respect. The teachers find that students nowadays tend to accept failure much more readily than they used to ten or fifteen years ago. These students do not seem to set standards for themselves. Nowadays, students will submit shoddy work, accept unsatisfactory grades, say "O.K." and walk away from it. This kind of behavior completely nullifies the strategies and efforts of many of the teachers because they try to build everything by appealing to the students' pride, self-respect and desire to achieve.

**Intended Mathematics Majors
of Top High School Seniors**

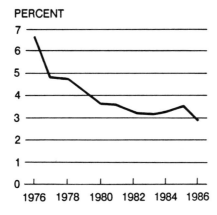

Figure 9. Intended Mathematics Majors[1]

How can you make a student take pride in learning to read, write and think mathematics when the student does not value such pride? How can you convince a student that majoring in math or getting a B.A. degree in math is a worthwhile education when the student does not care to have such an experience? How can you make a student work hard to pass a math course when the student is just happy to fail

[1] Reprinted with permission from *Everybody Counts: A Report to the Nation on the Future of Mathematics Education.* Copyright 1989 by the National Academy of Sciences. Courtesy of the National Academy Press, Washington, D.C.

and walk away? How can you make a student participate in classroom activity, when the only way the student knows to participate is to watch (TV) and to sit passively in front of the teacher (or a TV)? These are some of the questions that are plaguing many of the veteran teachers at Potsdam. Many of the previously successful strategies do not seem to work on a large section of the present day students. For example, in the old days whenever a student is absent in class, the teacher would call the student and find out why. If the student was absent for any reason other than serious unavoidable circumstances, the student would be immediately apologetic, but nowadays the students would not care and would not even care to say "thank you" for calling or for showing concern.

Shifting Student Interests

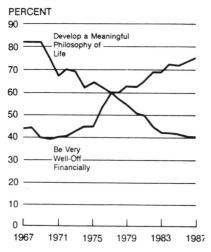

Figure 10. Shifting Student Interests[2]

In a society where broken families have become the rule rather than the exception, in a society where serious crimes like murder, rape and child abuse have been increasing in alarming proportions, and in a

---

[2] Reprinted with permission from *Everybody Counts: A Report to the Nation on the Future of Mathematics Education.* Copyright 1989 by the National Academy of Sciences. Courtesy of the National Academy Press, Washington, D.C.

society where almost every TV show dramatizes acts of violence, acts of passion and sexual aberrations and above all, acts of hatred, young boys and girls seem to be comfortable with "hating" things and often seem to take pride in saying things like "I hate so and so," "I hate such and such", and "I HATE MATH." It is not easy to convert a student who proclaims to hate math to love math. Yet "love of math" is a key to the success of the SUNY Potsdam. The math teachers at Potsdam try to motivate students by showing their love of math and by enthusiastically acting as role models of "love math" but such role playing do not appeal to hatred-prone youths of today.

For example, the quality of the freshman class at Potsdam, as judged by HSA, SATV, SATM and ACT scores, has been declining. Strong evidence of this is supplied by the declining number of freshmen invited to consider taking Honors Calculus I during their first semester at Potsdam. Such an invitation is extended to any freshman, regardless of intended major, who has HSA $\geq$ 90, SATV $\geq$ 450 and SATM $\geq$ 550 (or appropriate ACT scores correspondingly) and whose mathematics high school grades are $\geq$ 90 for each of four years of mathematics which include algebra, trigonometry and geometry. The invitations are extended during the summer, prior to the students' first semester at Potsdam. Whereas, in the past (the early eighties) it was possible to invite 15-17 % of the entering class (130 - 140 students) and have 50% - 60% of the invitees accepting and thus, creating two sections of Honors Calculus I, currently (in the last 5 to 7 years), only about 10% (about 80-90 invitees) of the class qualified for an invitation, and only about 30-40% of these accepted to form a single section of Honors Calculus I.

The College has had to "meet its quota" of a freshman class from a shrinking pool of college-bound New York high school seniors. It has had to accept more students at the lower end of the eligible applicants.

Changes in the Course Requirements for Graduation by the College. Starting in the fall of 1987, every freshman was required to take two quantitative courses during his/her first year: a statistical analysis course (essentially a discrete statistics course) and a problem solving/abstract reasoning course (which for most students meant a mathematics course.) The Department was called on to offer several sections of the introductory statistics course (MA 125 Probability and Statistics I) and several sections of introductory college-level mathematics courses other than Calculus I (MA 101 Elements of

Math I, MA 102   Elements of Mathematics 2 and MA 110 PreCalculus.) Many students who otherwise would have chosen Calculus I now chose one of these other courses, though they were prepared for Calculus I. Other students chose to start with meeting the statistics requirement first and were not allowed (or were advised not or chose not) to take Calculus I. Faculty advisers during Summer Freshman Orientation in general steered freshmen into taking only one quantitative course during the first semester, and if the students were timid about Calculus I, faculty advisers had plenty of other math courses to put freshmen in (who wanted a math course anyway.) The Department has significantly cut down on the number of sections of lower division courses other than Calculus I offered in the fall of 1992: freshmen are now required to take only one quantitative course during their freshman year.

The requirement that every student who desires to graduate from SUNY Potsdam must take a statistics course in the freshmen year has adversely effected the math enrollment because this requirement interrupts the math program. Previously the percentage of freshmen taking freshman calculus used to be as high as 64% and these students provided the fertile ground on which the math teachers sowed the seeds of love for math. With the present requirement freshmen do not like to enroll in Calculus because they consider statistics a math course. If they take Calculus, that would mean taking two math courses and would leave only three other courses to take. So they do not take Calculus and they are late getting started in the math program - as such, they think they are behind and they don't want to major in math.

In addition, the department is opposed to the idea of forcing undergraduates to take math courses because it makes many students hostile to math and creates an environment of hate. Like Steve, the department thinks that students should have the opportunity of taking math courses voluntarily so that they may learn in a more humane environment. Steve feels, and rightly so, that instead of pressuring students to take math courses by making it a requirement, students should be educated and advised by their respective departments as to why they should take a certain math course.

Changes in the Math Program.   In the Fall of 1989 the Department was asked by the Administration to come up with a proposal for a thirty-six semester hour mathematics major for the students in a certification 7-12 program (the students preparing to be high school mathematics teachers.) The reason given was that the (NY) State Education Department was about to institute such a requirement. The department proceeded to propose a single 33-hour major, for all mathematics majors. It was the case that up to that point almost 30% of mathematics majors were completing at least 33 hours (with the three hours beyond the 30 being an upper division mathematics course.) It was also the case that the mathematics major included no cognate requirements (and still does not.) So the increase from 30 to 33 was not deemed burdensome for the students.

However, the increase from 30 to 33 in the number of credit hours required to major in math is making mathematics less attractive to students seeking a degree in liberal arts education. This increase and the statistics requirement have somewhat blunted the earlier thrust of the math program among the students who are undecided about their majors or who are looking for possible changes in their choices of major.

Changing Face of the Department. Because the beginning of the decline in the enrollment coincides with the retirement of Clarence Stephens, it seems natural to suggest that the departure of Stephens as well as the retirement or resignation of other faculty members may have had some bearing on the decline.

Here are some changes that took place in 1987. C. F. Stephens retired as chair and V. C. Cateforis took over in June. Patricia Beaulieu was appointed full-time secretary to the Department of Mathematics in the summer. David Wycoff was appointed the Calculus coordinator in place of Cateforis, who had held that job since 1974. K. Chapman, a harmonic analyst, was hired (1987) to fill the vacancy created by Stephen's retirement.

Then C. L. Smith retired at the end of 1988, after thirty years of service to the Department. He had contributed critically to the success of the Potsdam mathematics program. During 1987-88, a search to fill the vacancy created by Smith's retirement was unsucessful. A person with a Master's Degree who is homesteading in the North Country was hired for one year, 1988-89.

David Wycoff resigned to leave at the end of 1989. He was a mathematical physicist and a great friend of the students. Drs. Cheryl C. Miller, a logician, Laura Person, a topologist, and David Spellman, also a topologist, were appointed to the department in 1989. Dan Kocan retired at the end of 1990. He was a functional analyst who was providing a special dimension to the program with his personality and teaching style. John Koker, who fit right in with the program, resigned in April 1991 to return to Wisconsin. Arnie Dunn retired at the end of 1991. He was one of the "original" members of the Potsdam Mathematics Department. A functional analyst, a great friend of the students, a hunter, a fisherman, a former baseball pitcher, he added much to the program both with his personality and his style of teaching. Wes Mitchell, a harmonic analyst, went on leave without salary for 1990-1992. He had added much to the program with his expertise in algebra, topology and analysis and his own brand of gentle but firm teaching style. He later resigned in 1992.

Thus, one by one the old guards are leaving the department and the face of the department is changing quite a lot. Even though the department has been able to replace some of them with younger teachers who seem to fit well with its program and who are equally committed to carry on the tradition that has been established so firmly, yet these changes may have taken its toll on the enrollment figures. The current chair, V. Cateforis, does not believe so. He believes that the commitment on the part of the new teachers to teach "the students that we have and not the students we wish we had" is as high as it has always been in the department; it may seem that the task of teaching our students has recently become harder but it was never easy, though always a pleasure."

Decline in the enrollment of students majoring in computer science. Several members of the math department at SUNY Potsdam are also of the opinion that the failure of the computer science department to attract students to Potsam College has contributred to the decline in the number of math majors [see Figure 11]. They point out that a large number of computer science majors also majored in math, so if the enrollment in the computer science department goes down, it is bound to affect the number of math majors.

This seems to be a valid point because students majoring in computer science find it helpful and useful to take a large number of math courses - they usually take so many math courses, that by taking two or three more courses they can usually major in math as well. Many industries also prefer computer science majors with math background and vice versa. Because of this trend, many colleges and universities like the University of Rhode Island offer undergraduate math programs that require a substantial number of credits in computer science. In short, a good program in computer science is very essential to support a good math program and conversely.

Year	All Bachelors	Math Majors	CIS Major	CIS and Math Majors
1978	890	58	97	11
1979	760	60	92	27
1980	655	73	100	20
1981	712	81	131	25
1982	780	69	149	24
1983	770	96	180	46
1984	738	124	189	33
1985	821	184	219	61
1986	845	213	165	64
1987	745	182	118	43
1988	658	131	88	27
1989	640	119	63	21
1990	585	83	46	13
1991	659	64	27	7

Figure 11. Distribution of Math and Computer Science majors

Unhappiness in the department. In a document circulated to the members of the department of math on March 9, 1981, Professor Stephens warned, "Although we have taken more than 10 years to develop our present mathematics program by dedicated and hard work, our program can be destroyed very easily. This result can be achieved by inadequate administrative support or by faculty members taking out their frustrations on students." Unfortunately, there is some evidence that this trend of inadequate administrative support and of faculty frustration, has already begun.

The dedicated services of the members of the math department have been acknowledged by the administration from the Dean of the Arts and Sciences of Potsdam College to the Governor of New York. Thus, we read, "The dean told me of the time he was walking across the campus late one Friday afternoon when spring had just broken out and everyone had fled home early - except that as he passed the mathematics building he happened to look up and there were the professors still at work at their desks"[9]. These members have but attracted only drops of the merit increments awarded to the faculty at Potsdam. According to data prepared by a member of the math department, it ranks 13th among the departments of Potsdam College in receiving merit increments for years 1983-90 (Figure 12). It is sad that the department, which during the last fifteen years has produced 15% of its graduates and has brought prestige and glory to Potsdam College that cannot be matched by any other department, should receive such treatment (so little in merit raises) from its adminstrators. In addition, the last time a member of the math department received a Chancellor's award for excellence in teaching was in 1977, and in the last 25 years only two members of the department have received this award - not very encouraging statistics for a department which is being acclaimed as one of the best in the country.

It seems that Potsdam College has a strange mechanism of evaluating candidates for merit, promotion, teaching excellence and sabbatical leave. The mechanism demands such self-propaganda and self-glorification that many self-respecting teachers say, "heck with it, I can't be bothered with all that nonsense."

In any case, there is evidence to suggest that the math department, which has been receiving national and international attention for over a decade as being an exemplary one, and which has been singled out by the mathematics community of America as a successful program, has only attracted lip service from its own adminstration.

This kind of inadequate administrative support or unfair treatment threatens the good work done by the department. This has created some unhappiness among the veteran teachers and some fear among the new faculty. It is bound to reflect on their relationships with students and bound to tell upon the extra effort which had been instrumental in attracting students to major in mathematics. Also, it may stand in the way of recruiting and/or retaining the kind of teachers that the Potsdam math department likes to have. A case in point is the resignation of a younger member, who wrote in his letter of resignation, "I grew tired of insufficient reward and recognition for the Department's (unsurpassed) efforts at nurturing and maintaining a program offering true excellence in education in mathematics. Apparently, the State of New York is doing even worse than when I left at finding adequate resources to support quality education."

Rank	Department	Total Amount	Average size	Ratio
1.	Sociology	14,000	7	2,000
2.	Pol.Science	11,000	6	1,833
3.	Geology	9,000	5	1,800
4.	English	23,300	16	1,456
5.	Psychology	19,500	14	1,395
6.	Chemistry	10,500	8	1,312
7.	Art	9,500	8	1,187
8.	Economics	13,000	11	1,180
9.	Anthropology	7,500	7	1,071
10.	Foreign Languages	10,000	10	1,000
11.	Biology	9,500	10	950
12.	History	4,500	5	900
13.	Mathematics	12,000	15	800
14.	Physics	4,500	6	750
15.	Dance & Drama	3,500	5	700
16.	Computer Sc.	5,900	9	656
17.	Philosophy	3,000	5	600

Figure 12. Merit increments For years 1983 - 90 in the School of Liberal Studies ranked according to the ratio of total to size

It is indeed admirable that the Potsdam math teachers do the job they do inspite of administrative neglect, nonrecognition, nonsupport, etc., as true professionals. In this regard, the words of the same member of the department who resigned recently are very revealing, "I have the highest regard for my colleagues in the Department, and have enjoyed a professional relationship with the Department that would be difficult to duplicate at another institution. I have the highest regard as well for the students of the College, in particular those that choose to educate themselves in the Department."

Rumour that Potsdam College may be shut down. Add to this the recent rumour that the Potsdam College may be closed.

"Gov. Cuomo has proposed cutting funding to SUNY by three percent this year and 15 percent next year. That would result in the loss of $178 million in revenues for the SUNY system over the next two years.

SUNY Chancellor Bruce Johnstone has said there is a real possibility of massive layoffs, higher tuition, lower enrollments and even campus closings.

Mr. Johnstone has declined to release the names of the SUNY institutions on that list of campuses that could close their doors.

There is speculation — and that is all it is at this point — that Potsdam College could be on the short list of schools being considered for closure."

[The *Daily Courier-Observer,* Friday, December 13, 1991].

This widely circulated rumour is bound to cause decline in the enrollment of able and ambitious students, who were the bread and butter of the math program, at Potsdam College. Of course, the state of New York and therefore, the SUNY Potsdam is now going through serious financial difficulties. It has very seriously effected the math department. There has been a hiring freeze. So the math department had to take recourse to such stop gap arrangements like hiring retired professors, hiring instructors on very short term basis, etc.

Therefore, it is very likely that in the coming years, the world may see a decline in the number of math majors produced by SUNY Potsdam. Then it will be wrong to put a pointing finger to the department. The success of a department cannot be measured by the number of its graduates alone. As long as the math teachers of the SUNY Potsdam continue to do the job with the same spirit and dedication as they have been doing for more than two decades, the Potsdam math department will remain an example of math teaching at its best.

Chapter 9

MEETING A CHALLENGE OF NUMBERS

The authors of *A Challenge of Numbers* [16] have declared, after giving many facts and figures,

"• The workplace is changing as jobs require higher-level skills and greater adaptability. Mathematics-based jobs are leading the way in increased demand.

• If present patterns persist, most socioeconomic and demographic trends indicate that fewer students will study mathematics and choose mathematics-based careers.

These trends point to an increased demand for and a shrinking supply of mathematical scientists and other mathematically educated workers. The nation must recognize this critical condition, and understand the major challenge it poses for U.S. education in general and for college and university mathematical sciences in particular" [16, p. 73].

They also talk about issues that are raised by several questions, among which are the following:

• How can national needs for mathematically educated workers be met?
• What changes are necessary to attract more students to the study of mathematics?
• How can colleges and universities prepare graduates who are more valuable and effective in the nonacademic workplace?

From what we have described in the previous chapters, it is clear that the mathematics department of SUNY Potsdam has already met this challenge of numbers with considerable success. It has convincingly shown a way to meet this challenge. Therefore, the question may be posed how other colleges and universities can emulate Potsdam in establishing a successful mathematics program. Here are some thoughts on this question.

In our opinion the success of the Potsdam math program is very clear in three areas:

(1) In producing a large number of math majors,
(2) In making the program truly gender-independent, and
(3) In the quality of its math graduates. The math graduates of Potsdam go out with a sense of accomplishment, and they prove their accomplishment in later life by obtaining Ph.D. degrees in math, by becoming good math teachers, by proving their worth in the jobs they take, etc.

Therefore, by achieving a level of success as that of Potsdam, I shall refer to only three areas, namely, increasing the number of math majors, making the program gender-independent and improving the quality of math majors as reflected in their sense of accomplishments and actual accomplishments in later life.

Increasing the Number of Math Majors

Potsdam math majors may be divided into three types:

(1) the typical students, who are good in math and who are committed to study math,
(2) the brilliant math students who had taken calculus in high school and are happy to get into a more challenging math program, and
(3) students who were not originally thinking of majoring in math but were attracted to it after coming to Potsdam.

Almost all schools have their own share of students of type (1), so perhaps nothing much can be done to increase their number. However, other schools may perhaps do something to increase the number of students of type (2) and of type (3) by imitating SUNY Potsdam. As a matter of fact, it is desirable that the mathematics community follow the leadership of Potsdam in these directions.

First, since more and more high schools are nowadays teaching Calculus to meet the demands of brilliant math students, it is desirable to give these students the opportunity to get into a graduate math program early. The four year B.A./M.A. program does it very well and can surely be implemented by other schools. Such a program may actually boost the graduate program of a school by increasing the number of students in its graduate courses.

Secondly, more emphasis need to be placed on the liberal arts nature of mathematics. The mathematics community has, in general, been ignoring this aspect of mathematics. Most of the undergraduate and graduate programs in mathematics are geared towards producing math teachers, mathematicians and individuals for applied areas.

Potsdam has shown that a large number of students, who are just interested in getting a bachelor's degree in an area of liberal arts, may be attracted to do so in math. These students get worthwhile education by majoring in math and take pride in their accomplishments. Even in the job market, there are increasing demands for such graduates. This has been beautifully portrayed by Sue Bauer, a math graduate of Potsdam now working for Eastman Kodak, "The value of a liberal arts education right now is through the roof! You've been recognized as really hot stuff. And the reason is that businesses need to look for well-rounded individuals. I'm not talking about well-rounded as in how many societies and sports teams and clubs you're involved in. That's important, but more important today is that industry needs technical people who can understand the non-technical business needs, and who can speak a language other than their own particular technical jargon, who can relate to the other departments, because no technical department is an island. The technical departments are there to serve the line organizations, whatever they might be: if it's a manufacturing company, they're there to serve the manufacturing line; if it's an accounting or consulting firm, the technical research departments are there to serve the people going out and making money. You need to be able to talk to those people and find out what it is they need in terms of your support. Businesses are looking for people who can express themselves, verbally and in writing. You are getting practice in both in your mathematics program"[1].

This brings the difficult question, how the math department at SUNY Potsdam is able to attract liberal arts students to math. There are two things that seem to help. First, the efforts of the department to make the students aware of the professional opportunities in mathematics. Second, the emphasis the department puts on the liberal nature of mathematics and the way they teach the math courses that students take as freshmen. To achieve the first, the department publishes quite a few pamphlets.

Department Publications

The mathematics department at SUNY Potsdam maintains a good stock of pamphlets for the students to read. These are always available in the department and a student can take a copy of any of the pamphlets, free of charge. On occasions, like the freshmen orientation, these are given to the prospective students and some of them are also sent to selected high schools. These pamphlets are a big help to the students to plan their studies both before coming to the college and also, while pursuing their studies in the college. Some of the information is helpful even to students who are not majoring in math. The pamphlets are easy to read and easy to understand and they reflect the concern of the math department for the well-being of the students. These pamphlets are also instrumental in attracting students to study mathematics. It assures them that their math study is not going to be in vain. We give here a list of these pamphlets with a summary of its contents:

(1) *Advanced Placement Credit for High School Calculus Courses.* [This pamphlet gives the criteria by which the department grants advanced placement credit in calculus.]

(2) *Academic Advising for Mathematics Majors.* [This pamphlet contains two parts. The first part describes the math programs and lays out a year-to-year plan for courses to be taken by a math major. Part II describes the methods of teaching. This part has been reproduced in chapter 6 of this book.]

(3) *Why Mathematics ?* [This pamphlet describes, in a nutshell, various career options ope to a mathematics major. It not only gives an overview of the connections of mathematics with other disciplines but also states in very clear terms which course will be useful for which area of study or which profession. We are reproducing this booklet in Appendix 1.]

(4) *Why Graduate Mathematics ?* [This useful pamphlet gives an insight into the graduate programs in mathematics including a rating of graduate programs of the leading institutions in the country made by the American Council on Education. The second part tells how one should prepare for graduate schools during one's undergraduate years.]

(5) *Four-year Bachelor's-Master's Degrees Program in*

Mathematics. [This outlines the four-year two-degrees program of Potsdam College mathematics department. It is possible for a qualified student to complete in four years the requirements for both the B.A. and the M. A. degree in mathematics without overload or summer school attendance.]

(6) *Undergraduates in Graduate Mathematics ?* [This contains exact copies of letters from the chairpersons or faculty members of several institutions describing what they do about enrolling undergraduates in graduate courses. The main purpose of this pamphlet is perhaps to tell the students in the four year B.A./M.A. program that they are not alone and that they are a highly talented select group. It was also used to convince a skeptical college adminstration that the B.A./M.A. program is feasible.]

(7) *Why do Mathematics ?* [This is the invited address delivered by Dr. Kathryn Weld, now a math professor of Manhattan College, at the Fall Induction of the New York Phi Chapter of Pi Mu Epsilon on October 27, 1984. This inspiring story tells how and why Dr. Weld, who came to study English at Potsdam College, switched to math and how she has found happiness working with mathematics.]

(8) *Thoughts on the Real Value of a Mathematics Education* [This is the invited address delivered by Sue Bauer, a Systems Analyst at Eastman Kodak, at the Fall Induction of the New York Phi Chapter of Pi Mu Epsilon on November 14, 1988. This is a delightful account of how her math education at Potsdam has helped her in the business world. She also gives a very positive view of how math education can help one to cope with the real world.]

In these pamphlets, some very pertinent facts are presented in a very lucid and matter of fact manner. The style definitely reflects the stability of the department's programs and the department's desire to give the students a definite direction in life. They also contain a good share of assuring comments like, "We care about our students and encourage each to achieve to the maximum of his/her ability. Every effort will be made to advise students to elect the course in calculus which will be of greatest benefit to them. Students will be challenged but our goal is to help our students succeed."

Every student I met at Potsdam claimed to have read all these pamphlets and claimed to have benefitted by reading them. There is no doubt that these pamphlets have been instrumental in attracting some students to study mathematics. On principle, I think this kind of straight information is of immense value to the students to get a good perspective of their mathematics education. The Department's efforts in publishing these pamphlets are highly commendable.

A summary of the most important aspects of the pamphlet *Why Mathematics ?*   are displayed on the walls of the corridor of the math building. This summary shows how a mathematics major could prepare for careers or for graduate and professionsl studies in actuarial science, business adminstration, computer science, economics, medicine, operations research, statistics, and more. Copies of this pamphlet were mailed to all high schools in New York state. This is perhaps the reason why almost half of the mathematics majors in Potsdam are double majors.

Year	All Bach	Math Bach	Second Major	%	CIS	Educa	Econ	Psych	Phy	other
1978	890	58	34	59	11	17	1	0	3	2
1979	760	60	35	58	27	5	2	1	0	0
1980	655	73	49	67	20	14	3	1	10	1
1981	712	81	42	52	25	10	3	0	1	3
1982	780	69	36	52	24	6	4	0	1	1
1983	770	96	55	57	46	2	3	2	0	2
1984	738	124	50	40	33	4	2	1	4	6
1985	821	184	95	52	61	16	7	1	5	5
1986	845	213	112	53	64	31	5	1	4	7
1987	745	182	95	53	43	25	14	4	3	8
1988	658	131	69	53	27	31	4	2	4	1
1989	640	119	69	59	21	35	3		3	7
1990	585	83	36	44	13	13	6		3	1
1991	659	64	29	48	7	16	3	1		2

Figure 13. Distribution by second majors

The double majors represent almost all the major departments in the college. For example, some of the departments represented are anthropology, art, economics, English, French, history, music, philosophy, psychology, computer science and all other sciences (see Figure 13). Therefore, it is not surprising that mathematics majors of

Potsdam later earned Ph.D. degree in economics, statistics, computer science etc., or have earned graduate degrees in medicine, management, engineering, etc. It will perhaps be worthwhile to mention here few cases as to why liberal arts students chose to major in mathematics after coming to Potsdam and that I have come to know. (All the names, except that of Kathryn Weld, are fictitious.)

One who felt put down in another course. John came here to major in computer science. But in a computer course that John was taking, the teacher did not like John's way of asking questions in class. According to his classmates, John's questions usually were pertinent to what was being taught in class, but they were quite numerous. In any case, the computer science teacher started becoming annoyed with John's questions and started to put him down and finally threw him out of the course. In his math class, John also showed the same behavior of asking repeated questions. The math teacher never put John down and always led him through his questions to what was going on in class. So, John switched from computer science to math.

One for whom none but the math representative waited during freshmen orientation. Linda was originally thinking about majoring in psychology. During freshmen orientation Linda and her parents were a little late in coming. However, the math teacher taking part in freshmen orientation, waited patiently for Linda while the representatives of all other departments left. This had a profound influence on Linda's mind and she took a math course with the teacher. Linda became convinced that the math teachers really care for the students and that a math degree will be more meaningful to her. So instead of psychology, she decided to major in math.

One who could not afford to go to an expensive school. Joan was completely lost when she entered Potsdam College as a freshman. She was good in math and wanted to be an engineer. But she could not afford to go to a university with an engineering program. She wanted to get a degree that would help her to get a job. She tried computer science and others but they could not hold her interests. While taking the required math course, she was straightened out - math made more sense to her than any other course she was taking. So, she decided to major in math. After getting her B.A. in math, Joan again faced the same problem. She did not know what to do - more so because she could not get a job.

So she decided to become an electrical engineer. Again the confidence she gained in her math courses was sufficient to convince her that she could do it. Joan is finishing her electrical engineering degree at Clarkson this May. Even before she finished her finals, Joan has already three good jobs lined up. Does she feel bad that she wasted a few years majoring in math instead of going straight to electrical engineering? "No", not a bit because they helped her to become an electrial engineer.

One who was drawn by the unique combination of the ideas, the content, and the rigorous thought found in a freshmen Calculus course. Then we have the case of Kathryn Weld, who tells, "I came to Potsdam to study English and, in particular, the craft of writing. At that time, it was almost fashionable to have several changes in one's major field of study, and I was no exception. My disenchantment with English was the result of having taken several classes with teachers who might best be described as nonrigorous thinkers. I should say that I later heard reports of excellent teaching in the English Department, but by then my choice had been made. I turned to Philosophy. There I found that in modern philosophy, the emphasis seemed more on correct argument than on content. Since I was initially interested in Philosophy for the sake of ideas, and since the method of study did not seem to serve the subject matter, I began to look for something else.

At that time I was a junior, and taking a Calculus to satisfy my math and science requirements. To my surprise, I found myself drawn by the unique combination of the ideas on which the subject is based, that is to say, the content, and the rigorous thought which is the means by which the ideas came into flower"[36].

[Kathryn (Weld) Brown switched to math, graduated in 1977, and then completed her Ph. D. in mathematics from the City University of New York. At present, she teaches mathematics at Manhattan College. She was recently tenured and promoted to Associate professorship.]

Catalyst. Perhaps good reports about the mathematics program as given by present math majors and alumni to their parents, former teachers and friends do more to attract students to the program than anything else. In this context, here is an example as told by Steve: "A few years ago a young woman entered our college from a high school from which we did not usually recruit students. She stated that she had been admitted to MIT, but was not financially able to attend MIT. She was successful in some challenging mathematics courses during her freshmen year. She was one of the students who completed our Theory of Sets course as a freshman. The next year she met me on our campus and told me that she had brought 5 freshmen from her former high school to Potsdam State and all of them planned to major in mathematics" [32].

Making Mathematics Gender-Independent

During the last 23 years Potsdam has produced more female math graduates than male math graduates. This in itself is quite remarkable because very few schools, if any, can match this success. Everywhere we hear about math avoidance by females and math anxiety among females. Workshops and all kinds of programs have been run by other schools to encourage more females to math courses. It seems that Potsdam College has outdone everybody else without making any effort to attract female students. I think the reasons for this success are:

(1) Potsdam does not administer placement tests and does not emphasize SAT scores, both of which are now known to be discriminatory against women.

(2) The math teachers at Potsdam genuinely try to recognize and to nurture the intellectual potential of every student. Their belief that everyone can do mathematics is especially assuring to females and other minority students.

(3) The way math teachers try to teach by building students' self-esteem leaves no room for math anxiety. For it is known that the key to alleviating math anxiety is to let the person gain confidence and self-esteem [4].

(4) Potsdam mathematics curriculum has stayed away from the high tech approach of using sophisticated calculators or computers. In this connection, it will be worthwhile to describe an incidence as told by its present chairman, Vasily Cateforis, "I received a call from a transfer student, entering in the fall of 1992 and transferring to Potsdam from a

community college. She wanted to know whether our program requires the use of sophisticated calculators because she was about to invest in an expensive one at her community college and if we did not use such calculators, then she would rather not spend the money. She had asked Patty (the math department secretary) all this and Patty, had on my instruction, assured the student that no such calculators were in use by us. Well the student was skeptical, and politely asked to talk to me. I assured her of the correctness of Patty's information. Several days later, on a request by the admisssions office, I called an incoming student who had a question about our program. It turned out it was the same young lady. She said, 'You have already answered my questions. But since you called me, I must tell you that my teachers here at the community college are questioning whether I am transferring to a mathematics program which is as advanced as the one we are having here at my community college.' I assured her that all was fine and sent her literature on us."

Producing Accomplished Math Graduates

After spending a year at Potsdam, after talking to numerous students and math graduates, and after observing the math teachers, I have come to the conclusion that three aspects of the Potsdam experience have contributed immensely in producing accomplished math graduates, who believe in their own accomplisments. Fortunately, these three aspects may easily be duplicated elsewhere. First, the emphasis on treating the students with love and respect have paid large dividends. Second, the emphasis on making the students independent by making them able to read and understand mathematical texts seems to have done wonders for the students. Third, the use of the course Set Theory and Logic as a bridge to get over to new areas of interest has also proved very fruitful.

Treating students with love and respect. As mentioned before, at SUNY Potsdam math department, the emphasis on treating the students with love and respect is not merely a lip service, but a very commendable way of communicating with students. Of course, that one should treat the students with love and respect has been known to mankind since the days of Aristotle and Plato but how it has to be put to practice has not been documented very well. The Potsdam math gurus have demonstrated it in many different ways. From providing comfortable chairs for waiting students to honorable mentions in newsletter, the love and respect that the math department shows to its students manifests itself in every possible way. Let me mention some of these manifestations that I have direct knowledge of.

Student after student have told me how they feel so comfortable in their math classes because the teacher never puts them down. The teachers and the Department take the utmost care to see that the class time of a math class is no way interrupted or wasted for unnecessary reasons. They regard this as a show of disrespect to the students. Every teacher takes a personal interest in every student and makes genuine efforts to know them by name.

Even the math department secretary and her helpers go out of their ways to be polite and helpful to the students. [I am told that this is a tradition by Joyce Flint, whom everybody praises as being very instrumental in creating the healthy environment in those glorious years when Steve was pushing hard to put the program on top.]

The emphasis on making the students independent. At SUNY Potsdam, the emphasis is on making the student able to read and understand a math book. Time and again, past students have praised this approach. This has been eloquently described by Sue Bauer, "one of the things I like best about the philosophy of the mathematics program at Potsdam is that the faculty believe that you should be able to read a math book. And they not only believe it is possible, they are able to teach students to do it. This appealed to me on a kind of a base level when I was here because I liked the idea that I was getting more out of my $20 or $30 investment in a book than a few homework problems and a sore arm from carrying it around. . . Potsdam's mathematics program, with the way courses are taught, the way assignments are given, and with the math lab and the tutoring that's done, is a program that fosters a lot of self-motivation and independence in the student. Assignments are given in some of the upper level courses, either in teams or individually, with instructions: 'Here it is, and here are the resources. Go away, figure it out, and come back and present it to us all.' And that is done in gradual steps through the upper division courses. It goes a long way in fostering self-confidence in the students to be independent, and gain the ability to go out and get things done on your own. Those are key elements to success and promotion in any field. Independence is right up there next to resourcefulness, I might add, part of which is being able to look things up. Those dimensions are key elements on which performance is rated at Kodak, and I would venture, at every other company"[1].

The use of the course Set Theory and Logic. The central driving force in the Potsdam teaching is the idea that mathematics is the art of discovering and proving theorems. Therefore, math majors are required to take a course on Set Theory and Logic. Usually, math students take the course on Set Theory and Logic in their sophomore year. One good thing about this course is that it requires no background material. Therefore, the course can be introduced with a very fresh view of mathematics — and this is exactly what is done in Potsdam. They use this course to help the students acquire facilities in understanding and using the language of mathematics, and help them to get a good grip in the logic of proofs. In addition, through the formalities of Cantor's theory of Infinite sets, the students are led to the wonderful and rich world of creating, formalizing and applying concepts. This course enables the students to encounter, at an early stage, the mathematical way of searching for a way to describe an intuitive concept like infinity. The way this course has inspired many students at Potsdam to find new directions of studies speak well about the usefulness of such a course in a math program.

One important thing to bear in mind, and Steve reiterates it again and again, is the fact that there have been many reports, many committees and many scholars who have been producing many theories on how to improve teaching mathematics and on how to attract more students to the study of mathematics. But what has happened at Potsdam is no theory, but a true story of success. Therefore, there is no point theorizing whether this would work or not. That this approach would work has been demonstrated by Potsdam for over two decades. Therefore, what one should try to do is to find the essence of the Potsdam example and try to adopt it as best as one can. We have, therefore, tried to capture the esence of the Potsdam example without making theories and hypotheses. It is up to the math teachers, math departments of different colleges and universities to figure out ways how they may benefit from this example. For the benefit of math teachers, we are giving below an overview of the documented accounts of how others have benefited from the Potsdam experience.

Recommendations to Emulate the Potsdam Experience

The most elaborate plans to emulate the Potsdam success has of course been made by the ETM group (for Experiment in Teaching Mathematics) of York University of Canada under the leadership of Pat Rogers. Supported by grants from the Social Sciences and Humanities Research Council of Canada, the ETM group adapted and applied some of the methods that have made Potsdam program renowned as one of the top undergraduate program in the country. The ETM published newsletters, organized social activities bringing the students and faculty together in informal setting, initiated awards for outstanding math students, provided peer teaching, arranged invited talks etc., as detailed in the York University mathematics department report entitled *Experiment in Teaching Mathematics, 1988-90.* However, the report does not indicate what effects the ETM groups efforts had on the math program at York. For example, it does not indicate if their efforts resulted in more math majors.

Gould [10] believes that there are certain principles employed by the department which contribute to its outstanding program. These principles are: student-oriented teaching, high goals, group-oriented guided problem sessions and self-confidence building. According to him, "These are not novel ideas peculiar to SUNYP. Portions evidently go back in some form to the one-room school-house of Colonial times". . . However, the novel feature for the SUNYP math department appears to be its outstanding success through a dedicated application of such principles, as shown also in articles by Poland (1987) and by Rogers." So, Professor Gould also decided to apply those principles to a calculus-based second-semester introductory physics class. This is how he describes his experiences,

> "I hesitated to begin the semester in this way because of my fear that I would not be in control of the class as much as when I was engaged only in lecturing. Anyway, after a few weeks I began the "experiment" by explaining to the students that I would no longer just lecture because I believed they should take more responsibility for their own progress; that they should therefore be sure to read the book and attempt the homework problems; that they will be working problems with each other as an integral part of the class period; and that attendance is mandatory.

As a result, I found that I was even in more control of the class. I had contact with students that I never experienced by just lecturing. I could gently probe to test their understanding, urge them on with compliments for any progress they made, and felt more confident about their grasp of the physics principles.

The students in turn seemed less reticent to express their views in class. Through working in groups there was a spirit of cooperation and a desire to help each other in overcoming some of the hurdles in problem solving."

The secret of Potsdam's success is not in reforming curriculum or in concerted efforts to increase the number of math majors but in the environment it has created and what the teachers do with the students in and outside the classroom. For example, as Lynn Cominsky narrates, the Sonoma State University Physics and Astronomy Department has been doing many things like newsletter for majors, lots of publicity for accomplishment, and tracking of alumni etc., yet 'how to attract more majors' is a topic raised often in their department meetings. Lynn Cominsky finally decided to use Dr. Stephens' advice in her calculus-based physics course and this is what happened,

"During the next class, I divided the students into groups of three and gave each group a different question to work on from an old exam. These questions were very difficult, and I did not expect the students in this class to be able to solve them if they worked individually on the problems. Much to my delight, they were very excited by the opportnity to work harder problems, and to see what kind of material they were expected to master for their next exam in two weeks. They were so enthusiastic about this change in style and the chance to practice what I was preaching that I continued to run this way until the exam. The improvement in the understanding and attitude of the students was much more than I had expected. The subsequent improved performance of this group of students on the next exam (which I made harder than the problems they had practiced) convince me that Dr. Stephens is correct"[2].

In my opinion the single most important factor responsible for the success of Potsdam is that it has succeeded in creating a humanistic environment for learning math. Therefore, if anybody else wishes to duplicate Potsdam's success, the institution will have to strengthen all the ingredients of humanistic environment that have been defined and refined by the Potsdam math department and that we have outlined in Chapter 2. This can be done, not easily, but with some sincere efforts. If the chairman of a math department is able to give the leadership in collecting a good band of dedicated teachers or is able to make the members of his department work with the same spirit and dedication as the math teachers of Potsdam, then success is bound to come. Of course, the math teachers must make sincere efforts to imbibe the spirit and the dedication of the teachers at Potsdam. Such an effort by the department needs a great deal of support from the adminstration. The adminstration and the department will have to be aware of the reasons which are now causing harm to the Potsdam program and will have to find ways to negate such adverse effects.

I have made several recommendations to the math department of the University of Rhode Island to bring it closer to the Potsdam model. With the belief that most of these recommendations are valid for many other colleges and universities in the country, I am listing the recommendations here.

1. Introduce a four year B.A./M.A. program like that of Potsdam to encourage the excellent students to get into graduate studies early.
2. Introduce a course on Set Theory and Logic that will be required of every math major.
3. Prepare a booklet describing every math course offered by the department for the benefit of the students, the advisers and the members of other departments. This should contain a brief description of the goal of each course, the importance of the course and the areas where the knowledge of the course may be useful.
4. Try to assign all the freshmen and sophmore level courses in the same building. [The math department at this university had one of the nicest math buildings in the country with several beautiful well-lit classrooms, wrap-around blackboards and well-located windows. But all these lecture rooms, save one, are now used either as computer labs or math offices. So, now math classes are held all over the campus. This situation hampers the interaction between math teachers and students and interaction among students and makes it difficult to create a

humanistic environment.]

5. Replace the placement exam by a diagnostic test, which will be taken by all students registered in freshmen level math courses, on the first day of class or earlier. The test will consist of two parts. Part 1 will be on essential mathematics and part 2 will be on algebra. To be eligible to take precalculus, a student must pass both part 1 and part 2. To be eligible to take take freshmen level math courses for liberal arts students, a student must pass part 1. For the students in a freshmen level calculus course, the diagonistic test will be on precalculus material (like the final examination of a precalculus course.)

The diagnostic test will be traditional and will be corrected by the instructor in whose section the student is enrolled. The instructor will tell the student whether his or her background is satisfactory or what area he or she is deficient. The instructor will take the responsibility, if the student so desires, of helping the student learn the material that the student is deficient in. The instructor, in consultation with the student, will make the final decision whether to let the student continue in the course or to send the student to take a remedial course.

The department shall publish an announcement giving the reasons for the diagnostic test, the topics to be tested on, and a set of sample problems.

Unfortunaetly, our department did not like the above recommendation and instead it accepted the following:

(Alternative Proposal) The placement exam will be multiple choice and computer graded, but the students will be given answer books, where they will show their work. The placement exam will consist of two parts. Part 1 will be on essential mathematics and part 2 will be on algebra. To be eligible to take precalculus, a student must pass both part 1 and part 2. To be eligible to take take freshmen level math courses for liberal arts students, a student must pass part 1. For the students in a freshmen level calculus course, the placement exam will be like the final examination of a precalculus course.)

If a student fails to qualify to stay in a course and petitions to stay in the course, his or her instructor will look at his or her answer book and decide whether to approve or not to approve the petition.

6. The department should request that the requirement that every student must take a three-credit math course be dropped. Instead the department should offer two or three courses for liberal arts students. These courses should be designed by asking various other departments as to what kind of math skills may benefit their students. The content, philosophy and usefulness of these courses must be printed in the department booklet, suggested in 2. The advisers and members of other departments should advise the respective majors why they should take a math course, and guide them as to which math course they should take. Let the importance of math be emphasized by the department in which the student is majoring. The math department should point out through its publications what it offers and how each course may help the student - a publication like *Why Mathematics ?* (see Appendix 1) of Potsdam College is strongly recommended.

7. The math department should make course assignments for the permanent members well ahead of time (at least a year ahead). Also, course assignments should be made so that every teacher teaching the remedial courses or the calculus sequence teaches the follow-up course in the succeeding semester.

8. The department should organize workshops and seminars to make the teachers and the graduate students aware of innovative teaching methods like that initiated by Clarence F. Stephens.

Rationale For My Recommendations: The rationale for recommendations 1 - 4 have been mentioned in earlier chapters. The rationale for recommendation 5 is because the math department of the University of Rhode Island gives a compulsory placement exam to every incoming freshman. The placement exam is a standardized multiple choice test. On the basis of the students' answers, the computer assigns a number 0, 1, 2, 3 or 4 to the students. A score of 4 allows the student to take calculus, a score of 3 allows a student to take precalculus, a score of 2 allows the student to take a freshmen level math course for liberal arts student or to take a non-credit remedial course on algebra and trig, and a score of 1 or 0 sends the student to a non-credit course on remedial math.

This kind of placement exam may be very scientific, but it creates so much hostility that it becomes very difficult to teach math to these students. I have direct knowledge of this because I have been in charge of the remedial math courses for the last five years and I have also been involved in considering the petitions of the students to override the placement exam score. There are many reasons why this kind of placement exam is very unfair to the students. But my main objections to the placement exam are the following:

(1) The scores do not correlate with the students abilities and do not indicate to the student what area the student is deficient in.

(2) It allows the department or the teacher to throw some students out of a course that the students want to take and send them down to a lower-level or non-credit course, but it does not allow the teacher to take the responsibilty of teaching the students. As a matter of fact, hardly any teacher in the department is given the responsibility to teach these students. Usually, one teacher and some graduate teaching assistants are assigned to teach the remedial courses, where the enrollment is often more than a hundred. Usually, the department assigns graduate assistants, who it feels cannot teach a regular class, to the remedial courses. Often the graduate students assigned to teach remedial courses are foreign students, who have just landed in the country.

(3) The placement exam creates fear among the students and so destroys the self-respect of some that they start experiencing math anxiety. Several times, I have met students in the algebra and trig lab, who have already had precalculus in high school and who seem to be competent. If I discover them in the beginning of the semester, I try to send them back to a precalculus class, but they get so afraid of precalculus that they are reluctant to do so.

The rationale for recommendation 6 is that it is not a very good idea to force every student to take a math course on the pretext of making them acquire "quantitative thinking skills". This again creates hostility and fear among some students and which rub onto others. The Potsdam scenario is a good example. Potsdam math department was able to attract a large percentage (often as high as 64%) of its freshmen students to take calculus when such a requirement was not there. However, in recent years after the college imposed a requirement that every freshman take two quantitative courses during his/her first year: a statistical analysis course (essentially a discrete statistics course) and a problem solving/abstract reasoning course (which for most students meant a mathematics course). This was done in spite of strong opposition by the math department. As a result, its enrollment in calculus and the number of math majors have been decreasing ever since this requirement was imposed (this has been discussed in Chapter 8 on Present Realities).

It is true that many incoming students nowadays may not have sufficient or minimal math skills. But by imposing the math requirement to force these students to take a math course, we are actually hurting a large majority of students, who already have these skills and who could profit more by taking a math course that enhances their analytical and quantitative skills or by taking a more profitable course in another discipline. So what I am suggesting is education instead of compulsory requirement. Students should be educated to take math - a compulsory requirement is not the way to do it. Such a requirement usually makes everybody look for a math course that would be easy. It does not help them to acquire any significant math skills.

Rationale for recommendation 8, the most important factor of a humanistic environment for learning math, is perhaps the teachers. To be successful like Potsdam, math teachers will have to acquire the attitude, the spirit and a sense of commitment shown by the Potsdam teachers. Teachers must be able to demonstrate love for mathematics, respect for the students and the sense of joy in acquiring the mathematical way of thinking the way math teachers at Potsdam do. As suggested by Poland [22], if the majority of mathematicians do not wish to devote their efforts to such a program, then a group of caring teachers could form an effective relay team across the core mathematics courses in the early years. Even if a group is not easily formed, willing teachers may do a lot individually. For this we need to make the teachers aware of what is being done in Potsdam so that there may be open discussions about how one can benefit from the Potsdam experience. This can be achieved through workshops, seminars and lectures on about the Potsdam model. We will discuss this in the next chapter through my classroom experiments and the details of a workshop presented at the University of North Carolina, Chapel Hill.

Chapter 10

TEACHING MATHEMATICS
THE POTSDAM WAY

During my stay at Potsdam, one evening I went to my office to pick up something. I was really surprised to see Professor S, who had his office right across from mine, pasting cards from a deck onto a big piece of cardboard. When I asked what he was doing, he answered, "Dilip, you are not going to believe this. I am teaching this course on elementary statistics and I have been doing all these problems about drawing cards. But, it never dawned on me that some of them might not have ever seen or played with a deck of cards. I would have never thought of it. Today, one student very honestly told me in class that she was having trouble because she did not know what was in a deck of cards. So, I just asked if there were others who had not seen or played with a deck of cards, and you would not believe there were quite a few raised hands. I felt bad because how can they do card problems when they don't know what the cards are? So, I just bought a deck of cards and I am pasting them to this board. I am going to take it with me to class every day for the students to see. Do you think it is a good idea?" I was very much moved by Professor S taking so much trouble to familiarize the students with a deck of cards. But I realized the importance of not taking anything for granted and of acquainting the students with the deck of cards. I also felt guilty because I have been teaching a similar course (finite mathematics) at the University of Rhode Island almost every year for the last 25 years and have never ever asked the students if they knew a deck of cards. So I made up my mind that the next time I teach a course in finite mathematics, I would surely do something like what Proffessor S was doing.

Luckily I did not have to wait long because soon after my return to Rhode Island, I had to teach finite mathematics during the summer of '92. This was a very small calss of only 9 students so it was easy to create a friendly and humanistic environment in the class. So I started experimenting.

Experiments with the Postdam Style of Teaching

Remembering Professor S and the cards, I asked the class if everybody knew what was a deck of cards and what was a die. True enough, there were some who had not and some who said things like "I have seen a pack or what you say a deck, you see, I never knew it, I don't exactly know what the different cards are, I have never rolled one". So, I made it a point of carrying a couple of decks of cards and a few dice of different sizes and colors with me. Every time I discussed a card problem, I would pass the cards and let them figure out what was being done in the problem. Similarly , I used the dice to actually demonstrate the problem. I could not believe how easily the students were able to understand and do those problems.

Also, in reply to my question of what they expected to learn in that course, one of the students had said that she read the newspaper daily but she could not understand all those graphs and charts so she would like to learn about them. Another student told me that she would like to know more about the polls that were on the headlines almost every day (this was because of presidential election). Taking a cue from those comments, to make the students participate in the class, I turned the course around - instead of starting with set language or permutation and combination, I started the course with topics like mean, mean deviations, making histograms and pie charts etc. of descriptive statistics [5]. I also passed out questionaires which they later had to prepare class stastistics about heights, weights, age, SAT scores, liking for math, math fears, grade point average, weekly expenses, etc. Also, after every test, I would read out the scores of the students and ask them to figure out the mean, the mean deviation and decide how they were doing.

Even with these statistics, they were asked to probe such questions as: does the SAT discriminate against females, are women more afraid of math than men, what should be a reasonable normal weekly expense of a student, etc.

The results were immediate - students were involved in the course from day 1. Since this was a small class, I introduced everybody in the class to one another and let them get to know each other — and told them that I would like them to help one another even in doing homework. But I told them that nobody should allow others to copy homework, but instead teach what is involved and how to do them.

Also, the random selection process was introduced soon after they were acquainted with probability. After that I made it a rule that I would randomly select someone to do randomly selected problems from homework on the board. I would write each of the homework problems on a separate sheet of paper, fold them, put them in my hat and pass the hat around for the students to pick one each - with the rule that nobody could look at what he or she got untill everyone finished picking one. - This became almost a regular fun routine in class.

Almost all the students in that class told me that they learned a lot in that course and that they never thought math could be so interesting. One student told me that she had been avoiding math all her college life but she felt so good about math after taking that course that she wanted to take another math course. When I told her that I was teaching precalculus in the fall, she enrolled in that course. In any case, I saw the benefits of creating a humanistic environment in the classroom.

The other course that I was teaching that summer was an introductory course on differential equations. In the course, I decided to experiment with making the students independent learners. I was using the text written by my colleagues Finizio and Ladas [8]. The text proved ideal for the purpose because in every section it had many applications of differential equations to different areas. I decided not to teach any of those applications but to assign them as independent study. I made a list of selected topics from those applications with one or two corresponding exercises and assigned one each to the students to be presented in class. Every day I set aside the last twenty minutes for those presentations. Usually three or four were able to finish the presentations every day. I was available to help them prepare for the presentations. If they came for help, they were well prepared and knew exactly what they did not understand. In all, every student in the class made three presentations during the semester and they were given homework points on the basis of the presentations. To make sure everybody learned the material in the presentations, I asked every students to select five of each set of presentations and submit them as homework. The other thing I did was to make them find their mistakes in the hour tests and to give the corrected answer for credit. For the first test, I gave them 50% of the points they lost, after the second test the corrections were worth 40% of the points lost, and after the third test it was 25% of the points lost. Towards the end of the course, most of the students really became very capable of reading and learning differential equations on their own and I was able to cover more material than usually accomplished in the course. Not a single student failed the course and several did extremely well.

Bouyed by the success in the summer courses, I decided to teach all my courses in the fall in what I call "the Potsdam way". Creating a humanistic environment in the classroom, adopting a participatory style of teaching, forming study groups, trying to help students become independent learners and alwaays treating students with kindness are the essential elements of teaching mathematics the Potsdam way.

In a precalculus course that I taught in the Fall of '92, this is how I implemented the Potsdam way of teaching.

On the first day of class, I found that the students had a very hostile attitude towards learning math. Most of the hostility was because of the placement exam; some of them were mad because they had failed the course earlier. To diffuse the hostility that they might have had thinking that they were wrongfully placed in that course, I told them that the placement exam was not fair and asked if anybody felt he or she could go into calculus, and that I would help. Three students responded "yes". I set up appointments for them with me (two of these students were allowed to go into calculus).

I identified my goal with theirs by saying that my goal was to get them ready for calculus and that they would all receive a grade better than they expected. I told them about me, my background, my year at Potsdam and the Potsdam mathematics program.

I asked the students to fill in cards giving me the necessary information. I told them about the goals of the course and gave them an idea about the content of the course. I listed some of the background material that they were expected to be proficient in. Then I asked them to tell me which of those topics they had difficulties with; we discussed those topics in a conversational style in the first two classes.

I made a class directory and formed six study groups of four each. How these groups were formed and other things that I did in that course, I will put on hold for the moment. The success of the students were beyond my expectations. Since this was a coordinated course and there were thirteen other sections of the course taught by others, all the hour tests and the final were departmental. In the first test my section did as poorly as other sections but by the end my section did better than other sections. Out of 24 students, 4 students failed and almost everybody got a grade better than he or she had expected. Three of the four students who failed did not cooperate at all, and in spite of my best efforts, I could not make them come to class regularly, do homework or come to the study groups. The other student who failed participated in everything but always remained very passive. It seemed that she believed that by being there she would somehow or other pass the course. She had no motivation to learn. To my utter surprise, I found that she did not even need to take precalculus, and she expected to get a grade of D or F. Unfortunately, I found these things towards the end of the semester when I could not do much. On the last day of class, I asked them to give me their addresses if they wanted me to mail out the grades. When I mailed out the grades, I wrote a few appropriate lines commenting on their performance and offering them my help in future math courses that they might be taking. Below are few samples of my letters.

(1) Congratulations! Your score in the final exam:170/200

Final course grade: A-

How could you think that you were a 'C' student? - I hope it is your modesty and not a low opinion about your abilities. You were a wonderful student. Your systematic approach to the subject, your sincere efforts and your positive attitude to math were all very exemplary. In the future, I hope to point to you as a role model. So, keep up the good work and if you have any difficulty with any math course, please do come and see me.

(2) Congratulations! Your score in the final exam: 150/200

Final course grade: C₊

I am very pleased with the improvement you made in learning to understand Math during the last semester. So, keep up the good work and if you have any difficulty with any math course, please do come and see me.

I wish you a very Merry Christmas and a Happy New Year.

Good luck with QBA 102 or MTH 131.

(3) Congratulations! Your score in the final exam: 150/200

Final course grade: B-

I thought you would do better. In any case, you should not be disappointed. Just try to be little more careful and more thorough with the material in your next math course.

It was a pleasure having you in class and in the study groups. So, keep up the good work and if you have any difficulty with any math course, please do come and see me.

All these helped to create a very humanistic environment and most of them stopped by the following semester to thank me. In addition, there was a student from another section, who often sat on the table, which was on a common area, when some of the groups were meeting. She was attracted by the Potsdam way of teaching and asked me what I was teaching the following semester. Since I was teaching an introductory course on linear algebra, I told her even though students just finishing precalculus were not usually allowed to take linear algebra, I would let her in if she was prepared to do some studying on her own. She agreed and she became one of the top students in my linear algebra class.

After these experiences, I became convinced that even individual teachers can really improve their teaching effectiveness by adopting the Potsdam style, and that there is more to the guiding principles of Clarence Stephens than meets the eye. Therefore, in the following semester, I organized a workshop for the precalculus teachers. Later in the same semester, I was invited by the Center for Teaching and Learning at the University of North Carolina, Chapel Hill to present a workshop on the Potsdam way of teaching math. So instead of saying more let me give the ideas that I presented at a day long workshop at Chapel Hill.

A workshop on Teaching Mathematics The Potsdam Way

[What follows is an account of the workshop on innovative approaches to teaching college mathematics sponsored by the Center for Teaching & Learning and Math Department, University of North Carolina, Chapel Hill, and a summary of the presentation the author made at the workshop. The workshop held on Saturday, February 13, 1993 from 10:00 am - 3:00 pm, was divided into four sessions.]

Workshop Schedule

Session I. Workshop Goals & Classroom Realities
10:00 - 10:50
> Review of goals for Math 10, 16 & 31
> Discussion of classroom realities at UNC
> New ideas from the math program at SUNY Potsdam

Session II. Classroom Strategies
11:00 - 11:50
> Creating a humanistic environment in the classroom
> Getting students to participate actively in the learning process
> Organizing study groups
> Helping students become independent learners

12:00 - 12:50   Buffet Lunch

Session III. Creative Teaching
1:00 - 1:50
> Making lesson plans
> Preparing interesting reading materials
> Teaching students to find answers to their questioions

Session IV. Student Perspectives
2:00 - 2:50
> Math Anxiety: how to help students overcome it
> Marginalized groups: misconceptions and suggestions
> Summary: putting ideas into practice

Classroom Realities at University of North Carolina

Concerns of the TAs (as indicated in writing by the TAs present):

1. Getting the attention and interest of those one or two students who don't seem to be/want to be involved.
2. When teaching precalculus keeping students from having that remedial feeling.
3. I had many students last semester, when I taught Math 10, who obviously believed they would never use what they were learning. How do you convince them otherwise?
4. Some of the students have not had math in several years, and in some cases, 15 - 20 years have gone by since their last math class. These students seem convinced that they are incapable of really "getting math", they are just trying to get through the class to fulfill a requirement, just hoping to pass. How do you combat this kind of mentality? What do you say to make them believe that they can do it?
5. Some students in my class often asked very simple questions and wasted lots of class time.
6. Students do not have the habit of reading the textbook.
7. My math class is so large that I find it difficult to feel connected to them during class.
8. The biggest problem seems to be motivating any sort of justification for mathematical ideas. Anything that even begin to look like a proof immediately terrifies the students.
9. Students are generally more concerened with preparing specifically for a test or exam, rather than just keeping up and doing their homework and assignments.
10. I am sometimes surprised at how basic knowledge is missing (e.g. 1 minute = 60 seconds), and I don't expect it and therefore don't mention it in class.
11. The class seems to be divided into a group which is improving, and one that is falling behind more and more.
12. Many of the students seem to prefer memorizing formulas to reasoning through problems.
13. The poor students are unwilling to ask for help.
14. Many students are not interested in math. How can I get them interested?

15. How many homework problems should I give?
16. A lot of students seemed to be afraid - they have had too many bad experiences in the past.
17. I never knew what to do with students who really don't want to be there.
18. Some students seem to understand and do not ask questions. But in the test, I see they don't understand at all.
19. Few students come to my office hours. I guess some students do not make an effort, skip classes, but show up in quizzes and exams.
21. Lack of dedication. Students don't do the homework unless it's collected.
22. Lack of respect for other students. For example, homework solutions that are posted outside of my office are often taken.
23. Problems in grading and organizing group projects.
24. Difficulty in getting students to volunteer answers without being asked.

Concerns of the Department and the Center of Teaching and Learning

1. TAs should improve their ability to discuss and explain mathematics in a more "conversational" style.
2. A frequent comment right now is: "The TA talks and talks, and I have to ask my roommate the same question."
3. TAs should learn strategies of raising student awareness of the difficulty of the course and the need to work and ask questions. That is, TAs need to be able to point to some form of study method and learn how to get students to study more effectively.
4. TAs should develop some skills at group problem solving or other interactive methods.
5. TAs should improve their ability to work problems in front of the class. They should be comfortable using specific example and they should know when to be specific and when to use abstract proofs.
6. TAs should gain some insight into how they can more effectively interact with students so that classroom communication is more of a two-way process.

7. TAs should learn the importance of reviewing previous material and fitting all material into context.

8. TAs should gain some insight into the "chilly climate" for women and minorities in math. This would include examining their own preconceptions and how they affect classroom behavior and getting the perspectives of some undergraduates.

In my presentations, I shall try to address the above concerns by telling you the way math teachers at Potsdam teach mathematics. Of course, these are my observations. They are based on my year-long study of the Potsdam model during the academic year 1991 - 92. It is my sincere belief that every teacher in Potsdam consciously or just naturally follows some guiding principles that Professor Clarence F. Stephens has been propagating during his long career as a math teacher. Since these principles form the very core of the approach I will take let me list them here.

Guiding Principles of Stephens

Definition of a GOOD MATHEMATICS TEACHER (accepted by Clarence Stephens):

"A good mathematics teacher is one who uses his knowledge of math as well as his love and respect for his pupils to lead them to an enjoyment of the study of mathematics."
[John Egsgard, Former President of National Council of Teachers of Mathematics]

A. Create a humanistic environment in and around the classroom. "Know your students well - their names, what they know, their hopes and fears." Tell them about yourself so that the relation becomes more intimate. Develop love for math and genuine affection for the students. Assure the students that you love and care about them. | BE KIND |

Believe in your students - everyone can do mathematics. You cannot push the students from only the bottom; you must also raise them up from above.

You can best achieve your goal as a teacher by helping the students to learn to think for themselves, to read mathematical literature independently with understanding and enjoyment, and to become free from the need of a teacher.

B. Protect and strengthen the self-esteem of every student. Find the area that the students are having trouble with and discuss them thoroughly. "Build students' confidence by giving them problems they can do."

C. AIM HIGH "Set high standards of achievement for your students. The standard should be as high as you can inspire and help your students to be successful in achieving."

Caution: "High standards do not mean having unrealistic expectations so students feel that they have failed." So, be more concerned about promoting a favorable environment in which students can learn than about protecting academic standards.

D. Make it your primary goal to make the students INDEPENDENT LEARNERS. Adopt a participatory style of teaching so that you are not the only one to talk. Plan strategies to make the students take active part in class.

E. Be creative in teaching. You can use your creativity in preparing lesson plans, in writing reading materials, in creating role models, etc. "It is not the responsibility of the students to learn in the style that the professor wishes to teach; it is the teacher's responsibility to teach the students in the style in which they can learn." GO FAST SLOWLY

F. Teach the basic concepts well. If a student learns the basic concepts of the course well and learns to work independently, the student can learn additional subject matter rapidly.

Give only a reasonable amount of homework. Write tests carefully - know what your average student can do; and what your best student can do. Give a balanced test."

G. Provide easily accessible and available support system.

DO NOT PUNISH anybody for anything but REWARD good effort and good work.

H. Form relay teams to teach the calculus sequence.

I. Make the students feel that they are part of a big family.

How to create a humanistic environment in classroom

By humanistic environment in the classroom, I mean a pleasant environment for the students where they are comfortable, where they have a teacher who cares about them, where they have friends, where they are loved and respected. To create such an environment one may try to do the following:

1. Diffuse the hostility that students have towards learning math because of the placement exam or because of past experiences, weight and price of texts, etc.

2. See that the students know their teacher well. So you must tell them about yourself - not just your name and office hours, but also other information that will help the students to know you as a person. Do not hesitate to tell them about your hobbies, about your educational background or about a problem you may have - like back ache, allergies from chalk dust, etc. Tell them why you love math and why you enjoy teaching.

3. You must know the students and the students should know one another. Prepare a class directory by asking them to fill up cards. Hand in blank cards and ask every student to give you the following information:
Name; campus address; phone number; math courses he or she has completed, dropped or failed; math course he or she would like to take after completing this course; proposed major; what areas in math are difficult for him or her; something about himself or herself.

4. In very simple and clear terms set some goals for yourself and the students. For example, you may say, "My goal is to help you learn the material of this course well and enjoy doing so. My goal is to see that after completing this course you will be able to think better, understand math better and love math more." Identifying your goals with theirs is very encouraging. For example, you may say that if each one of them gets a grade better than he or she expects, you will also feel rewarded. You should ask the students to set goals, but tell them that they should not think of just a good grade in this course but they should try to find how it can stimulate them to think

better, learn better, and help them build a better future for them and others.

5. FACE THE REALITY — these are the students you have. Don't waste your time thinking about or talking about the kind of students you wish you had. Try to find the strengths and weaknesses of your students. Ask them what they find difficult or the kind of math they might have had trouble with in the past [This is somthing you can ask them the first day, and in a casual manner discuss some of these trouble spots like polynomial divison, factoring, solving quadratic, etc. Students will never forgive you if you anyway imply that they are not the kind of students you expected or that they should have been better prepared.]

6. DO NOT PUT ANY STUDENT DOWN. Even if sombody asks a very simple or elementary question, do not in anyway imply that it was a dumb question or that the answer is easy. Remember your duty is to TEACH and not to pronounce judgements.

7. Love and respect the students with all your sincerity.

8. It is very important that you put great value in the class hour. You must never be late, never let the class out early, never keep them a second past the class hour. Do not miss a class, do not cancel a class, if you have to miss a class for some reason, let the class know ahead of time and make definite arrangements for somebody else to take the class. There are lot of reasons for these suggestions. Most important is that being late, letting them out early, or cancelling a class gives them the signal that the class hour is not important. You must hold the class hour very sacred, you should not allow any interruptions by others, nor should you waste any minute of your time together. Above all students do not respect a teacher who does not fully utilize the class hour .

Utilizing the class hour does not mean that you have to lecture for the whole hour. On the contrary, it is more humanistic to let the students take active part in the class hour instead of passivley listening to you for the whole period. The experts say that nobody can pay attention to a lecture for more than 20 minutes. Therefore, you should not lecture for more than 20 minutes at a stretch — instead you should devise ways to allow the students to actively participate in the class hour.

9. Make a class directory and form groups. Give one hour a week of your office hour to each group. If a student misses a class or group session, ask why just to show you care.

10. Mail grades in with your comments and assurance to help them in future math courses they take. Try to teach a section of the next course in the sequence.

How to Get Students to Participate Actively in the Learning Process

The basic strategy is simple — make the students aware that you want them to become independent learners, which means they must learn to read and understand mathematics on their own, and apply them. The following are strategies you may try :

(1) In teaching any section of the text, you should always ask the students to give it a reading before coming to class. In class, you should discuss what it is all about - what are the basic concepts, what are the customary symbols and notations. You should write down the important formulas, important theorems and important properties, do one or two illustrative problems from the exercises and ask them to try some in class. Ask them to help one another, and you should go and help them, too. If somebody finishes a problem, send him or her to do it on the board for the class.

(2) Do not go over worked out examples in the text. They are good as reading assignments.

(3) Do not go over the details of the proof of a theorem. Just outline the proof and let them read the rest.

(4) Encourage students to ask questions but do not answer them. Ask if somebody in class has the answer. If somebody asks you to do a problem in class, ask the class first. If anybody knows the answer, let him or her answer. You should answer only if nobody knows the answer.

(5) Do not go over sample tests. Assign it as homework. Then give the worked out answers. Sample tests should be given just before the test.

(6) Do not review answers to test. Instead ask them to find their mistakes and correct them - assign this as homework for credit.

(7) Try to create role models.

(8) Mark some of the homework problems as 'to be presented in class'. Then select students at random to do one each of these problems.

(9) Make up some short snappy questions that test the understanding of the subject matter, and assign one each at random to be presented in class.

RANDOM SNAPPIES

1. An inverse function of a function F exists if and only if :

2. If an inverse of F exists, then it is denoted by :   , which is read as:

3. The function F and its inverse must satisfy the following two conditions:

4. To determine the inverse of F:

5. The graph of the inverse of F is obtained by:

6. If (a,b) is a point on the graph of F then the corresponding point (b,a) on the graph of inverse of F is obtained by:

7. The inverse of $F(x) = a^x$ is:

8. The inverse of $F(x) = \ln x$ is:

9. The inverse of $F(x) = 10^x$ is:

10. An interval in which sine function is one - to - one is:

11. An interval in which the cosine function is one -to -one is

12. An interval in which the tangent function is one- to -one is:.

13. An interval where the sine function will have an inverse is:

14. An interval where the cosine function will have an inverse is:

15. An interval where the cosine function will have an inverse is

16. An interval where the tangent function will have an inverse is:

17. The coordinates of the point on the unit circle and on the terminal side of the 30° angle are:

18. The coordinates of the point on the unit circle and on the terminal side of the 60° angle are:

19. The coordinates of the point on the unit circle and on the terminal side of the 45° angle are:

20. The number x such that $\sin^{-1} x = 30°$ is:
21. The number x such that $\cos^{-1} x = 60°$ is
22. The number x such that $\tan^{-1} x = 45°$ is:
23. The number x such that $\sin^{-1} x = 60°$ is:
24. The coordinates of the point on the unit circle and on the terminal side of the 150° angle are:
25. The coordinates of the point on the unit circle and on the terminal side of the 240° angle are:
26. The coordinates of the point on the unit circle and on the terminal side of the 315° angle are:

How to Organize Study Groups

Most of the teachers at Potsdam encourage the students to form groups and study together. The consensus is that the group method does work very well in lower-level courses as well. However, one should take a slightly different approach in the lower-level courses.

In the lower-level courses, every student usually tries to determine how much math he or she can handle on his or her own, and the teachers are usually trying to decide the potential of each student individually. Therefore, it is better if the teacher acts as the leader of each group in the initial stage. This is what I do: I write down 5 or 6 hours a week (including my office hours) and tell the class that I would like to break the class into several groups so that I can meet with each group one hour each week. Then I ask them to tell me which hour is most suitable for them. After the first meeting, I tell each group to meet at least once a week at another time without me. In the group sessions, I try to play an advisory role and try to get them to help one another. Towards the end of the semester, my role diminishes almost to nothing.

In my precalculus class, I had tried to get the students to form groups voluntarily. But it did not seem to work. The same is the experience of some of my colleagues teaching precalculus. Of course, you may also try some of the strategies used by Potsdam teachers as discussed in Chapter 6.

Helping Students Become Independent Learners

One of the primary goals of freshmen level math course should be "to teach students to read independently mathematical literature with understanding and enjoyment, which means that students must read with paper and pencil in hand". The teacher should exploit every situation to make students read and explain. For example, if a student asks the teacher to do a problem, the teacher should ask the student to read the problem aloud (in class or in group or while meeting individually) and then ask him or her to explain what is being asked.

(1) Reading assignments may be of the following type:
   (a) Light reading (at home) of the section that you are going to discuss in the next meeting.
   (b) worked out example (often in class).
   (c) Easy or straightforward sections, which you will not discuss in class.
   (d) Prepared notes on difficult concepts or topics.
(2) In an algebra or precalculus course, students may be asked to fill in the logical steps in a proof or solution. Trig identities are a lot of fun for this method. Whenever I do a trig identity in class, I always skip every other step, which the students must figure out.
(3) Asking students to prepare summary sheets of important formulas of each chapter of the text also works well. The good students usually do it anyhow.
I usually allow students who are struggling to prepare such a summary and let them look at the summary during quiz. The rules that I usually follow are:
   (a) The summary must be written in the students' own handwriting (copy of pages from textbook or somebody else's summary are not allowed).
   (b) The summary cannot contain any example or explanation. The idea is to force the student to read and decide what is important. If this process is repeated for each chapter he or she will be well under way to becoming independent.
(4) Freshmen courses are very good to set the students on a research path to find the true meaning of things like "constants, variable and parameter", "Limits", "asymptotes",

"graphing function", etc. Limits delimited is an example of how sending students to find answers to their questions can be very productive.

Limits delimited. This had to do with the following problem on limit.

$$\text{Lim}_{x \to 2} \frac{x^2 - 4}{x - 2} = \text{Lim}_{x \to 2} \frac{(x + 2)(x - 2)}{x - 2}$$
$$= \text{Lim}_{x \to 2} (x + 2) \qquad \text{since } x \neq 2.$$

$$= 4 \quad (\text{putting } x = 2).$$

One of my students Mark complained to me saying, "First we simplify by saying $x \neq 2$, and then in the next step we put $x = 2$. These problems are very easy. I can do them but it is all a trick. I can't see the logic."

I told him that if he really understood the concept of limits then he would have no difficulty understanding why that process worked. In any case, Mark was convinced that his main problem was with the concept of limits, which historically was a difficult concept. When he asked me how he could learn limits, I told him that I did not know anything better than what was in the textbook, but with his help we might be able to clear the air a little. So, I set him on to do some searching himself. I asked him to read his text and see if he could get some answers to the questions that he had raised before me, namely:

1. What limit is all about?
2. Why study limits?
3. Why does one need to know the definition of limits?

Mark came back with some answers with which he was not satisfied, so I gave him two other calculus books. Anyhow, after meeting and discussing with me what he thought about limits, he was quite happy and started enjoying calculus more. One remarkable thing was, Mark discovered for himself that the concept of limit is necessary to study the behavior of a function near a point, which may not be in the domain of the function. Since his motivation to study limits came from that point of view, it gave me a new idea about doing limit problems by using the following theorem:

THEOREM A: If $f(x) = g(x)$ for all x in a deleted neighborhood of $x = a$, then $\text{Lim}_{x \to a} f(x) = \text{Lim}_{x \to a} g(x)$.

It is needless to say that Mark became an independent learner. After Mark, I have had several students with similar trouble with limits. As a matter of fact, every time I taught the introductory calculus course, there would always be many students who would be driven to anxiety by limits. With each one of them I do the same thing I did with Mark, that is, to set them on a research path to find some motivation for themselves and then do limit problems, wherever possible, by using Theorem A in two stages: first find a function which equals the given function in a deleted neighborhood of the given point, and then use the second function to determine the limit.

Making Lesson Plans

Remember, it is not necessary for you to explain every section of the text or to do every problem the students ask you to do. The students will learn better if you make them read and try the problems themselves first.   A student will learn more by doing one problem himself or herself than by watching you do fifty problems.   Don't do anything to make them passive learners.

(1) Ideally a lecture should be divided into

> Review or introduction : 5 -10 minutes
> New Material: 10 - 20 minutes
> Problem solving by students: 15 - 20 minutes
> Doing problems on the board both by the teacher and the students:15- 20 minutes.

> Before you go to your class, you should mark the problems you are going to do in class (if you have the experience of blacking out in front of the blackboard, you should actually write the complete solution before going to class), the problems you are going to assign as homework and some problems that you are going to let them try in class.

(2) In reviewing or introducing a new topic, the teacher should focus on the importance of the topic in the stated goal of the course.

(3) In introducing a new concept, the teacher should very clearly write the definition of the important concept, the meaning of each symbol and notation, and give examples that are easy to understand and are illustrative.

(4) Give a few problems to make them get used to the new idea, symbols and notation. Then move on to introduce additional notations and problems.

(5) You should not finish a class abruptly in the middle of lecturing or in the middle of doing a problem. You must always keep your eye on the clock. End your class by showing them how to do a problem they could not do, by telling them what they should read or what kind of problems they should try. Remember, if you close the class in time and in a well-rounded manner, it gives the students a sense of accomplishment.

(6) In preparing the lesson plans, it is important to keep in view the most important part of the chapter and to use the so called spiral method, in which the lessons are planned to expand the subject systematically in such a manner that the students never lose sight of the important part. In this method, with every new topic, the student gets an opportunity to look at what the student had learned before.

Here is an example of a lesson plan for a whole week, which I have used:

     Topic: Function, dependent and independent variable
        Notations to be taught: f, f(x), graph of f

Introduction: If somebody asks me what is calculus, without any hesitation, I will say that calculus is but the study of functions. Therefore, it is very important that you learn about functions very well. Now let me try to describe what is a function. In the real world, we always encounter quantities that are interdependent. If we know the first or the independent quantity, we can determine the second or the dependent quantity. A function is a tool to study such interdependence of two quantities.

For example, let us say, you are driving at an average speed of 60 m.p.h. So if we know how long you have been driving, then we can figure out how far you have travelled. We can tabulate this interdependence or express it using ordered pairs in the following way:

Time in minutes	distance travelled in miles	ordered pair
1	1	(1, 1)
2	2	(2, 2)
3	3	(3, 3)
x	x	(x, x)

Here, time is the first or the independent quantity, and distance travelled is the second or the dependent quantity.

For another example, let us look at squares of different sizes. If we know the length of a side of the square, then we know the area of the square; in other words the area of a square is a function of the length of its sides.

length of a side in ft	Area in ft^2	ordered pair
1	1	(1, 1)
2	$2^2 = 4$	(2, 4)
3	$3^2 = 9$	(3, 9)
x	x^2	(x, x^2)

Definition of f and function formula f(x).
    Do problems: 1,2/p.107
    Let class try problems: 3,4,5/p.107

    Graph of f:
        Do problems: 12, 13, 19/p.117
        Let class try problems: 15 - 21/p.117
Graphing linear function (only two points are necessary) and quadratic function.

    Vertical and horizontal shifting of graph. Introduce $|x|$, $\dfrac{1}{x}$

Determining the vertex and the line of symmetry of a function whose graph is a parabola. Review completing a square.
    Do problems: 5, 6, 7/p.128
    Let class try problems: 8 - 12/p.128
    Graphs of other functions: x^3, $\dfrac{1}{x^2}$

        Dom f, Range f
            Introduce: $\sqrt{x}$, $\sqrt{a^2 - x^2}$
        Do problems:
            Let class try problems:

Reading assignment: Vertical line test, symmetry about axes.
Homework: 8/p.107, 12/p.113, 14/p.128, 12,16/p.141.

In the above example, the important part of the topic is identified as consisting of the concept of a function f, the function formula f(x), the graph of a function and function algebra. Acquainting the students with some common functions and their graphs is recognized as the main goal of the chapter so that students will later be able to learn about log, exponential and trig functions. First, students are motivated with two simple examples of functions. After, the formal definition is given, students are familiarized with linear and quadratic functions. Graphing of functions is introduced next, illustrating first with linear functions and then with quadratic functions. Vertical and horizontal shifts are then introduced with some more functions like $f(x) = |x|$, $f(x) = \dfrac{1}{x}$.

With vertical and horizontal shifts again all the functions known so far are looked at. The subject matter is then expanded by telling them about domain and range of functions and by introducing some more functions like $\sqrt{x}$, $\sqrt{a^2 - x^2}$ and so on.

Preparing Interesting Reading Material

One of the things a creative teacher can do is to create interesting examples or reading material to clarify difficult concepts or to make the students think for themselves. I do not wish to infringe upon your creativity. But I would like to emphasize not be afraid to try something new and do not be afraid that there may be something wrong in what you write. Present it to the class as something you have made up and ask them if it helps them or if there is anything wrong. So without saying anything more, I will like you to look at two examples.

The one about limit is what I gave to my class based on an actual conversation. The second about the graph of function, is from Jan Terwel's article in *Cooperative Learning in Mathematics* [6], which is a very resourceful book. Another resourceful book that I may recommend is *Calculus*, produced by the Consortium based at Harvard and funded by National Science Foundation grant, published by John Wiley.

Mike: You say that (x → a) means x approaches a. But how does x approach a, on foot, by car or what?

Teacher: No, no we do not mean approach in that sense, we mean the value of x is near a.

Mike: That makes some sense. (After a brief pause) But what should the value of x be to qualify that it is near a. My grandpa says his house is near the post office and the post office is two blocks away.   Is two blocks "near" enough?

Teacher: No, no that is too much.

Student 1: How about one foot ?

Student 2: No, that is too much, maybe an inch.

Student 3: No, that is too much, maybe a centimeter?

Mike: I think even a centimeter will be too much, I think we should settle for one millimeter.

Student 4: What is a millimeter? I don't understand all the metric stuff, you know the centimeter, millimeter stuff.

Teacher: I see, we have a problem here.   The problem is that we do not have an accepted definition of "'near". So we must clarify what we mean when we say x is near a. From your arguments about foot, inch, centimeter, etc., it is clear that to clarify nearness, we need to specify distance or in this case the difference between x and a. Do you agree?   Do you agree that this difference should be small?   But how small is the question.

Students: Yes.

Teacher: Now, what if I say x is near a if the difference between x and a can be made smaller than any given number?

Mike: What exactly do you mean?

Teacher: For example, let us say x is near 1.   If you say, can you make the difference between x and 1 to be less than 1/10, I will say yes by taking x = 1 + 1/100. In which case the difference between x and 1 is 1/100, which is less than 1/10 .

Martha: What if I say one over a million (1/1000000).

Teacher: Fine. Then I will take x = 1 + 1/10000000. Then the difference between x and 1 is less than one over a million.

Student 3: I sort of get it.   But will you please write it down.

Teacher: Before we write down, we of course have to make a
             distinction between x approaching a from the right
             and from the left.

$x \rightarrow a^+$ (*Read* x approaching a from the right) means $x > a$ and $x - a$
can be made smaller than any given positive number.

$x \rightarrow a^-$ (*Read* x approaching a from the left) means $x < a$ and $a - x$
can be made smaller than any given positive number.

$x \rightarrow a$ (*Read* x approaching a) means $x \rightarrow a^+$ or $x \rightarrow a^-$, that is, $x \neq a$
and $|x - a|$ can be made smaller than any given positive number.

Teacher: So Mike, do you think your grandpa's house is near the
             post office according to our definition?

Mike: No, because we cannot make the distance less than two
             blocks. Wait till my grandpa hears it. Every day he
             takes a walk to the post office and back. He will have
             a heart attack if I say that the post office is no longer
             near his house.

Teacher: No, no. Please don't do it. I mean don't apply your
             mathematical ideas everywhere. All I am trying to
             say is that in mathematics words have definte meaning
             and you have to understand the mathematical meaning.
             So Martha, are you near the door, I mean in the
             mathematical sense ?

Martha: Not if I am sitting down- but I can be if you let me
             stand up and allow me to move.

Teacher: Good thinking. Now please read the definition one
             more time and see if you understand the meaning of the
             statement: $\lim\limits_{x \rightarrow a} f(x) = L$.

The following is a good example of an interesting reading material.
It illustrates graphing functions with a topic that is close to every
student.

CYCLING[1]

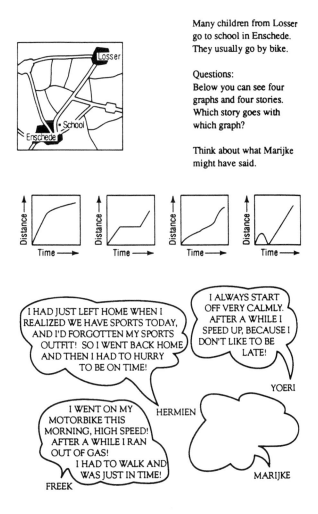

Many children from Losser go to school in Enschede. They usually go by bike.

Questions:
Below you can see four graphs and four stories. Which story goes with which graph?

Think about what Marijke might have said.

Teaching Students to Find Answers to Their Questions

It is true that you must encourage students to ask questions and that you must answer them. However, you do not have to answer every question. You should definitely answer anything that is pertinent to what you are discussing that lecture hour. Then there are other questions, which you should not answer. The strategy should be to set them to find answers to their questions, take help of his or her study group and read the text. Here is a sample of such questions with answers.

1. *Question:* Will you please do problem so and so?
   Answer: (a) Have you tried it — Please read it to me.
   (b) Has anybody done this ? Will you please do it on the board?

2. *Question:* What is the meaning of the word asymptote?
   Answer: I never thought of it—will you please check the dictionary and tell us.

3. *Question:* Will you please telll us how to find Limits?
   Answer: Do you know what is a Limit? Do you know what you are supposed to do to find the limit of a function?

4. *Question:* I am really confused about what is a constant, what is a variable and what is a parameter. Will you please clarify these terms?
   Answer: That is a very good question. I must admit I do not really know how to answer it. Maybe we can take it as a class project and find acceptable definitions of these terms. This is what I want you to do - read your text and other texts on algebra or calculus. Write down what you think are the true meanings of these terms. I will do the same and then we will have a discussion.

5. *Question:* Will you please show me how you get the difference of squares formula?
   Answer: I think that is something your group members can show you. If they can't, I will show you when your group meets the next time.

What to do About Homework

(1) Homework should be reasonable 10 simple problems or 5 harder problems. It must be collected on time, corrected and returned on time. It is better that the instructor corrects homework himself or herself. Grading of homework should be fair and strict and mistakes should be pointed out with red pen.

(2) Assign homework during the last class of the week. Collect them first thing as the students come in during the first class of the week. Do not allow late handins. Tell them that you will give more than 100 points worth of homework so if they miss one or two, it would not hurt them because you are going to take the best 10.

Do not allow them to write homework in classs — even if they say they are just copying their own answers. Insist homework must be done at home.

(3) It is better to mark the homework problems when you prepare your lesson -- these should be the problems without answers. Make sure similar problems have been discussed or done in class.

When you return the corrected tests, you may assign corrected tests as homework for 20 points or so.

If you give sample tests or review problems, they should also be assigned first as homework. In addition, if you had designed any random presentation for the class, the whole thing may be assigned as homework.

The final exam may be assigned as a 100 point make-up for homework.

(4) Do not review homework problems in class - it is better to discuss homework during group sessions - point out mistakes they made, go over common mistakes just to focus on important material. [It is always better for you to do the homework answers first before correcting, and correct before copying].

(5) In the study group, discuss homework problems, help them by doing a similar problem or by explaining what the problem is all about, and what they should know to do the problem. The strategy ahould be such that they are getting help in their homework.

What Is Math Anxiety and How to Help Students Overcome It

In the workshop on math anxiety a panel of four students, three undergraduates and one graduate, narrated their feelings towards math, math courses and math teachers as follows.

Student 1: I used to be very intimidated by the idea of taking math courses especially in junior high. Math was my weakest subject and I always did average on it though I was doing very well in everything else. Though I liked math, I was very afraid of it. I was afraid of thinking deeply about it and trying to make use of the knowledge I was learning. Then it got to a point where my parents both took a notice of it since they were both in math they took the time to work with me, helped me figure out why I was so afraid. Basically I was intimidated by my teacher who seemed to FOCUS ON BOYS AND EXPECTED THEM TO DO BETTER. I think Calculus was what saved me. It was a fresh start for everybody and when I realized that everybody else were as scared as I was about the topic, I gained more confidence and then I decided to major in math.

Student 2: Math has, in my memory, always been a difficulty for me. I have more of a positive grasp of addition and multiplication than I do of subtraction and division SUBTRACTION IS THE BASIS OF MY MATH DIFFICULTIES. As the math became more intense, so did my anxiety. I do well in quiz type situations but major tests and exams always posed difficulties. Though I was anxious about math, I have always had good relationships with my math teachers. They were willing to help me after classes and before major tests. In their presence, I was able to understand, but on my own I faltered. I am avoiding math here at Carolina.

Student 3: Uninteresting, classes were very monotonous. Cold, not much relation to other things outside the class. Hard to pay attention to. My calculus professor was fairly unsympathetic to changes in her grading system. Rigid in her approach. Tests were strange because they would require only one method answer. That I don't believe how reality is. O.K. as a game, but not for life outside the classroom.

Student 4: Math courses are usually difficult for me. I am not afraid of math, I just don't enjoy it, therefore, I usually don't do as well in it. As for my experience with math course, I feel it is important for teachers to go at a pace where all students can keep up. Teachers should encourage those experiencing difficulty to come by their office hours.

After the panel's written statements were read out, the TAs were asked to start a dialogue with panel members to figure out what was wrong and what can be done to correct the situation. During these dialogues it was clear that the the anxiety, apprehension and ill-feeing of the panel members were more intense than what came out in their written statements.

Now, I would like to ask you two questions. Do we want these students to graduate with these feelings about math sticking to their resourceful mind? Do we want them to pollute the minds of their friends, relatives, children, grandchildren and what not with this kind of ill-feeling towards math and math teachers?

I am sure many math teachers will say that there is something wrong with every one of them. The teachers may say let these students take the placement examination, put them in remedial courses and throw them out if they can't handle it. No, we don't want to do that. We do not wish to say that there is something wrong with them. They are normal people, they are experiencing math anxiety. They can also learn math. They just need some help.

Somebody ought to help them - who else, but people who teach freshmen level math courses? But these math teachers must be aware of what math anxiety is and how to help students experiencing math anxiety. Actually, the experiences of student 1 indicate to us that yes, these people may be helped and they can learn math. She is lucky that her parents, both good math teachers, took the trouble of helping her. Isn't it wonderful that somebody who was afraid of math at junior high school is now a math major in a reputed university. Her case should be an eye opener, we should be like her parents. How?? Let me tell you something about math anxiety and certain strategies.

In short, math anxiety refers to the anxiety that a person experiences or may experience in a math related situation. This is an upsetting emotional state which is marked by tension, irrational behavior and a search for some eacape. Like many other kinds of anxiety math anxiety is caused by a threat to the person's self- respect. When a person is unable to do math he or she is likely to doubt the efficacy of his or her intellectual abilities and the tendency will be to surrender to emotions. In our view, the best way to counter such a surrender to emotions of math anxious person is to help build his or her self - confidence. The key is in the guiding principles of Stephens, "PROTECT AND STRENGTHEN THE SELF-ESTEEM OF EVERY STUDENT."

What Causes Math Anxiety?

Learning math or building math skills is akin to constructing a brick wall - if some bricks are missing in lower parts of the wall, the upper wall is shaky and may crumble at any time. Math anxiety is caused when there are some missing blocks in the lower wall. One way this can happen is when the student fails to master certain concepts, facts, symbols or notations. For an example, we can look at student 2, for whom the negative sign is the biggest hurdle. Since she is not sure of it, she is going to experience anxiety anytime she is confronted with problems containing the negative sign. Let us call this the math type. Math anxiety of this type is triggered by certain symbols (the negative sign in the case of student 2), certain mathematical concepts or terms which for some reason or other create mental blocks in the process of learning. Since the symbol, the concept or term in question make that person uncomfortable, the person is not able to go any further.

For another type of math anxiety we look at students 1, 3 and 4. In case of 1, the math environment she was in tried to make her feel that math was for boys only. In case of 3 and 4, the background or the environment they have been accustomed to have made them create mental blocks towards learning math. The unsympathetic teacher or the rigid grading system in the math class have made the situation worse. We call this the socio-cultural type. Math anxiety of this type was experienced by student 1 and to some extent students 3 and 4 are experiencing it. This is the kind of anxiety that Ms. Tobias and others have been discussing. As observed by Tobias, and as our experiences show, common causes of this type of anxiety are:

(1) The female fear of competing on man's turf
(2) The myth that boys naturally do better in math than girls

(3) Distrust of intuition, especially as applied to math, a science

(4) Common myths about mathematical ability

(5) Illusion of math as an exact science

(6) Individual experiences in school, at home, or society in general

(7) Traditional background that leads to misconceptions about math.

Any one or more of the above may cause a person to experience math anxiety.   Of course, there are other social and cultural factors which may cause math anxiety.

In addition, we have a third type of math anxiety, which we call the handicap type. This is caused by physical or mental handicaps like dyslexia, motor difficulties, shaky hands, etc. It is imperative that the math teacher be aware of it, be sympathetic, and devise strategies to help the student. Just to give an example, a couple of years ago, I had in my linear algebra course a bright young man, who was crippled by a car accident. When he was taking the first test, he first read the test very carefully and commented, "This looks like a very fair test, I am going to do well." But after about half an hour, everything changed, his face became all red, he sweated profusely as he tried one thing after another, and he looked very sick. I went over and asked if he was feeling alright, and told him that if he wanted to quit, I could arrange a make-up for him at another time. He said he was alright and he just made some mistakes somewhere and the answers he was getting were not checking out. Since he insisted on trying, I left him alone. I knew that even though he was confined to the wheelchair, he enjoyed being in the class and doing everything the way others do. When I was correcting the test I noticed that he had difficulty rounding up letters like O, 0, 9, 6 etc. Especially, in several places, it was not possible to distinguish whether he was writing 6 or 0. He made mistakes taking one for the other. I pointed this out to him and suggested that he should do his test on a personal computer as we had good arrangements in the math building for that. With this arrangement he was able to do well in the course.

In short, three types of math anxiety are defined by the factors which cause them. They are:

I.   *Math type*   is caused by mental blocks in the process of learning math.

II. The *socio-cultural type* is the result of socio-cultural factors.
III. The *handicap type* is caused by physical or mental handicaps.

A math teacher should be aware of math anxiety and be able to distinguish between these types. With a sympathetic attitude and care, strategies may be developed to help these persons learn math. Of course, the first step in this direction is to create a humanistic environment in classroom. It is only in a humanistic environment, where the students feel that their self-respect is protected (remember anxiety results when a person's self-respect is threatened) that the students feel comfortable to express their true difficulties.

Fortunately, the handicapped cases are nowadays diagnosed early enough. The student or the counsellors usually inform the teacher when such a handicapped student is in class. However, it is not very easy to identify students experiencing math anxiety of the first two types. Often it is difficult to distinguish between the two. Here are some of our observations. [4]

If a person is experiencing math anxiety of Type II that is because of some socio-cultural factor, then usually the reaction to math is severe. The person is likely to make statements like:

"I can't do math."
"I just don't understand math."
"Math makes me sick."
"Complete blackout."
"So and so is super bright, he is really good in math."
"You would not believe it, math makes me throw up."
"I may think thirteen but write fifty one."
"I will always stay away from math. I hate math."

Key phrases are "HATE MATH"; "MATH MAKES ME SICK." Such a person is likely to show exteremely irrational behavior towards math or mathematicians. As Ms. Tobias suggests, there is usually a moment of SUDDEN DEATH, when these people felt that "as far as math was concerned, they were through."

People experiencing this type of anxiety will usually talk about their moment of sudden death, about friends and relatives who are good in math and about tricks they played on math teachers, whom they hated. These math anxious people always do stay away from mathematicians and anybody who is good in math. It is almost impossible to get them to talk to a math teacher or to take them near a math building. They show signs of anxiety even if they enter the office of a math teacher. The best strategy is to take help of counsellors or advisers of the student, who should try to reduce the global anxiety to local difficulties in math and refer the student back to a sympathetic teacher who would help him or her with math.

It is to be noted that a math teacher cannot usually help a person experiencing math anxiety of the socio-cultural type. First, because the teacher may not be trained to handle emotional problems; secondly, time or resources may not be available to attack socio-cultural problems on an individual basis. Therefore, all suspected cases of socio-cultural type should immediately be referred to the counsellors. The approach is to reduce the persons global fear about math to a local learning problem about learning some math well. For example, people like students 3 and 4, should be told about the true nature of math and about the importance of math. This cannot be done by a math teacher since they are not likely to listen to or believe a math teacher. Collaboration of a mathematician and a counselor permits the two origins of math anxiety to be identified and dealt with mathematical deficiencies and psychological block.

It is seen that many students have serious misconceptions about the nature of mathematics and about why to study math. Misconceptions about mathematics are deeply rooted in home and social background, and are often enhanced in schools and playgrounds. Comments like "Math is very abstract", "I am never going to use it", "Math is not relevent to real life", "Math is all computations", "Math is very boring" are frequently heard from students. This kind of attitude of misconceptions do produce stumbling blocks to learning math and are bound to create anxiety sooner or later.   The air should be cleared right in the beginning of a course.

The approach we take is to convince the students, through counsellors or advisers or parents, that math is a very different process of acquiring knowledge, and that the mathematical process teaches us a very definite way of thinking and applying knowledge to practical situations.   It is, therefore, not just a subject for school but an activity for life.

Then we usually confront the students who think "math is not relevant to my life" or "Cold, not much relation to other things outside the class" by pointing out various applications of the real numbers: to counting, measurement, etc., and point out other applications of mathematics in areas like music, art and architecture. We point out to them that in today's world, math literacy is indispensable for a person to be regarded as educated. Mathematics is the foundation of science and technology. Applications of mathematics in the social, biological behavioral and environmental sciences are growing every day. Mathematics is "No longer just a tool for the physical science, mathematics is a language for all disciplines." I tell them, stop kidding, everybody needs math.

The reaction is not so severe in case of students expperiencing anxiety of Type I. The students will make statements like:

> "I used to be good in math."
> "I like geometry but I get lost in algebra."
> "I had a really bad math teacher in eighth grade."
> "Calculus is so abstract."
> "I always got into arguments with the geometry teacher. Could not see the meaning of invisible points and lines."
> "I tried to read through the book, made me sick, went out and had a beer."
> "I understand what you are saying, but I don't see the meaning, I am sorry."

Key phrases are: "SORRY" and "I TRIED". Reaction is mild and often of disappointment. There is a period of SLOW TORTURE when the student tried to learn something but could not understand it.

People experiencing this type of anxiety usually complain about the teacher, about the textbook and something that has to do with classroom experience. The same student may complain about the foreign accent of his teacher or the glare of the classroom blackboard or if nothing else, he or she may blame his or her own eyesight.

These are the people who get into a course and then find some excuse to drop the course. They are constantly looking for some escape to avoid repeating the experience of slow torture.

These people are always eager to talk to math teachers who are willing to listen. They are not afraid of math and they do not necessarily hate math or math reachers. They really need help and a math teacher can usually help them.

A math teacher can often single out math anxious students in a math classroom. The math teacher should try:

(1) to determine whether it is a case of Math type or socio-cultural type;
(2) to identify the source of the anxiety;

(3) to figure out the strengths and/or weaknesses of the math anxious person.

A math biography of the student prepared with the help of a set of carefully selected questions does help to achieve the above objectives. The math biography may be prepared by the teacher in an informal session with the student or by the student himself or herself in a math anxiety workshop. Often, it is possible to identify students with anxiety and to determine the source of the anxiety even in a fairly large classroom. One way is to assign problems to be completed in class and then walk around helping the students. Soon the troubled students and their troubles become clear.

Once the source of the anxiety has been determined the math teacher's strategies should include the following:

First, the teacher should study the topic or the symbol that is causing the anxiety very thoroughly from various angles such as the underlying concepts, the historical background, its inherent difficulties, etc. This topic or symbol should be mastered by the teacher.

Second, the math teacher should try to reduce the pressure that the anxiety might bring to the person. The teacher should talk with sympathy and let the person feel that he or she cares. The teacher should try to avoid using the symbol, concept or topic that is creating the problem till such time as the person becomes comfortable with it. The person should constantly be assured that it is possible to overcome math anxiety.

Third, the math teacher should find out communication skills of the math anxious person. Some people like to communicate with written words, some with pictures and graphs, some with sound and so on. The teacher should try to exploit the medium of communications the math anxious person is most skilled in.

Fourth, the teacher should then devise a method to teach the material in a way that would reduce the burden of the student and yet remove the sore point.

For example, to help student 2, I will note down the following facts:

(1) Yes, negative numbers and the symbol "-" is a big source of trouble for many students.

(2) She is not alone. I have known many people who had trouble with negative numbers. Even Newton had trouble with negative numbers. He had a hard time accepting the rule that

the product of two negative numbers is a positive number. Cardan regarded the negative numbers as fictitious.

(3) The formal definition of negative numbers were not known till the nineteenth century.

(4) It is only with the group theoretic approach that we can give a logically acceptable definition to negative numbers. This means that in the freshmen level, we must clarify it without using group theory but immitating its approach.

(5) Added to the above is the problem that the symbol " - " is used to mean several different things. For example,

- 3 (means opposite of 3) ,

a - b (means a + (-b)), that is, to a add the opposite of b, so it stands for subtraction)

a^{-n}(reciprocal of a^n; negative exponents are a big source of math anxiety),

9 - 16 (9 through 16).

(6) There is nothing negative about negative numbers. Negative number is just a name.

Therefore, my approach will be to tell her all the above facts and assure her that her deficiency is very normal and that even genius like Newton had problems with it. Then I will try to make her understand the negative numbers. For example, -2 is a number whose sum with 2 is 0, and so on. Then I will talk about opposites. The approach I take is to emphasize 0 as a great matchmaker, which pairs every number and its opposite and I will show some of these pairs like, (1, -1), (2, -2), (.5, -.5), ... Then I will tell her that putting the negative sign in front of a number simply means we are talking about its opposite. Thus -(-1) = 1. This way, she will perhaps get used to the idea of why two negatives give positive. After making her comfortable with the negative sign, then other properties or formal rules involving negative numbers will be introduced.

I give below a list of common causes of math anxiety among students in lower-level math courses. If any student is having trouble with any of these, the teacher better be careful.

(1) Transition from arithmetic to algebra.
(2) Clarification of frequently used terms like:
       (a) constant, variable, parameter
       (b) greater, bigger, larger, higher (when to use which)

(3) Using the same symbol to denote different things : the symbol " - " , the parentheses is used for grouping, ordered pairs and describing intervals.

(4) Using symbols without proper clarification, often contradicting results. The greatest offender is the symbol '∞'. You will perhaps understand this if you try to answer the following questions.

Is ∞ a number?
Is ∞ a point ?
What is ∞ ?

∞ is not a number because it does not satisfy the axioms for number.

∞ is not a point because if A and B are two points then the lines joining A and B to ∞ will intersect at ∞ , which of course will rule out that the lines may be parallel.

If ∞ is not a number nor a point, then how can it exist?

Actually, in freshmen level courses, ∞ is a convenient symbol used to explain certain behavior of variables or to express limiting concept. It has meaning only with limits:

x → ∞ means x is greater than any given number

f(x) → ∞ means F(x) is greater than any given number.

$$\text{Lim}_{x \to \infty} F(x) = L \quad \text{means} \quad F(x) \to L \text{ as } x \to \infty$$

$$\text{Lim}_{x \to a} F(x) = \infty \quad \text{means} \quad F(x) \to \infty \text{ as } x \to a$$

$$\text{Lim}_{x \to 0} \frac{1}{x^2} = \infty \quad \text{means}$$

$$\text{Lim}_{x \to 0^+} \frac{1}{x^2} = \infty \quad \text{and lim}_{x \to 0^-} \frac{1}{x^2} = \infty$$

This is not in agreement with the definition of limits because we say:

Lim $_{x \to a}$ f(x) exists if Lim $_{x \to a^+}$ f(x) and Lim $_{x \to a^-}$ f(x) exist and are equal. But equality of ∞ is not properly defined.

Expressions like [0, ∞) or (-∞ ,0] are very misleading because they seem to treat infinity as a number. I think one should express them simply as {x | x ≥ 0} or {x| x < 0}. Similarly, one should not talk about extending a 'line to ∞ ' that seems to indicate ∞ is a point, which it is not. It is good enough to say extending the line in this or that direction.

(5) What is the meaning of equation of a (line, circle , etc.)?
(6) Definition of function and graph of a function .
(7) Unnecessary harrassment with problems that are not really of importance to understand the subject or for future applications. For example, (a) graphing crazy rational functions (b) All kinds of tests of symmetries (c) Finding slant asymptotes, (d) graphing trig functions with complicated phase-shifts. (e) ambiguous word problems.
(8) Square roots
(9) The concept of limit. The concept of limit should first be explained geometrically and only gemetrical problems should be emphasized first. This will help in graphing as well.
(10) Treacherous methods like the one narrated in Limits delimited.

In conclusion I would like to say that as math teachers, we can really help math anxious students if we:

1. Recognize the fact that math anxiety is real.
2. Identify some of the sore points of mathematics that cause anxiety and devise methods to make them more meaningful.
3. Try to distinguish between the various types of math anxiety.
4. Seek help for socio-cultural cases. We should not try to be psychoanalysts. For handicapped cases, get all the facts and information about the handicapped person. Make arrangements with sympathy. Try to arrange separate tests and help sessions, and make arrangements for the handicapped student as the situation may demand. Thus, for example if a student has difficulty writing, you may ask him to key in answers on a PC.

For math type cases, it may be fun discovering new things, devising new methods and imparting new knowledge.

With a little patience, some awareness about math anxiety and a sincere effort to help the students, a math teacher may obtain wonderful results. Personally, I found my work with math anxious students to be very rewarding. The most cherished moments of my 25 year teaching career have been the overwhelming reactions of math anxious students that I have helped.

Putting Ideas into Practice

The TAs and the teachers present were asked to give written answers to the following questions:
1. Write down one or two things that you learned today that you feel you can apply to your teaching.
2. What do you need to do to implement these ideas?
3. What can the Center for Teaching and Learning or the Math Department do to help you?

The following is a sample of answers (unedited):
"I will immediately begin asking the students to do more problems in class, and at the board. With some planning, I will start forming groups."
"I like the idea of assigning some homework problems to be presented in class & the idea of letting students help each other in groups."

"I think organizing sessions like this are great. I enjoy finding out new creative ways of teaching through literature & through meetings like this. Thank you for organizing this & having the extra literature available."
"Respecting the class hour. I haven't always done this in terms of (1) letting them out early or (2) keeping them late. Continuing & expanding my use of the index cards. Incorporate more student work/participation in classroom."

"The importance of "forcing" students to learn by themselves has come up repeatedly today, & I think it can be incorporated into most anyone's course organization.
To implement this idea, I think it would be best to have a bunch of class time set aside to discuss how you go about "teaching yourself", & to fill in the gaps once the students ask questions about the assigned reading material.
I think the math dept shouldn't push such a structured & fast paced syllabus. Some students have such a hard time learning math that the fast pace is very intimidating & discourages learning."
"Get away from lecture-only-oriented teaching by assigning reading and advance problems for discussion in class.

Organize my lectures differently, get the students involved, assign homework more carefully."

"Let students do problems in class. Be more close to students." "I think that explaining why we do math as a teacher and as a student will help motivate the students."

"Ideas for groupwork. Smaller class size. Rethink the placement policy for Math 10, that is, does everyone really need to be there? Why not offer multiple sections of Math 16, 17, 18?"

"I can try to break the class up into groups for some activities. Have the students do more in class. Just make a few changes in my lecture notes.

Make sure our classes are in good rooms with good chalkboards. They usually are, but I have been stuck in a horrible room in the past (in Gardner)."
"The center for T & L could provide literature on innovative teaching methods for TA's (& Profs) to read. These references and/or articles should preferably be in Phillips. Also more discussions/workshops would be a good way to discuss teaching ideas.

The math dept could also participate in sponsoring these workshops. It would be nice to see Profs taking more of an interest in teaching. The math dept could reduce our teaching loads so we have more time to spend on our teaching."

"Telling the students something personal about myself to personalize the class more.

Provide seminars such as this to introduce new ideas. The math dept could offer some sort of TA training program which brought up ideas and methods that current teachers find effective."

"Give the students assignments and to let them learn on their own. Ask students to work out problems on the blackboard. Focus more on the most important things. Try to form study groups for the students.

Need the support of the math dept. Need time. More workshops."

APPENDIX - 1

WHY MATHEMATICS?

[This is a complete reproduction of the Spring 1991 version of the pamphlet *Why Mathematics ?* published by the mathematics department of SUNY at Potsdam. We have not made any changes except in format. This innocent looking pamphlet is, in the words of a student, "a dynamite" that opens their eyes to the world ahead of them and presents a very clear avenue of success in life through mathematics education.]

GENERAL PROGRAM

All mathematics majors complete a basic sequence of courses that leads to a high level of competency in mathematics. Through appropriate course selection, several paths are available - a career as a mathematician, in business, government, or industry; a career in teaching or further graduate study.

Our basic undergraduate courses include Calculus, Set Theory and Logic, Linear Algebra, Modern Algebra and Advanced Calculus. A wide selection of elective courses includes applications of mathematics to contemporary problems.

SPECIAL PROGRAMS

Honors Program:

Qualified students may enter an Honors Program at the beginning of their junior year. Students successfully completing this challenging program are recognized at graduation and by appropriate notation on their transcripts.

Bachelor-Master Degrees Program:

Students who enter the Honors Program may also qualify for the Two-Degrees Program. All students in this program are expected to complete the requirements for the Bachelor's Degree in four years. Since the program is adapted to the needs of each student, the time required to complete both the Bachelor's and the Master's Degrees ranges from four to five years.

OTHER INFORMATION

Competent and concerned teachers contribute to an atmosphere designed to help you succeed.

We have a mathematics lab where free tutoring is available.

Near our classrooms and offices you will find a reading room with our own collection of books and journals where students study together and a coffee room for informal conversations with other students and staff.

Cross-registration courses are available at three other schools in the area.

Our graduates have been awarded assistantships and fellowships for further study at leading universities. These include Cornell, Illinois, Michigan, SUNY at Binghamton, and the University of Wisconsin.

We care about our students and encourage each to achieve to the maximum of his or her ability.

FURTHER INFORMATION

Write to: Chairman
                   Mathematics Department
                   State University College
                   Potsdam, New York 13676

Requirements for Majors:

Regular Major..33 semester hours
    (Includes 12 hours of lower division and 21 hours of upper
    division courses.)

Required Courses (8)   sem. hrs.

    3620-MA-151 Calculus I.............................. 4
    3620-MA-152 Calculus II............................ 4
    3620-MA-253 Multivariate Calculus............... 4
    3600-MA-340 Set Theory & Logic................. 3
    3610-MA-375 Linear Algebra I..................... 3
    3610-MA-423 Modern Algebra I.................... 3
    3620-MA-451 Advanced Calculus I................ 3
    3600-MA-460 Problem Seminar.................... 3

Elective Courses (2)
    I. Any mathematics course at the 300-500 level. 3

> NOTE 1: MA 547 Theory of Sets may be elected only
> upon recommendation of mathematics
> faculty.
> NOTE 2: A student who is also preparing to be a
> teacher should choose either MA 404
> Elements of Geometry or MA 553 Concepts
> of Geometry to satisfy this elective.

II.   One course from the following list to be taken only
after the student has completed 3600 MA 340, 3610
MA 375, 3610 MA 423 and 3620 MA 451 or with
permission of the instructor............................3

    3610 MA 524 Modern Algebra II
    3610 MA 526 Linear Algebra II
    3620 MA 452 Advanced Calculus II

The requirements for the regular mathematics major are minimal by comparison to national practice, but they are consistent with the basic philosophy of a liberal arts education and the philosophy of our mathematics department. These requirements allow the student to complete a second major or pursue other interests in relative depth. More than half of our mathematics majors complete a second major. A wide selection of elective courses are available which include applications of mathematics to contemporary problems. Therefore, through appropriate course selection, several paths are available - a career as a mathematician in business, or industry; a career in teaching, or further graduate study.

Mathematics Honors Program

Admission. Students usually enter this program at the beginning of their junior year. Their grade point average is expected to be at least 3.0, with a grade point average in mathematics of 3.25 or better. Two letters of recommendation are required, one of which must be from a member of the mathematics faculty from whom the applicant has taken a course.

Curriculum. A major who graduates with honors in mathematics must complete the honors curriculum and the honors examination, which will be both oral and written. A student who maintains a cumulative average of at least 3.5 in his or her mathematics courses will be exempted from the written examination. The oral examination will cover primarily the work of the student in Independent Study courses but may include questions on areas from the honors curriculum courses.

Graduate with honors in mathematics. The Mathematics Department must approve all persons recommended for graduation with honors in mathematics. Students who successfully complete the Mathematics Honors Program will be given proper recognition at commencement, on transcripts and on diplomas. A student who has completed the Honors Curriculum but who is not recommended for Departmental Honors will be considered to have completed the regular mathematics major.

Honors Major............................33 cr hrs
(includes 12 hours of lower division and
18 hours of upper division courses.)
Calculus I...................................... 4 cr hrs
Calculus II..................................... 4 cr hrs
Multivariate Calculus....................... 4 cr hrs
Set Theory and Logic....................... 3 cr hrs
Modern Algebra I............................ 3 cr hrs
Linear Algebra I.............................. 3 cr hrs
Advanced Calculus I......................... 3 cr hrs
Independent Study I.......................... 3 cr hrs
Independent Study II......................... 3 cr hrs

One course from the following list to be taken only after the student has completed 3600 MA 340, 3610 MA 375, 3610 MA 423 and 3620 MA 451 or with permission of the instructor....................3

3610 MA 524 Modern Algebra II
3610 MA 526 Linear Algebra II
3620 MA 452 Advanced Calculus II

A student who completes these core requirements with high grades and good recommendations should be able to continue his studies successfully to the graduate level in mathematics.

Double Degree in Mathematics

The Mathematics Department, through its double degrees (B.A./M.A.) program, offers to well qualified students an opportunity to develop their mathematical abilities to a high level and to progress towards the frontiers of mathematics as rapidly as their abilities and motivation will permit. A person who wishes to know more about this program should refer to the Department's brochure "Four-Year Bachelor's-Master's Degrees Program in Mathematics."

Actuarial Science

Actuaries are involved in all aspects of insurance and related businesses. They - design and price life insurance plans - design company pension plans - recommend procedures for determining who is a good risk and who is not.

Persons interested in becoming Actuaries should take the following courses as a minimum. If you have the time and interest, additional courses in business and economics would be useful.

Principles of Microeconomics   Principles of Macroeconomics
Financial Accounting I   Financial Accounting II
Probability & Math Statistics I (MA-461)
Probability & Math Statistics II (MA-562)

Students may want to take MA-125 as a prelude to Probability & Math Statistics I. Familiarity with a high level programming language (such as Pascal) and courses in computer science to include Numerical methods, Operations Research I and II are also recommended.

Biology

Mathematics and mathematically trained people are becoming increasingly important in the field of Biology. Careers in both government and business are open in medical research, toxicology, neurobiology and so on. For those in Biochemistry there are many openings in the development of synthetics, development of fertilizers and drug research.

Persons interested in careers in Biology should take the following courses as a minimum. If you have the time and interest, additional courses selected under advisement would be useful.

Biomathematics I   Probability & Math Statistics I
General Biology I   General Biology II

Other biology courses should be selected through consultation with chairman of the Biology Department.

Business Administration

Business Administration as a career can be both lucrative and challenging. In nearly every facet of government, business or educational activity there is a continuing need for able administrators. People with solid mathematical/technical backgrounds who also are trained in administration are always in short supply. Continued training to the level of MBA (Master of Business Administration) is particularly useful with respect to finding an interesting career.

Persons interested in careers in Business Administration should take, as a minimum, the following courses.

Fortran for Liberal Studies	Numerical Methods
Microeconomics	Macroeconomics
Introduction to Econometrics	Accounting I
Probability & Math Statistics I	

Students may want to take MA-125 as a prelude to Probability & Math Statistics I.

Computer Science - BA Level

Computer science is a relatively new field and one whose employment outlook is better than average both in the United States and Canada. Government, at all levels, and business expect a continuing demand for scientific and business applications programmers, systems programmers, systems analysts and so on. The computer manufacturers need capable people in customer service, marketing and sales, and design.

Persons interested in careers in Computer Science should take the following courses as a minimum. Additional courses selected under advisement would be useful.

Introduction to Computer Based Information Systems
Introduction to Problem Solving
Programming Structures
Discrete or Data Structures
Assembly Language Programming
Applied Fortran
Probability & Math Statistics I

Computer Science - Graduate School

As in most fields, it is becoming increasingly important that people interested in Computer Science have advanced degrees. Many of the jobs that were formerly held by persons with BA degrees are now reserved for persons with graduate training. Typical of such jobs are design and manufacturing positions and computer administration.

Persons interested in graduate training in Computer Science should take the following courses as a minimum. If you have the time and interest, additional courses selected under advisement would be useful.

Introduction to Computer Based Information Systems
Introduction to Problem Solving
Programming Structures
Assembly Programming
Numerical Methods
Applied Fortran
Differential Equations

Dentistry

Many Dental Schools require for admission a background in Mathematics at least through Calculus. A Mathematics major who is interested in Dentistry can prepare himself/herself for Dental School by choosing electives wisely. The following are typical requirements for admission to a Dental School (specifically Columbia).

8 hours of English   8 hours of Organic Chemistry
8 hours of Inorganic Chemistry   8-12 hours of Biology
9 hours of Physics

Students who are interested in a career in Dentistry should consult with the Career Services and the Biology Department.

Economics

Mathematics is becoming increasingly important in the field of Economics. The collection and classification of data and deducing the significant trends therein is a job for people with strong mathematical backgrounds. Business applications of Economics are carried out in studies of Agricultural Economics, Market Studies, Pricing Policies, Insurance Risk Studies and Bank Loan Policies. Government applications include labor supply studies and National Economic Policy.

Students interested in careers in Economics should take the following courses as a minimum. If you have the time and interest, additional courses selected under advisement would be useful.

Principles of Microeconomics	Principles of Macroeconomics
Econometrics	Managerial Economics
Income, Employment, Growth	Theory and Practice

Education

For those persons planning a career in Elementary Education the requirements for the Mathematics Major and the College of Education are sufficient to qualify them for certification. Those students interested in Secondary Education may be similarly certified. However, High School Mathematics Teachers are increasingly expected to teach courses in Computer Science and Probability. Therefore, the following courses are recommended.

Introduction to Computer Based Systems	
Fortran for Liberal Studies	Probability and Statistics I
Probability and Statistics II	History of Mathematics

Persons interested in careers in Education should contact the School of Education concerning the requirements for certification in New York State.

Law

There are no specific majors which prepare students for Law Schools. Any student with a strong liberal arts background may apply to and be accepted by a law school. There are certain courses offered at Potsdam that students interested in a Law career find useful.

American Government   Constitutional Law
Civil Liberties   At least a year of English

Medicine

Modern medicine is making increasing use of quantitative techniques. A person with a solid mathematical background can become qualified to enter Medical School if he or she uses electives properly. The following is a list of requirements for a typical medical school.

6-8 hours of Physics   16-18 hours of Chemistry
6-8 hours of English   12-16 hours of Biology (with Lab)
plus courses in Comparative Anatomy, Genetics and Microbiology.

Operations Research

Operations Research is concerned with scientifically deciding how to best design and operate man-machine systems, usually under conditions requiring the allocation of scarce resources. Many positions are available in management consulting firms and in military or other government agencies.

Persons interested in careers in or should take the following courses as a minimum. If you have the time and interest, additional courses selected under advisement would be useful.

Introduction to Computer Based Systems
Numerical Methods   Applied Fortran
Operations Research I   Operations Research II
Differential Equations

Physics

The science of Physics is involved in nearly every area of technological advancement. Industrial and Product research, Biophysics and its relation to Ecological studies, astronomy and various engineering fields (Mechanical, Electrical, Acoustic) are some of the careers available to Mathematics majors with a background in Physics. Persons wishing a career in Physics should go to graduate school, but a B.A. in Physics combined with geology, mathematics, computer science, or engineering usually will lead to employment. Physics combined with an applied science is good.

Differential Equations	General Physics I
General Physics II	General Physics III
Modern Physics	Mechanics

Statistics

Statistics is a branch of applied mathematics concerned with the organization and analysis of data. It is rapidly expanding and as such the job picture is quite good. Careers for trained statisticians are available in medical research (particularly drug firms), agriculture (testing new grain varieties, for instance), and government regulatory and research organizations. Moreover, virtually all large corporations maintain a statistical division to help analyze economic conditions, pricing policy, etc.

Persons interested in careers in Statistics should take the following courses as a minimum.

Probability and Statistics I, II } (discrete)
Linear Algebra II
Advanced Calculus II
Probability & Mathematical Statistics I, II.

THE NEWSLETTER

[We have mentioned before that Potsdam College math department has succeeded in creating a large family of its math graduates and the math teachers. The department makes sincere efforts to give its students a sense of belonging to this close-knit family. This contributes a lot to creating a humanistic environment for learning math. The newsletter, published annually, plays a major role in keeping this family together. Therefore, to give the readers a glimpse of the activities of this family, we are reproducing here the 1992 newsletter with apologies to the math family of Potsdam since we have not been able to reproduce the beautiful and pleasant get-up, the display and the formatting of the newsletter. In any case, we do hope that the contents of the newsletter, as presented here, will give a good insight into what goes on outside the classrooms at Potsdam and how the math graduates of Potsdam prove their worth in the real world.]

POTSDAM COLLEGE

OF THE STATE UNIVERSITY OF NEW YORK

THE NEWSLETTER 1992

M.A.A.E.M., New York Phi Chapter of Pi Mu Epsilon and the Department of Mathematics

FALL 1992   CIRCULATION 2,600

171

TABLE OF CONTENTS

DEPARTMENT OF MATHEMATICS

Chair of Department .... Vasily C. Cateforis
Secretary ....Patricia A. Beaulieu

FACULTY:

Mark Armstrong, B.A., M.A., Potsdam College, SUNY; Visiting Instructor; AMS

Vasily C. Cateforis, B.S., Morgan State College; M.S., Ph.D., University of Wisconsin; Algebra; Professor; MAA; AMS

Kerrith B. Chapman, A.B., Assumption College; M.S., Ph.D., Kansas State University; Harmonic Analysis; Associate Professor; AMS; MAA

Dilip Datta, B.A., Cotton College (India); M.A., Ph.D., University of Delhi (India); Differential Geometry; Adjunct Professor; AMS, MAA, Indian Math. Society, Tensor Society, Japan

Hector B. Foisy, A.B., St. Michael's College; M.A., University of Illinois; Ph.D., George Peabody College for Teachers; Mathematics Education; Professor; MAA

Jerre F. Kilroy, B.S., M.S., SUNY at Albany; M.A., University of Illinois; Algebra; Associate Professor

Ramesh M. Kulkarni, B.S., M.Sc., Wilson College (Bombay University); M.A., Ph.D., Indiana University; Functional Analysis; Associate Professor

James C. Magee, B.S., St. Lawrence University; M.A.S., Harvard University; M.S., Notre Dame University; Ph.D., Clarkson University; Functional Analysis; Professor; AMS

S. Kazem Mahdavi, M.S., Tehran University, Iran; M.A., Ph.D., SUNY at Binghamton; Algebra; Professor; AMS; MAA

Cheryl Chute Miller, B.S., John Carroll University; Ph.D., Wesleyan University; Logic; Assistant Professor; AMS; MAA; AWM; CMS

Wesley J. Mitchell, (On leave 1991-1992), B.A., University of Rochester; M.S., Purdue University; Ph.D., University of Colorado; Harmonic Analysis; Associate Professor; MAA

James Parks, B.S., University of Wichita; M.S., Wichita State University; Ph.D., University of Houston; Algebraic Topology; Professor; AMS; MAA; SIAM

Laura Person, B.S., M.A., Ph.D., University of California at Santa Barbara; Topology; Assistant Professor; AMS; MAA

Irene Schensted, A.B., Radcliffe College; M.A., University of Minnesota; Ph.D., University of Michigan; Mathematical Physics; Associate Professor; MAA

William N. Sloan, B.S., M.Ed., St. Lawrence University; M.A., University of Illinois; Mathematics Education; Associate Professor

Charles L. Smith, B.S., Rensselaer Polytechnic Institute; M.S., Syracuse University; M.A., University of Illinois; Ed.D., Columbia University; Mathematics Education; Professor; MAA

David Spellman, B.A. (History), University of Texas at Austin; B.S. (Mathematics), University of Texas at San Antonio; Ph.D., University of Texas at Austin; Topology; Assistant Professor; AMS; MAA

Armond E. Spencer, B.S., M.S., Ph.D., Michigan State University; Algebra; Professor; AMS; MAA

Key:
AMS = American Mathematical Society;
AWM = Association for Women in Mathematics;
CMS = Canadian Mathematical Society;
MAA = Mathematical Association of America; and
SIAM = Society for Industrial and Applied Mathematics

DEPARTMENTAL AWARDS AND RECOGNITION OF STUDENTS
Departmental Scholar
Institutional Membership to the American Mathematical Society, the Mathematical Association of America and the Association for Women in Mathematics
Susan DeWitt Kaiser Award

M.A.A.E.M. (Mathematics Alumni Award for Excellence in
Mathematics)
Pi Mu Epsilon
C. F. Stephens Mathematics Scholar
Mathematical Achievement Scholarship
AMTNYS (Association of Mathematics Teachers of New York State)
Award

July 1, 1992
Dear Mathematics Alumni,
    Mathematics Majors,
    Parents and Friends:
We are pleased to send you the 1992 Newsletter.

You will find depicted in the pages that follow one aspect of the life of
the Department for the year 1991-1992: the documented aspect.

As usual, a lot of space is given to the achievements of the mathematics
majors that walk the hallways of MacVicar Hall now. And that is as it
should be.

You will also read about the faculty that look after these mathematics
majors, though, as you know, our task is made easier when we all, students
and faculty, work together.

And I hope that the Alumni section will provide you with as much
enjoyment as it provides us here in the Department. You will notice in the
Pi Mu Epsilon section that our alumni continue to make our induction
ceremonies quite special and always memorable. And there is an interesting
tale in the MAAEM section.

The number of mathematics majors who are also in a certification
program, preparing to teach in our primary and secondary schools has
increased significantly over the past five years. So we have created a
special section for them.

As you know, there is much more to the life of our Department - more
than what we have documented here. And it has to do with feelings:
feelings of satisfaction from good math classes; from correct proofs; from
solving a difficult problem after many hours (or days, or months) of work;
from making lifelong friends.

    Keep writing to us.
Sincerely,

V. C. Cateforis, Chair
Department of Mathematics

GRADUATES

MATHEMATICS MAJORS
70 baccalaureate Degrees Awarded
August 1991 (3), December 1991 (25), May 1992 (51)

Allgaier, Eric George
** PME
Presidential Scholar
Other Major: Physics
Schenectady
Colonie Central High School

Avila, Erwin Delizo
Minor: CIS
New York
Newtown High School

Barber, Laurie Lynn
Glens Falls
Lake George Central School

Beaulieu, Gina Marie
(LaFave) PME
Other Major: Education N-9
Brasher Falls
St. Lawrence Central School

Blackburn, Pamala Jeanne
Other Major: Education N-6
Gouverneur
Gouverneur High School

Bourgault, Steven James
*** PME
BA/MA
Troy
Tamarac High School

Bracken, Lynn Ellen
Ilion
Ilion Junior-Senior High School

Burke, Ronald Patrick
*** PME
Other Major: Education 7-12

Canton
Hugh C. Williams Senior High School

Carswell, Brent Joseph
*** PME
Presidential Scholar
BA/MA Math
Other Major: Physics
Whitehall
Whitehall Junior-Senior High School

Catanzarite, Christine Lynn
Other Major: Education 7-12
Massena
Massena Central High School

Clemons, Lisa Ann
(Collins) Hannawa Falls
Potsdam Central High School

Converse, Elizabeth Susan
* PME
Other Major: Education N-9
Massena
Massena Central High School

Cooke, Jana Lee
*** PME
Other Major: Education 7-12
Philadelphia
Indian River Jr.-Sr. High School

Crane, Kristie Ann
Other Major: Education N-6
Harrisville
Harrisville Central School

Cuddeback, Heather Anne
*** PME
Other Major: Education N-9
Auburn
Auburn High School

D'Agostino, Melissa Anne
Minor: CIS
Liverpool
Liverpool High School

D'Ambrosi, Patrick Lee
Minor: Health Science
Turin
S. Lewis Jr.-Sr. High School

Davidson, Andrew E.
Fairport
Fairport High School

Defone, Laurie Anne (Rowsam)
Other Major: Education N-9
Lowville
Lowville Academy and Central School

DeRoche, John Thomas
** PME, Minor: CIS
West Hurley
Onteora Central Jr.-Sr. High School

Dissanayake, Rohana
Springfield, OH

Dix, Patricia Ann
* PME
Other Major: Education N-9
Watervliet
Watervliet Junior/Senior High School

Dixon, Stephen Michael
Other Major: Physics
Syracuse
Westhill High School

Drake, Andrew Thomas
* PME
Other Major: CIS
Clifton Park
Shenendehowa Central School

Dunkelberg, Lisa Marie
* PME
Other Major: Education 7-12
Gouverneur
Gouverneur High School

Edick, Kathleen E.
** PME, BA/MA Math
Other Major: CIS
Croghan
Beaver River Central School

Emburey, Susan L.
PME, Other Major: CIS
Potsdam
Potsdam Central High School

Emerson, Timothy O.
Minor: Biology
Rochester
Churchville-Chili Sr. High School

Ewell, William Todd
Rochester
Ellsworth J. Wilson Sr. High School

Fenwick, Christopher Richard
Minor: CIS
New Windsor
Newburgh Free Academy

Flett, Melissa Quinby
* PME
Minor: Business Economics
Cape Vincent
Thousand Island High School

Frank, Kevin W.
Minor: Business Economics
Schenectady
Notre Dame-Gibbons High
School

Glasgow, Ellen Julia
Other Major: Education 7-12
Canton
Colton-Pierrepont Central
School

Goodwin, Ervin Ellsworth
Other Major: CIS
Antwerp
Indian River Jr.-Sr. High
School

Gorman, Matthew James
West Monroe

Green, David Christopher
Other Major: Education 7-12
Adams
Belleville Henderson Central
School

Griffith, Stacy Thomas
Minor: Health Science
Ogdensburg
Lisbon Central School

Gunn, Gregory Carl
** PME
Other Major: Education 7-12
Auburn
Auburn High School

Hall, Andrew Joseph
* PME
Other Major: Physics
Endicott
Whitney Point Sr. High
School

Harned, Raymond Todd
Other Major: Education 7-12
Clay

Cicero-N. Syracuse High
School

Hoen, Cyd Marie
Rensselaer
Bishop Maginn High School

House, Melissa Marie
Other Major: CIS
Parish
Pulaski Academy and Central
Jr.-Sr. School

Humphrey, James P.
PME
Minor: Business Economics
Poland
Poland Central School

Jones, Tracey Ann
Other Major: Education 7-12
Canton
Hugh C. Williams Sr. High
School

Kelly, Colleen Bridget
Other Major: Education N-6
Westerlo
Greenville Jr.-Sr. High School

Lagoy, Rene Lynn
Amsterdam
Bishop Scully High School

Larue, James Patrick
*** PME
Other Major: Education 7-12
Massena
Thomas High School

Lyndaker, Loren Donald
*** PME
Other Major: Education 7-12
Lowville
Lowville Academy and Central
School

MacKinnon, Heather Jan
Other Major: Education N-6
Gouverneur
Gouverneur High School
Maier, David Anthony
Other Major: CIS
Rochester
Brighton High School
Merlino, Michelle Ann
Other Major: Education N-9
New Hartford
New Hartford Sr. High School
Miller, Christian Edward
Lancaster
Lancaster Central High School
Monaco, David Michael
Other Major: Education 7-12
Gouverneur
Gouverneur High School
Muscolino, Patrick Francis
Other Major: Education 7-12
Chittenango
Chittenango Senior High
School
Nagle, Scott Allen
Minor: CIS
Binghamton
Chenango Valley High School
Newton, Debra Lee
** PME
Other Major: Education N-9
Potsdam
Potsdam Central High School
O'Neill, John Clifford
** PME, BA/MA
Presidential Scholar
Other Major: Drama
Albany
Bishop Maginn High School

Ovando, Leslie Marina
** Other Major: Education 7-12
Beaver Falls
Beaver River Central School
Panczyszyn, Frank T.
* Other Major: Education 7-12
Rochester
McQuaid Jesuit High School
Pate, Tina Marie
*** PME
Other Major: Education 7-12
Castorland
Beaver River Central School
Pauquette, Paul M.
*** PME, Other Major: CIS
Earlton
Coxsack Athens Jr.-Sr. High
School
Pierce, Laura Anne
PME
Other Major: Education N-9
Lowville
Lowville Academy and Central
School
Pitaniello, Anthony Louis
Clifton Park
Shenendehowa Central School
Pokorak, Eric Gerard
Other Major: Biology
Endwell
Maine Endwell Senior High
School
Schneider, Kelli Jean
* PME
Other Major: Economics
Massena
Massena Central High School

Schofell, Tammy Lynn
Other Major: Education N-9
Lisbon
Lisbon Central School
Shaffer, Gail M.
* PME, BA/MA Math
Waterloo
Waterloo Senior High School
Siebels, Christopher G.
Other Major: Education 7-12
Gouverneur
Gouverneur High School
Smith, Mary Elizabeth
PME
Other Major: Education N-9
Ballston Spa
Saratoga Springs Senior High
School
Taub, Audrey Felicia
** PME, BA/MA Math
Minor: Business Economics
Beacon
Beacon High School
Tisdale, Marquis William
Chazy
Chazy Central Rural School
Trauffer, John David
** PME
Other Major: BA in Music
New Paltz
New Paltz Central High
School

Vatter, Jean Marie
Minor: Business Economics
Jamesville
Bishop Grimes High School
Vine, William Michael
Other Major: Education 7-12
Ogdensburg
Lisbon Central School
Waldruff, Christina Dawn
Other Major: Education N-9
Gouverneur
Gouverneur High School
Wilber, Pamela Louise
PME
Syracuse
Thomas J. Corcoran High
School
Williams, Robin Marie
* PME
Minor: CIS
Waverly
Tioga Central School
Woodrow, Tamra Anne
Hermon
Hermon-DeKalb Central
School
Zehr, Barbara Anne (Fayle)
Other Major: Education N-9
Lowville
Lowville Academy and Central
School

Graduate Key
***Summa cum Laude   **Magna cum Laude   *cum Laude
+ with distinction   **CIS** — Computer and Information Sciences
BA/MA — Student completed 4-year Bachelor's-Master's degrees in
                Mathematics
PME — membership in New York Phi (campus) chapter of Pi Mu
        Epsilon

Note: The following students who completed all the requirements for the BA degree with a mathematics major in 1991 were awarded the degree too late for inclusion in the 1991 Newsletter:

Meyer, Janene
B.A. Mathematics
Plattsburg
Plattsburg Senior High School

Washburn, Patrick J.
B.A. Mathematics
Norwich
Norwich Senior High School

Ramsay, Wendy Sue
B.A. Mathematics & Philosophy
Brockport
Brockport High School

The following mathematics graduates were President's Scholars:

Allgaier, Eric G.
Jeffery, Denise A.

Carswell, Brent J.
O'Neill, John C.

Six Master of Arts degrees in Mathematics were awarded at Commencement on May 10:

Bourgault, Steven J. + (BA/MA)
Edick, Kathleen E. + (BA/MA)
Shaffer, Gail M. (BA/MA)

Carswell, Brent J. + (BA/MA)
O'Neill, John C. (BA/MA)
Taub, Audrey F. (BA/MA)

The following student completed the requirements for the Master of Arts degree for the May 1991 graduation but was not included in the 1991 Newsletter:
Allen, Jr., Gilbert A.

The following students were awarded a Master of Science in Education, Secondary Mathematics during the period August 1991 - May 1992:

Ballard, Jeannine C.
Chase, Nelson W. III+
Mattingly, James R.+
Ross, Kathleen+

Capone, Andrew J.
Hollister, Kelly A.
McKeel, Lisa R.
Smith, Pamela F.

The following students were awarded the Master of Science in Teaching degree in Secondary Mathematics during the period August 1991 - May 1992:

Akins, Rebecca L.   Amo, Debra J.
Clemens, Glenn+   Clemens, Margaret +
Grover, Elizabeth M.   Grugan, Carolyn J.
Mackie, Pamela L.   Meyer, Janene K.
Mizgala, Heather   Norman, Donna M.
Richardson, Paul A.   Smith, Shane C.+

+With Distinction

(Students completing master's degree requirements at Potsdam College with a cumulative grade point average of 3.90 or higher are granted the degree With Distinction).

ACADEMIC ACHIEVEMENT: MATHEMATICS MAJORS
August 1991, December 1991, May 1992

College Cumulative *Averages*	*Number*	*Cumulative* *Number*	*Cumulative* *Percentage*
3.75-4.0 (Summa Cum Laude)	9	9	11.39
3.50-3.74 (Magna Cum Laude)	11	20	25.32
3.25-3.49 (Cum Laude)	9	29	36.71
3.0 -3.24	9	38	48.10
2.75-2.99	21	59	74.68
2.50-2.74	17	76	96.20
2.0 -2.49	3	79	100

Graduates with cumulative averages in the range 3.25 - 4.00 receive the designation of having graduated with honors if they have completed at Potsdam at least 60 academic semester hours of which at least 75% have been taken for a numerical grade.

DISTRIBUTION OF BACHELORS DEGREES

AUGUST 1991 - MAY 1992

	No. of Degrees	Awarded to Females	Awarded to Males	With Honors
College	770	488 (63.38%)	282 (36.62%)	167 (21.69%)
Mathematics	79	41 (51.9%)	38 (48.18%)	39 (36.71%)
Percentage	10.26%	8.40%	13.48%	17.37%

DISTRIBUTION OF BACHELOR'S DEGREES AWARDED WITH

HONORS

	Total Number	Cum Laude	Magna Cum Laude	Summa Cum Laude
College	167	78	66	23
Mathematics	29	9	11	9
Percentage	17.37%	11.54%	16.67%	39.13%

SECOND MAJORS COMPLETED BY THE GRADUATES
Total Second Majors: 48 (60.76%)

	Number	% Math Majors	% Second Majors
Education	34	43.04	70.83
7-12	(18)	(22.78)	(37.50)
N-9	(12)	(15.19)	(25.07)
N-6	(4)	(5.06)	(8.03)
CIS	7	8.86	14.58
PHYSICS	3	3.80	6.25
Other	4	5.06	8.33

(One each of BIO, DRAMA, ECON, MUSIC)

MINORS COMPLETED BY THE GRADUATES
Total Minors: 14 (17.72%)

	Number	% Math Majors	% Minors
Business Economics	5	6.33	35.71
CIS Minor	6	7.59	42.86
Health Science	2	2.53	14.29
Biology	1	1.27	7.14

EDUCATION AND JOB OFFERS

EDUCATION

Some of the graduates listed below received financial assistance for graduate study ranging from $8,000 to $14,000 (in addition to waiver in tuition or reduction of fees).

Pamala J. Blackburn
Potsdam College/Masters in
Reading
Steven J. Bourgault
Kansas State University/Ph.D.
in Mathematics; SUNY,
Albany/Ph.D. in Mathematics
Ronald P. Burke
Potsdam College/M.A. in
Mathematics; Syracuse
University/Law; SUNY
Buffalo/Law
Brent J. Carswell
University of Kansas/Ph.D.
Mathematics; SUNY
Albany/Ph.D. Mathematics;
SUNY Binghamton/Ph.D.
Mathematics
John T. DeRoche
SUNY Binghamton/M.A.,
Mathematics

Patricia A. Dix
St. Rose, Albany, NY/M.S.,
Special Education
Melissa Q. Flett
University of Michigan/M.S.,
Applied Statistics; Clemson
University/M.S.,
Mathematical Sciences;
University of Kentucky/M.S.,
Statistics
Gregory C. Gunn
Potsdam College/M.S. Ed.
Secondary Mathematics
Andrew Hall
North Carolina State
University/M.S. Physics
James P. Larue
Tulane University; Louisiana
State University; University
of Pittsburgh/Ph.D.,
Mathematics

Eric C. Lohr
College of Insurance,
Manhattan/MBA in
Finance/Actuarial Science

Loren D. Lyndaker
Potsdam College/Instructional
Technology and Media
Management

Christian E. Miller
SUNY at Buffalo/MA/Ph.D.
in Mathematics

John C. O'Neill
SUNY at Albany/Ph.D.,
Mathematics; University of
California at Santa
Barbara/Ph.D., Mathematics

John D. Trauffer
SUNY Albany/Ph.D. in
Mathematics

William M. Vine
Potsdam College/Secondary
Education/Mathematics

Christina D. Waldruff
Potsdam College/Elementary
Education

Barbara A. (Fayle) Zehr
Potsdam College/Elementary
Education

JOB OFFERS

Erwin F. Avila
Clemente Capital, Inc., New
York, NY as Trade Settlement
Administrator

Kristie A. Crane
Central Day Care, Buffalo,
NY, Teacher

James P. Humphrey
Kraft General Foods, North
Lawrence, NY, Lab
Technician

Loren D. Lyndaker
Lowville Central School,
Student Learning Center
Teacher

Kelli J. Schneider
SeaComm Federal Credit
Union, Potsdam, NY, Teller

Christopher G. Siebels
Thousand Island Central
Schools, Clayton, NY, Middle
School Remedial Mathematics
Teacher

Kimberly S. Spoor
Wendy's of Rochester,
Rochester, NY, Assistant
Manager

Barbara A. (Fayle) Zehr
3rd grade teacher, Beaver River
Central School

---

*Some of our graduating majors
shared with us education and job
offers received and accepted.
Beginning salary offers appear to
be keeping pace with inflation
and reflect the individual's
preparation as well.*

MATHEMATICS MAJORS IN EDUCATION

STUDENT TEACHERS DURING 1991-1992

FALL

Amo, Debra
Hermon DeKalb Central;
Edwards Knox Central

Beaulieu, Gina M.
(LaFave)   Lisbon Central;
Potsdam Middle School

Cooke, Jana L.
Gouverneur Jr. High;
Gouverneur High

Crane, Kristie A.
Joy Elementary; Denti
Elementary

Cuddeback, Heather A.
Alexandria Central;
LaFargeville Central

Defone, Laurie A.
(Rowsam)   School #30;
Eastridge Jr. High

Dix, Patricia A.
Madison School; Leary Jr.
High

Glasgow, Ellen J.
Gouverneur High; Morristown
Central

Harned, Raymond T.
South Jefferson; Alexandria
Central

Larue, James P.
Salmon River Central;
Salmon River Central

Mackie, Pamela
Perry Jr. High; Sauquoit Sr
High

Merlino, Michelle A.
Sauquoit Jr. High; Harts Hill
Elementary

Monaco, David M.
Canton Central; Canton
Central

Newton, Debra L.
Norwood Elementary;
Massena Jr. High

Norman, Donna
Brushton High; Brushton Jr.
High

Pierce, Laura A.
Forestport Elementary; Case
Jr. High

Siebels, Christopher G.
South Jefferson High;
Thousand Islands Central

Smith, Mary E.
Campus Learning Center;
Madrid-Waddington High

Thomas, Lisa
Malta Avenue School;
Saratoga Jr. High

SPRING

Blackburn, Pamala J.
A.A. Kingston Middle
School; Lawrence Avenue
Elementary

Burke, Ronald P.
Case Junior High School;
Watertown High School

Catanzarite, Christine L.
Salmon River Central School;
Ogdensburg Middle School
Chapman, Jr., Michael
Westmoreland Junior/Senior
High School; New Hartford
High School
Converse, Elizabeth S.
Madrid-Waddington Central
School; Potsdam Central
School
Defone, Laurie A.
(Rowsam) Albion Central
School
Dunkelberg, Lisa M.
Indian River Middle School;
Indian River Middle School
Forbes, Terese M.
Kennedy School; Ogdensburg
City Schools
Green, David C.
Copenhagen Central School;
South Lewis Central School
Grover, Elizabeth
Carthage Middle School;
Lowville Central School
Gunn, Gregory C.
Potsdam Central School;
Colton-Pierrepont Central
School
Johannes, Tamara L.
Paddy Hill Central School;
Kirkroad School
Jones, Tracey A.
Massena Central School;
Potsdam Central Schools
Kelly, Colleen B.
Lawrence Avenue Elementary;
Lawrence Avenue Elementary

MacKinnon, Heather J.
Calcium Elementary; Indian
River Middle School
McCarty, Robert
Heuvelton Central School;
Heuvelton Central School
Mizgala, Heather
Malone Middle School;
Immaculate Heart Central
School
Montondo, John A.
Morristown Central School;
Heuvelton Central School
Muscolino, Patrick F.
Gouverneur Central School;
Morristown Central School
Ovando, Leslie M.
Harrisville Central School;
Harrisville Central School
Pate, Tina M.
Lowville Academy & Central
School; South Lewis
Junior/Senior High School
Schofell, Tammy L.
Hammond Central School;
Hammond Central School
Shampine, Memorie L.
Philadelphia Elementary
School; Indian River Central
School
Vine, William M.
Indian River High School;
Indian River Middle School
Waldruff, Christina D.
Parishville-Hopkinton Central
School; Parishville-Hopkinton
Central School
Zehr, Barbara A. (Fayle)
Beaver River Central School;
Beaver River Central School

DEPARTMENTAL SCHOLARS

Teacher Education, N-6 Program:
Tamara L. Johannes   Terri Whitaker

Teacher Education, 7-12 Program:
Ronald P. Burke

Outstanding Student Teacher Certificate:

Debra Amo	Tina M. Pate
Heather A. Cuddeback	Christopher G. Siebels
Raymond T. Harned	Mary E. Smith
Michelle A. Merlino	William M. Vine

SUSAN DEWITT KAISER AWARD:

The Susan Dewitt Kaiser Award is given to the graduating mathematics major who has the highest academic average on record prior to the May graduation, who will also graduate with teacher certification, and who has also completed all academic years at Potsdam. The award was established by the family and friends of the late Susan Dewitt Kaiser, mathematics teacher, class of 1967.

1986 – Cheri Brunner	*1990 – Debra L. Zeiler*
1987 – Jennifer B. Every	*1991 – Gregory C. Gunn*
1988 – Donald C. Straight	*1992 – Elizabeth S.*
1989 – Kathleen D. Andrews	*Converse*

We are pleased to announce that the 1992 recipient of the Susan DeWitt Kaiser Award is **Elizabeth S. Converse**, a mathematics major in the N-9 certification program. Elizabeth was presented with a certificate and a check by Dr. James M. Parks at the College Honors Convocation, May 9, 1992, Snell Music Theater.

ASSOCIATION OF MATHEMATICS TEACHERS OF NEW YORK STATE (A.M.T.N.Y.S.) AWARDS

In the Spring of 1992 the Department established the AMTNYS Award to encourage prospective teachers of mathematics.

To be eligible for the award students must be juniors or seniors who have completed at least four courses in the Potsdam College mathematics major (or their equivalent) with an average of at least 3.25 in all mathematics courses taken (transfer grades in mathematics courses will be included in this average). In addition, the student must have declared a major in one of the mathematics teacher certification programs of the School of Professional Studies.

Recipients:

N-6	Margaret Scheitheir	N-9	Elizabeth S. Converse
7-12	Jennifer L. Ims		
	Ronald P. Burke		
	Tina M. Pate		

AWARDS TO MATHEMATICS MAJORS

Mathematics majors received awards and recognition at the School of Liberal Studies Honors Convocation, 4:00 PM, Thursday, April 30, 1992, Dunn Dance Theatre and at the College Honors Convocation, 1:30 PM, May 9, 1992, Snell Theater:

AMERICAN MATHEMATICAL SOCIETY MEMBERSHIP:

Steven J. Bourgault   Brent J. Carswell
Kathleen E. Edick   Christopher S. Hilt

ASSOCIATION FOR WOMEN IN MATHEMATICS MEMBERSHIP:

Monica L. Gabriel   Margaret Hagen

CLARENCE F. STEPHENS SCHOLARS: Monica L. Gabriel

MATHEMATICAL ASSOCIATION OF AMERICA MEMBERSHIP:

John T. DeRoche   Gregory C. Gunn
Charles J. Judge, IV

MATHEMATICS ALUMNI AWARD FOR EXCELLENCE IN MATHEMATICS

Graduating Seniors:	*Second Year Students:*
Steven J. Bourgault	Janet E. Anderson
	Jennifer L. Ims

Third Year Students:	
Eric Canfield	Monica L. Gabriel
Amy B. Dowett	Christopher S. Hilt

PI MU EPSILON AWARD: Brent J. Carswell

SUSAN DEWITT KAISER AWARD: Elizabeth S. Converse

POTSDAM COLLEGE FACULTY AWARD: (to a transfer student)
Instituted in 1992 to replace the Clarkson Memorial award, this is the highest award Potsdam College bestows upon at least two graduating seniors, one transfer and one not. This award is based on the student's academic achievement at Potsdam as measured by his or her GPA.

Loren D. Lyndaker

Mathematics majors were also recognized for their achievement with scholarships:

POTSDAM COLLEGE FOUNDATION SCHOLARSHIPS AND GRANTS:

Sylvia Levitt Angus Scholarship	Kathryn Longacker
Barrington Merit Scholarship	Meagan Brownell
Essay Award (Economics Department)	M. Somerset DePoint
Jessie B. Harman Scholarship	Nicole Cook
Jessie J. McNall Scholarship	Alexander Weissman
Married Student in Need Scholarship	Becky Montroy

Merit Scholarship

Eric Allgaier
Janet Anderson
Ginger Bassett
Brent Carswell
Patti Fadden
Christa Fahrenkrug
Monica Gabriel
John Hildebrand
Christopher Hilt
Michelle Houchin

Jennifer Ims
Denise Jeffrey
Jerry Jock
Tamara Johannes
Kathryn Longacker
David Lopez
John O'Neill
Scott Ozaroski
Christopher Smith
Angela VanAgs(Und-LP)
Julie Widelski

North Country Savings Bank Scholarship   Gloria Costello

Potsdam College Mathematical Achievement Scholarship

Steven Bourgault
Brent Carswell
Jerry Muir

John O'Neill
Gail Shaffer
Audrey Taub

Presidential

Eric Allgaier
Janet Anderson
Brent Carswell
Monica Gabriel

Denise Jeffery
Kathryn Longacker
David Lopez
John O'Neill

Scott Ozaroski
Crista Fahrenkrug
Michelle Houchin

Alan H. Stillman Memorial Award   Andrew Drake

Phi Kappa Phi

*Founded in 1897, Phi Kappa Phi is the largest and most respected
honor society in the country which is open to most students in all
academic disciplines. The Potsdam Chapter, one of the two in the State
University system, was chartered in 1991.*

1992 Inductees:

Steven J. Bourgault
Ronald P. Burke
Brent J. Carswell
Margaret Y. Hagen

Christopher S. Hilt
Tina M. Pate
Audrey F. Taub

Phi Eta Sigma

We are happy to congratulate the following mathematics majors for their induction into the national honor society Phi Eta Sigma:

1992 Inductees:

Meagan E. Brownell	Charles F. Rocca, Jr.
Todd D. Carpenter	Nicole G. Sayer
Mark G. Gilmore	Christy J. Smith
Susan M. Gregory	Katherine E. Swanson
Sara E. Malone	Robin M. Walpin

Past Inductees:

1991 Inductees:

Yi-Ming Chen	Karin Rodgers
Mark Eygabroad	Jacquline Ventura
Kathryn Longacker	Gregory Stevens
Steven Minnick	Nicole Cook
Todd Lorenc	Stacy Wetherby
Anthony Netto	

1990 Inductees:

Christopher Hilt	David Lopez
Tamara Johannes	Daniel Stoker
Harold Johnson	Aung Thu
Mark Lewis	Charlene Titus

Induction into Phi Eta Sigma is based on outstanding academic achievement during the freshman year and is the highest honor now bestowed upon sophomores at Potsdam College.

DEPARTMENTAL SCHOLARS

The Department of Mathematics named 12 senior majors Departmental Scholars in 1992. Each of the students designated had a mathematics average of 3.61 or better and college GPA of 3.40 or better. The highest mathematics average was 4.0 and was attained by one student. The highest college GPA was 4.0 and was attained by one Departmental Scholar, who was a transfer student.

Steven J. Bourgault	John C. O'Neill
Ronald P. Burke	Tina M. Pate
Brent J. Carswell	Paul M. Pauquette
John T. DeRoche	Gail M. Shaffer
Charles J. Judge, IV	Audrey F. Taub
Loren D. Lyndaker	John D. Tauffer

Additional senior mathematics majors with cumulative averages in the range for departmental scholars and who were among the group from which departmental scholars were selected:

Eric G. Allgaier	Gregory C. Gunn
Michael Chapman, Jr.	Andrew J. Hall
Elizabeth S. Converse	James P. Humphrey
Jana L. Cooke	Denise A. Jeffery
Heather A. Cuddeback	James P. Larue
Patricia A. Dix	Kelli J. Schneider
Andrew T. Drake	Robin M. Williams
Kathleen E. Edick	

Certificates were presented by Dr. K. Mahdavi at the School of Liberal Studies Honors Convocation held at 4:00 PM, April 30, 1992 in Dunn Recital Hall.

Mathematics majors were named Departmental Scholars by other academic departments:

Computer and Information Sciences: Christopher Hilt, Andrew Tate
The Crane School of Music: John D. Trauffer

Dance and Drama:	John C. O'Neill
Economics:	M. Somerset DePoint
Physics:	Eric G. Allgaier, Brent J. Carswell

The number of Departmental Scholars in a department may not exceed 5% of the total number of junior and senior declared majors (1st or 2nd) having attained a college GPA of 3.25 or better. There are a large number of mathematics majors deserving to be recognized as Departmental Scholars who are not so recognized because of the 5% restriction. In general, the Mathematics Departmental Scholars are chosen among the graduating senior mathematics majors.

PRESIDENT'S LIST

Students named to the President's List completed during the semester(s) at least 15 hours (12 of which were numerically graded) with an average of 3.50 or better.

Eighty-eight mathematics majors were named to the list during the 1991-1992 academic year. An asterisk (*) indicates those students named to the President's Honors during both the fall and spring semesters.

Eric G. Allgaier
Janet E. Anderson*
Matthew Archibald
Gretchen Bachner
Tina Bergdorf*
Anthony Betrus
Maureen Bouchard
Steven J. Bourgault*
Lynn E. Bracken
Meagan Brownell
Kelly Bulman
Ronald P. Burke
Sandra Campbell
Eric Canfield
Todd Carpenter
Brent J. Carswell*
Yi-Ming Chen
Nicole Cook*

Gloria Costello
Teresa Delgado
J. David Demattos
M. Somerset DePoint*
John T. DeRoche
Amy Dowett
Andrew T. Drake*
Thomas Dupee*
Mark Eygabroad*
Patti Fadden
Crista Fahrenkrug
Lori Felt
Melissa Q. Flett
David Furletti
Monica Gabriel*
Carrie Garris
Linda Gates
Mark Gilmore*

Susan Gregory
Mark T. Haggett*
Andrew J. Hall
Kelly Heberle
Kimberlee Hill
Christopher Hilt
Jason Horita
Russell Horita
Jennifer Ims
Kristen Iocco
Tamara Johannes
H. Dean Johnson
Tracey A. Jones
Shannon Jordan
Charles J. Judge, IV
Mark Lewis II*
Kathryn Longacker*
Todd Lorenc
Deborah Manhey
Julie Meloche
Christian E. Miller
Becky Montroy
Amy A. Nass*
John C. O'Neill*
Leslie M. Ovando
Scott Ozaroski*
Tina M. Pate

Paul M. Pauquette
Alicia Reed*
Christina Reilly*
Charles Rocca, Jr.
Karin Rodgers
Jason Rotella
Tamara Russell
Jessica Ryan*
Nicole Sayer
Edward Schneider
Kelli J. Schneider
Heather Scofield*
Gail M. Shaffer*
Christy Smith
Kimberly S. Spoor
Audrey F. Taub*
Marquis W. Tisdale
Charlene Titus*
Alexander Weissman*
Stacey Wetherby
Terri Whitaker*
Julia Widelski
Robin M. Williams*
Robin Wolpin
Georgia Wyatt

4.0 Grade Point Average

Students on the President's List who earned 4.0 in all their courses:

Janet E. Anderson (F)(S)
Brent J. Carswell (F)(S)
Monica L. Gabriel (F)(S)
Tamara L. Johannes (F)
Becky Montroy (S)
Audrey F. Taub (S)
Terri Whitaker (S)

Steven J. Bourgault (F)(S)
Patti Fadden (F)
Christopher Hilt (F)
Kathryn Longacker (S)
Tina M. Pate (F)
Alexander Weissman (S)

CLARENCE F. STEPHENS SCHOLARS

The Clarence F. Stephens Mathematics Scholar Award was established in 1987. This award is given annually by the School of Liberal Studies and the Mathematics Department to the nongraduating mathematics major who, by his or her achievement in mathematics, best personifies C. F. Stephens' vision of the mathematics student who is becoming all he or she is capable of being. The award is a $250 credit at the Potsdam College Bookstore. In addition, the recipient will be designated a Clarence F. Stephens Mathematics Scholar and his or her name will be inscribed on a plaque to be displayed in Carson Hall.

The recipients of the C. F. Stephens Mathematics Scholar award are chosen by the Mathematics Faculty

C. F. STEPHENS MATHEMATICS SCHOLARS

(The first two scholars were chosen by Dr. Stephens in consultation with the Mathematics Faculty.)

1987-88:	Donald C. Straight Massena	1990-91:	Charles J. Calhoun Greene
1988-89:	Lisa L. Carte Hudson Fall	1991-92:	Steven J. Bourgault Troy
1989-90:	Nga-Shan (Phoebe) Cheung Hong Kong		

The Mathematics Faculty named two C. F. Stephens Mathematics Scholar for 1992-93:

Monica L. Gabriel Delhi	Christopher S. Hilt Rochester

The students were presented with a certificate by Dr. Cateforis at the School of Liberal Studies Honors Convocation held on April 30, 1992 in Dunn Dance Theatre.

Monica Gabriel is a 1989 graduate of Delaware Academy High School in Delhi. It was there that her interest and strength in mathematics developed. After her freshman year of college, she decided to pursue the study of mathematics further.

Monica is a Presidential Scholar. During her sophomore year, she was inducted into Pi Mu Epsilon, the national mathematics honor society, as well as Phi Eta Sigma, the national honor society for freshmen. In recognition of her achievements in mathematics, Monica has also been awarded membership to the Association for Women in Mathematics. She entered the BA/MA program in the fall of 1991 and expects to meet the requirements for both her BA degree and MA degree by May 1993. Her plans for the future are uncertain, but further study is being highly considered.

Christopher Hilt is a 1989 graduate of Eastridge High school in Rochester, NY and chose to attend Potsdam based upon its reputation of both the Mathematics and Computer Science departments. In his freshman year, he took Theory of Sets and decided to enter the BA/MA program the following fall. He expects to complete the requirements for the BA and MA degrees in Mathematics next year, needing only to take Complex Analysis and Calculus III. He also plans to complete his Computer Science major.

In his time spent at Potsdam, he was inducted into Phi Eta Sigma, the national honor society for college freshmen, Pi Mu Epsilon, the national mathematics honor society, Epsilon Delta, the national honor society for the Computer and Information Sciences and Phi Kappa Phi, the largest and most respected honor society in the country. He was also the recipient of the Mathematics Alumni Award for Excellence in Mathematics in both his freshman and sophomore years. Academics are important to Chris, but he has always had an interest in helping people. As a result, Chris became a Resident Assistant in Fall 1990 and joined the Potsdam Rescue Squad in October 1991. After Potsdam, he plans to attend graduate school, but he is uncertain as to the field of study.

The following 15 students in addition to the chosen C. F. Stephens Scholars were considered by the Faculty for this award:

Janet E. Anderson	Tina Bergdorf	Anthony Betrus
Eric Canfield	Amy Dowett	Crista Fahrenkrug
Jennifer Ims	Tamara L. Johannes	Dean Johnson
Mark Lewis II	Robert Linscheer	David Lopez
Scott Ozaroski	Jessica Ryan	Alexander Weissman

M.A.A.E.M.

1976 FACULTY AWARD RECIPIENT:

Susan Hartwig Kirkey
Massena, NY

M.A.A.E.M. COMMITTEE:

Dr. Hector B. Foisy, Chairman
Dr. Vasily C. Cateforis, Vice Chairman

The M.A.A.E.M. senior award consists of a check and a framed certificate of award. The name of each recipient is also inscribed on a plaque that is on permanent display in the Mathematics Department area. Both the check and certificate are presented at the College Honors Convocation held in the Spring. It is customary for the Chairman of the M.A.A.E.M. Committee to make the presentation on behalf of members of the mathematics alumni and the department. Junior and sophomore M.A.A.E.M. awards consisting of credit at the College Bookstore and a certificate are also presented at this convocation.

SENIOR M.A.A.E.M. AWARD RECIPIENTS:

1975:	Emilio Casero		Utica
	Niagara Falls		Stephen O'Keefe
1976:	Paul Hafer		Rochester
	Potsdam	1982:	Nancy Ofslager
1977:	Philip Schwartau		Rochester
	Saranac Lake		Ronald Vienneau
1978:	Nancy Burger		Henrietta
	Vestal	1983:	Marcia Borden
1979:	Catherine McMillan		Boonville
	Webster		Sharon (Schacter)
	James Snyder		Shoemaker
	Tupper Lake		Middletown
1980:	Sue A. Bauer	1984:	Gregory VanSlyke
	Rochester		Riverhead
	Colleen Maloney		Karen Whitting
	Webster		Burnt Hills
1981:	Laurinda Corman		

1985:	Barbara Boytim		Japan
	Endicott	1989:	Ronald D. Bousquet
	Dwight Tuinstra		Champlain
	East Lansing, MI		Lisa L. Carte
1986:	Susan Doriski		Hudson Falls
	Fort Edward	1990:	Nga-Shan (Phoebe)
	John Kinateder		Cheung
	Wappingers Falls		Hong Kong
1987:	Stacy A. Miceli		Darwyn C. Cook
	Williamsville		Parish
	Carolyn Stisser	1991:	Charles J. Calhoun
	Lydonville		Greene
1988:	Donald C. Straight		Paula J. Golding
	Massena		Rochester
	Eichiro Tokutomi	1992:	Steven J. Bourgault
	Zama Shi, Kanagawa,		Troy

We are pleased to announce that the following were chosen to receive a M.A.A.E.M. award at the School of Liberal Studies Convocation, April 30, 1992, Dunn Dance Theatre:

Third Year Students:	*Second Year Students:*
Eric Canfield	Janet E. Anderson
Amy B. Dowett	Jennifer L. Ims
Monica L. Gabriel	
Christopher S. Hilt	

We are pleased to introduce the recipient of the Senior M.A.A.E.M. award, **Steven J. Bourgault**. He was presented with a certificate and a check by Dr. V. C. Cateforis at the College Honors Convocation, May 9, 1992, Snell Music Theater.

Steven J. Bourgault is a 1988 graduate of Tamarac High School in Troy. He entered the BA/MA program in his sophomore year and received both degrees in 1992. During his college years, he was inducted into the following honor societies: Phi Eta Sigma, the national honor society for college freshmen, Kappa Delta Pi, the national honor society in education, Pi Mu Epsilon, the national mathematics honor society, Phi Kappa Phi, the largest and most respected honor society in the country.

In both his sophomore and junior years, he was a recipient of a Mathematics Alumni Award for Excellence in Mathematics award while also receiving the Clarence F. Stephens Mathematics Scholar Award as a junior.

As a senior, Steve was a departmental scholar and was granted membership to the American Mathematical Society.

Steve has accepted a Teaching Assistantship position at SUNY Center at Albany where he will continue with his mathematics education in pursuit of his Ph.D.

THE TALE OF THE FIRST PRESENTATION OF THE M.A.A.E.M.

CERTIFICATE OF AWARD
by Joyce Flint

When I was a child and would ask my grandmother about something that happened when she was young, her brown eyes would twinkle and she would say: "W-e-l-l, it was a long time ago, but this is how I remember it..." Perhaps that would be a good beginning for "The Tale of the First Presentation of the M.A.A.E.M. Certificate of Award" because it happened a long time ago - as reckoned by graduations.

In 1974, Dr. Arnold Dunn, a member of the mathematics faculty at Potsdam State and the department's alumni, was charged with the responsibility of obtaining addresses for as many of the mathematics alumni as possible and sending each of them a letter soliciting a contribution of $1.00 with which to establish "The Alumni Award for Excellence in mathematics." Response to the appeal was generous and an account for the award was opened at the Credit Union on campus. Emilio Casero was selected to receive the first award - a check from the fund - in 1975.

It wasn't until 1978, however, when Nancy Burger (now Sousa) was chosen to receive the award (which by then had come to be known as "The M.A.A.E.M.") that someone had the idea that it would be nice if the recipient were given something in addition to the check, something he or she could keep, something that would be a cherished reminder of the award in later years. A Pi Mu Epsilon certificate of award to be used as a guide for the new certificate was sent to the printer and the M.A.A.E.M. certificate of award was created.

Academic awards were seldom made in appropriate ceremonies at that time. So it was that on a pleasant afternoon between the last day of the semester and graduation day, Dr. Dunn, chairman of the M.A.A.E.M. committee, Dr. Charles Smith, advisor to PME and the departmental secretary drove Ms. Burger to Tardelli's Restaurant at the edge of town where the trio toasted her academic achievement. After the toast, Dr. Dunn, with well-chosen words and solemn manner that befitted the occasion, presented the M.A.A.E.M. certificate of award for the first time. That is how I remember it.

PI MU EPSILON — NEW YORK PHI

The New York Phi Chapter of Pi Mu Epsilon was established on April 8, 1970 with the following charter members:

Students: Sandra Caloren
   Gayle Carroll
   William Cavanaugh
   Velda Chamberlain
   Judy Dasno
   Diane Degroat
   Marilyn Facenda

Milton Ferreira
Christine Fischer
Nancy Goetz

Faculty: James Calarco(Adviser)
Hector B. Foisy
Elmer E. Haskins

During 1991-92 the Chapter inducted 35 new members.

Officers 1991-1992:
   President: Eric Canfield *Vice President:* Pamela L. Wilber

The Pi Mu Epsilon Award: $100. value: The recipient may choose one-year membership in a professional organization, books or a combination.

Award Recipients:

1973:	Colleen Guinn	1980:	Sue A. Bauer
	Baldwinsville		Rochester
	Richard Gustafson	1981	Laurinda Corman
	Syracuse		Utica
1974:	Harris Schlesinger	1982:	Lydia Hardy
	Glen Cove		Pleasantville
1975:	Barney Watson		Nancy Ofslager
	Canton		Rochester
1976:	Paul Hafer	1983:	Marcia Borden
	Potsdam		Boonville
1977:	Ron Olsson	1984:	Carla Genzel
	Huntington Station		Carthage
1978:	Nancy Berger		Gregory VanSlyke
	Vestal		Riverhead
1979:	Peter Brouwer	1985:	Barbara Boytim
	Potsdam		Endicott

1986:	Susan Doriski		Champlain
	Hudson Falls	1990:	Heidi J. Learned
1987:	Kimberly Johannes		Sandy Creek
	Greece	1991:	Paula J. Golding
1988:	Donald C. Straight		Rochester
	Massena	1992:	Brent J. Carswell
1989:	Ronald D. Bousquet		Whitehall

We are pleased to announce that Brent J. Carswell was chosen to receive Pi Mu Epsilon's 1992 award. Dr. C. Miller, the chapter's faculty sponsor, presented the award at the College Honors Convocation held May 9, 1992 at the Snell Music Theater.

Other nominees for the award were:

Steven J. Bourgault   John C. O'Neill
Andrew T. Drake   Gail M. Shaffer
Thomas Dupee   Audrey F. Taub
Gregory C. Gunn   Robin M. Williams

Brent Carswell graduated from Whitehall High School in 1988 and came to Potsdam College in the fall of that year. He has earned his masters degree in mathematics and his bachelor's degree in mathematics and physics, Summa cum Laude.

Brent is a Presidential Scholar, and a member of Phi Kappa Phi, the largest and most respected honor society in the country, Phi Eta Sigma, the honor society for college freshmen, Pi Mu Epsilon, a national honorary mathematics honorary society, Sigma Pi Sigma, the national Physics honor society and the American Mathematical Society.

He will attend SUNY Binghamton in the fall to pursue his Ph.D. in mathematics. To his two mathematics advisors, Dr. Daniel Kocan and Dr. Kazem Mahdavi, he owes unbounded thanks.

Pi Mu Epsilon Officers - 1992-1993
President: Lori L. Felt   *Vice President:* Charlene V. Titus (Fall)
                            Matthew P. Archibald (Spring)
Treasurer: Raymond B. Cole   *Secretary:* Lisa A. Santoro

Dates to Remember (Tentative)
Fall Induction: November 15,1992 *Spring Induction:* April 4, 1993
Picnic: Fall date contemplated

New York Phi Chapter Active Membership 1991-1992

Eric G. Allgaier
Janet E. Anderson (F)
Matthew P. Archibald (S)
Gina M.(LaFave)Beaulieu (F)
Anthony K. Betrus (F)
Maureen J. Bouchard (S)
Steven J. Bourgault
Carol Brafman
Ronald P. Burke
Sandra J. Campbell (S)
Eric Canfield
Brent J. Carswell
Michael Chapman
Raymond B. Cole (F)
Nola L. Collins (S)
Elizabeth S. Converse
Jana L. Cooke
Heather A. Cuddeback
J. David DeMattos (S)
M. Somerset DePoint (F)
John T. DeRoche
Patricia A. Dix
Andrew T. Drake (F)
Lisa M. Dunkelburg
Thomas Dupee (F)
Kathleen E. Edick
Susan L. Emburey (F)
Lynn Everett
Crista Ann Fahrenkrug (S)
Lori L. Felt (S)
Melissa Q. Flett (S)
Monica Gabriel
Linda C. Gates (S)
Gregory C. Gunn
Margaret Hagen
Mark T. Haggett (F)
Andrew J. Hall (S)
Christopher Hilt
Judy Hoskins

Michelle Houchin
James P. Humphrey (F)
Jennifer Ims (S)
Debbie Ingersoll
Denise A. Jeffery
Tamara Johannes
Charles J. Judge, IV
James P. Larue (F)
Karen LaShomb (F)
Roseanne Laudisio
Mark Lewis
Rob Linscheer
David Lopez
Todd J. Lorenc (F)
Loren D. Lyndaker
Deborah L. Manhey (S)
Phillip Meashaw
Becky L. Montroy (S)
Stacie Myers
Debra L. Newton
Jeffery Niccum
Kathy (Reape) Noftsier
John C. O'Neill
Scott E. Ozaroski (S)
Susanna Palmer
Tina M. Pate
Paul M. Pauquette (F)
Laura A. Pierce
Jeffery Pyskaty
Jessica L. Ryan (F)
Lisa A. Santoro (F)
Margaret G. Scheitheir (S)
Kelli J. Schneider
Gail M. Shaffer
Mary E. Smith
Daniel J. Stoker (F)
Kathy Swanson (S)
Audrey F. Taub
Karen Timkey

Charlene V. Titus (F)   Alex Weissman
John D. Trauffer   Pamela L. Wilber
Randy Tripp (F)   Robin M. Williams
Kris Van Beusichem   F – inducted in the Fall
Kathryn Walser   S – inducted in the Spring

Requirements for Membership in the Chapter

To be eligible for election into the New York Phi Chapter of Pi Mu
Epsilon, students must be:

1. Sophomores who are majoring in or intend to major in
   mathematics, who have completed at least three graded courses of
   college mathematics including one semester of Calculus, and who
   have achieved a grade of 4.0 in all mathematics courses taken and
   an overall grade point average of at least 3.25 (4.0 is the highest
   possible grade obtained at Potsdam College).
2. Juniors or Seniors who have completed at least four courses in the
   Potsdam College mathematics major or their equivalent with an
   average of at least 3.25 in all mathematics courses taken and an
   overall grade point average of at least 3.0.
3. Graduate students whose mathematical work is at least equivalent
   to that required of undergraduates who have maintained an average
   of at least 3.25 in all mathematics courses taken during the two
   semesters (immediately) preceding their election.

*Fall Induction was held at The Gallery in Thatcher Hall at 12:00 noon,
November 17, 1991. The Chapter welcomed 19 students into
membership. The guest speaker was Roseanne Serafini Romanek.*

Roseanne Serafini Romanek graduated in 1976 from Chenango
Valley High School in Binghamton, NY.

She attended Broome Community College from September 1976
until May 1979 where she received an Associates Degree in
Mathematics and Computer Science and another in Business
Administration. While at Broome, she was a member of the Honor
Society for Junior Colleges.

Roseanne transferred to Potsdam in the Fall of 1979 and graduated
with a Bachelor's Degree in Mathematics and Computer Science in
1981. She was inducted in Pi Mu Epsilon in October 1980.

She attended Southwest Texas State University from 1982 - 1986 and received a Masters Degree in Business Administration.

Roseanne has been employed with Lockheed Missiles Space Company as a software engineer for the past ten years - ever since graduation.

The title of Roseanne's speech was "The Real World." She spoke about her journey "after Potsdam" in search of job satisfaction and her settling for life satisfaction. Her very thoughtful remarks, which were extremely well received, are being made into a departmental pamphlet ("The Real World"). It will be available soon.

The Chapter's Spring Induction was held on March 22, 1992 at 12:00 Noon at The Gallery in Thatcher Hall. The Chapter welcomed 16 students into membership. The guest speaker was Joel Lalone.

Joel Lalone attended high school at South Jefferson Central, in Adams, NY. After high school, he continued his education and achieved an Associates degree in Accounting from Jefferson Community College. With his degree, Joel worked for a year as an accountant. Joel then attended Potsdam and graduated in 1984 with a BA in Mathematics. Next, he attended Syracuse University, and graduated in December of 1985 with an MS in Mathematics Education. Joel began teaching at Jefferson Community College the following fall. Just recently, Joel became an Associate Professor of Mathematics. He was, also, the recipient of the Chancellor's Award for Excellence in Teaching for 1991.

Joel spoke without notes of his experience at Potsdam and the debt he feels towards his teachers at Potsdam who helped him overcome his self-doubts. [We are grateful to him, as well, for being such a good advertisement for our program and for sending us many good students from Jefferson Community College.]

Officers and members of the Chapter sponsored faculty-student mixers during the Fall and Spring semesters. The Fall mixer was held in the afternoon of September 26, 1991 in the Faculty Lounge in Carson Hall. Many students stopped by between classes. The Spring mixer was held at noon, January 30, 1992 in the Faculty Lounge again. This mixer also was very well attended, and much fun was had by all.

Pi Mu Epsilon sponsored three talks during 1991-92. One talk was given October 17, 1991 by **Dr. Richard Ringeisen**, Chairman, Mathematics Department, Clemson University. He spoke on "To Thrackle, Subthrackle or What"; he also spoke on graduate study in mathematics at Clemson. The second talk was given by **Prof. David Hanson**, Chairman, Mathematics Department, SUNY Binghamton, November 14, 1991. He spoke on "Unexpected Outcomes of Coin Tossing" and also on graduate schools. The third talk was given by **Philip Church** from Syracuse University, March 11, 1992. He spoke on "Can Chrysler Corporation continue to improve with the help of Calculus?". He also spoke about graduate schools.

The concept of a Spring Picnic will have to be rethought, as the weather of Potsdam in late April or early May is not very nice.

ALUMNI NEWS

The following Job Offer to one 1991 graduate was received too late to be included in last year's Newsletter.

JOB OFFERS

Paula J. Golding, ANSER (Analytic Services Inc.), Alexandria, VA/Research Mathematician; Empire State College, Rochester, NY/Math Instructor; Prudential Insurance Company, Rochester, NY/Financial Planner

1963
Sandra (Smith) Austin, 17 Corey Lane, Niantic, CT 06357, Home Phone (203) 739-5826, Office Phone (203) 739-6946. East Lyme Board of Education, East Lyme, CT. Computer Coordinator. Sandra works with teachers and students in incorporating computer use into the curriculum of their high school.

1965

Mrs. Carol (Litke) Dawley, 7851 Pebblebrook Circle, Hanover Park, IL 60103, Home Phone (708) 830-9298. School District U-46, Elgin, IL, Substitute Teacher - all grades including bilingual most of the time, though it is high school math. Volunteer work - campaign chair for the Tri-Village United Way - secretary for Hanover Park Sister City Committee (also state board sci member). Married 25 years. Husband (G. Victor) works for SORBUS/Bell Atlantic - computer repair. Two children - Pamela is a junior at University of New Mexico (Spanish education major), Sean is a senior in high school.

1972

Pauline (Becker) Graveline has been promoted to professor of mathematics at Canton College of Technology. She resides with her daughter, Sara, at 23 Buck St., Canton, NY 13617.

1977

Dr. Kathryn Weld Brown has been given tenure and promoted to Associate Professor at the Department of Mathematics and Computer Science, Manhattan College (CUNY). Kathy and Shelden Brown and children, Nathaniel and William, reside at 241 Lake Street, Pleasantville, NY 10570.

1978

Nancy Del Borgo, Alumni Relations, has shared with us some terrific pictures from the *Cortlandt Forum* of Mark Monasky, MD, performing a craniotomy. Dr. Monasky is a neurosurgery resident in Baltimore, Maryland giving some of his time to the R. Adams Cowley Shock Trauma Center.

Stuart and Kathleen (Hetzler) Riordan are living in Raleigh, NC. A son, Brian Patrick, was born on March 15, 1991.

We had a nice long letter from **Nance (Burger) Sousa** around Christmas. During the summer of 1991, Nance and Dave took a 42 day trip across the USA on their bicycles - 3,652 miles! Wow! Nance has a new job at Kodak as Product Unit Manager for 110 cameras and slide projectors. The Sousas are still at 17 Old Orchard Lane, Fairport, NY 14450.

1979

Paul Chabarek, ACAS, MAAA, 7435 NW 75th Drive, Parkland, FL 33067-3904, Office Phone (407) 994-1900 x299, Lynn Insurance Group, Boca Raton, FL 33431-6398, Chief Actuary, Assessing the financial implications of future contingent events, married August 1983 to Diane Holst (BM from Crane, 1980, Masters (M.M.) from Ithaca College, 1984). Diane is currently a full-time homemaker. Kaylee Marie Chabarek was born 4/18/89. (Very nice picture!)

Jeri Anne (Jerminario) Hall, Box 104, Knapp Hall, Cobleskill, NY 12043, Home Phone (518) 234-5167, Office Phone (607) 431-2029, Programmer Analyst, Sicas Center, Oneonta, NY, Sicas Center, Lee Computing Center, SUC @ Oneonta, Oneonta, NY 13820,

Terri (Kohlbrenner) Holder, Lafayette Road, Jamesville, NY 13078, Home Phone (315) 677-3651 and Mark are the happy parents of a daughter, their second child, Kimberly Ann, born May 2, 1992. (Congratulations!)

Jane (Matuszak) Hunt, 2250 Big Bend Dr., Carrollton (suburb of Dallas), TX 75007, Home Phone (214) 416-1433, Office Phone (214) 575-5733, Texas Instruments, Dallas, TX. Jane says "I'm a technical writer. My primary responsibilities involve the design and development of technical documentation and training for the Government Electronics group of T.I. I'm most involved in computer-based training (CBT) for internal T.I. use. I worked for Texas Instruments in the area of technical training from 1980-1983. In 1983 I resigned to stay at home with our first born, Jeremy. In 1985, our 2nd son, Brian, was born. I returned to work at T.I. in 1988 after a 6-year hiatus". (Of course, Jane, we passed your message to Dr. Spencer.)

Paul Newmann and his wife Alison are living in Bellport, NY. A daughter, Casey Erin, was born February 14, 1991. (Congratulations!)

Beverly (Hasch) Payne, 14411 Garden Rd., Poway, CA 92064, Home Phone (619) 486-3988, Office Phone (619-547-3096), General Dynamics, San Diego, CA, Software Engineering Specialist. Beverly is a Lead Engineer managing 8-10 people on a multi-year, multi-million dollar software contract for the Air Force. She was recently married (4/25/92) and now has a stepson, Brian (9), as well as her daughter, Caroline (4). (Best wishes!)

1980

We heard from **Anita K. Powley.** She is now Anita K. Planenshek (was Anita K. Laux) and resides at 716 Orlando Streets, Edison, NJ 08817. (Best wishes!)

Leonard Van Wyk, 435 Plaza Dr., 2-24, Vestal, NY 13850 has completed the work for his Ph.D. in Mathematics, in an area of combinatorial group theory, at the State University of New York at Binghamton.

1981

James J. Burton, 5779 Main St., Verona, NY 13478, Home Phone (315) 363-4296, Office (315) 829-2520, Vernon Verona Sherrill Central Schools, Verona, NY, Math Teacher, teaches 6 classes each day with a total of 148 students, Course 1 - Regents, Course 2 - Regents, Course 3 - Honors, AP Calculus, mans the tutoring lab for two periods a day, coaches boys volleyball and boys tennis and is the co-advisor of Dollars for Scholars (Local Scholarship Group). James sends his congratulations to Dr. Foisy on his award. He also says he is very happy teaching at his Alma Mater. There are hopefully some positive changes in the future of education. There is always room for improvement and innovation. He would like to hear from the Department about how they feel about their students preparation and where high schools could improve. James feels that Potsdam, and in particular, the Math Department, served him well and would like to return the favor.

Scott Franko married Eileen Walsh in September. Eileen, a graduate of Plattsburgh State College and Russell Sage College, is an industrial hygienist with the U.S. Department of Labor, Occupational Safety and Health Administration. Scott, who graduated from Clarkson, is employed as a program research specialist with the State Department of Health. They reside in Colonie, NY. (Best wishes!)

1982

Robert and Kim (Quible) ('83) Ingersoll reside in Lockport, NY. Kim received her M.B.A. from Niagara University and is employed by Harrison Radiator Division of General Motors. She is a product comptroller for the heat exchange products business unit. A daughter, Kallie Suzette, was born on June 20, 1991. (Congratulations!)

1983

Lori Blaha has moved. Her new address is 29 Monroe Parkway, Massena, NY 13662 Home Phone (315) 769-3707. She is employed at SUNY, Potsdam, Central Computing Services as a Senior Programmer Analyst.

Randall Brown is a Math Instructor and Hockey Coach at Canton High School.

Kim (Quible) Ingersoll, (see Robert ('82)).

1984

Pamela (Kline) Bell, Lt., USN, 102 Glen Lake Dr., Pacific Grove, CA 93950, Home Phone (408) 375-7779, Office Phone (408) 646-3079, U.S. Navy, Monterey, CA, currently assigned to naval postgraduate school, Monterey, CA, as a student working towards her masters in applied mathematics. Pamela was married in July 1988 to Lt. Harold Bell, a naval aviator and E. E. from Villanova University. They met while stationed in Pensacola, FL and have managed to move together to Jacksonville, FL and then to Naval postgraduate school. Harry is also working towards his masters, majoring in Electrical Engineering. His follow-up orders are to USS Saratoga out of Mayport, FL. Pamela says "No children yet - no time!".

Karen (Cinzio) Corman, 326 Baltusrol Dr., Coatesville, PA 19320, Home Phone (215) 380-0290, Office Phone (215) 648-8946, Allstate Insurance Company, Valley Forge, PA, Financial Analyst, provides graphic analysis of company's statement of income. Karen was married on September 6, 1986 to Warren Corman, CIS graduate of 1984. They had a baby boy, Michael Warren on November 15, 1991. She will be working on a part-time home/office status. (Best wishes and congratulations!)

Andrea (Moore) Gerlach Crouch, Bear, DE, teaches senior high math and science at Wilmington Christian School. Her husband, Andrew, a graduate of Virginia Technology Institute, designs and sells irrigation systems for Aqua-Flo Company. They were married August 12, 1989. (Best wishes!)

Joseph Dempsey, 18 Robinson Street, Silver Creek, NY 14136, Home Phone (716) 934-7024, Office Phone (716) 532-3325, Gowanda Central Schools, Gowanda, NY, Joseph teaches math and computer science for Gowanda Jr./Sr. High School. He is also a part-time Math instructor for Jamestown Community College, Jamestown, NY. Joseph says "I have my Master's Degree in Math Education from SUNY Fredonia. My wife Barbara and I live in Silver Creek, NY. We have one daughter (18 months) and will be expecting our second in the near future. I still consider Potsdam's Math Program one of the best anywhere, and I would like to keep in touch so I may better promote the program to any possible students who may be interested". (Thank you, Joseph!)

Joel LaLone, 226 William St., Watertown, NY, 13601, was a recent recipient of the Coffeen Memorial Award presented to graduates of South Jefferson High School who have demonstrated exemplary leadership, character and citizenship. Joel is an associate professor of mathematics at Jefferson Community College in Watertown, NY. He has been honored as the outstanding faculty member by the JCC chapter of Phi Theta Kappa, a national honor society. He originated and continues to coordinate the college's math lab, and he has been involved in course development. He has also presented various programs on teaching strategies to staff, and he has spoken about the college's math program at high schools in the area. Joel was the keynote speaker at our Spring PME Induction (see the PME section).

1985

Jeannine C. Ballard, P.O. Box 147, Potsdam, NY 13676-0147, Home Phone (315) 287-4982, Norwood Norfolk Central, Norwood, NY, Jeannine is a Math 8 Teacher and advisor to the Math Club, 7th-8th. She has coached various sports presently reffing Girls Basketball. Jeannine graduated with Masters in Mathematics - Secondary Education, August 91 from Potsdam College. (Congratulations, we are proud of you!)

James Bash, Maplewood, NJ, recently left his position of six years with AT & T Bell Laboratories and is currently on a 18-month voyage around the world.

Paula (Wainwright) Easton had a daughter, Kristen Elana, born on July 21, 1991. (Congratulations!)

Kathy Purdy is back at Syracuse University (Mathematics Department) after her stint with the Peace Corps. She is into Applied Mathematics and very busy. She can be reached at 105 Dorset Rd., Syracuse, NY 13210.

1986

Cheri (Brunner) Boyd has completed her work for her Ph.D. in mathematics at the University of Rochester. Her thesis' title is "A type number formula for orders of level p2r+1M", a topic in Algebraic Number Theory. Dr. Boyd has accepted an appointment as Assistant Professor in the Department of Mathematics at the University of Scranton, beginning in the Fall of 1992. (Congratulations, we are proud of you!)

Paul and Virginia (Filiaci) Brunetto are living in Buffalo, NY. Paul is a mathematics instructor at Medaille College. Virginia is a senior biostatistician at Roswell Park Cancer Institute.

Christine Gladstone was married on September 1, 1991, to Randy Willmart. Christine is employed by Computer Science Corp. as a program marketing representative. Randy, a graduate of Clarkson University, is a terminal equipment technician at Glens Falls Communications Corp. They reside in Lake George, NY. (Best wishes!)

John and Kimberly (Johannes) Kinateder are living in Hilliard, OH. John is a statistician with the Battelle Memorial Institute, a Columbus-based research firm. Kimberly, who completed her Ph.D. in probability in three years at Michigan State University, teaches probability theory at Ohio State University. (Congratulation. We are proud of you!)

William J. Martin, Waterloo, Ontario, has completed his work (defended his thesis) for a Ph.D. in Mathematics at the University of Waterloo. His thesis was on combinatorics and optimization. He was married on August 19, 1989, to Jennifer Sly. (Congratulations! We are proud of you and best wishes!)

Sherrie L. Seaman was married on June 9, 1991 to Sonny Brar. Sherrie is employed by Pioneer Savings Bank in Troy, NY. Sonny, a graduate of Hudson Valley Community College, is employed by India Tea Co. They reside in Albany. (Best wishes!)

Sarah Jo Smith married Daniel Cullen in October 1991. (Best wishes!)

1987

Stanley Buyce, Maple Knoll Apts., Apt. I-50, Johnstown, NY 12095, Greater Johnstown Schools, Johnstown, NY. Stanley is a grade 7-8 Math teacher at Knox Junior High School, Johnstown, NY. This is his fourth year with the district.

David E. Colesante married Deborah A. Schneider on September 7, 1991. David is a technical support manager at Western Pacific Data Systems in Dallas, TX. Deborah is attending Mesa College in San Diego. They reside in Plano, TX. (Best wishes!)

Cheryl (D'Ambrosi) Goebel has moved to 56 Joann Court, Monmouth Junction, NJ 08852.

Eric Krauss, San Francisco, CA, has been consultant at the NASA Ames Research Center in Sunnyvale, CA since completing his dissertation.

Mary Alice Mooney, 120 W 44 St., Apt. 807, New York, NY 10036, Home Phone (212) 840-0322, CUNY Graduate Center, New York, Mary is pursuing a Ph.D. in Educational Psychology doing research in learning and teaching mathematics.

Daniel Royce, 3210 Klingle Rd, NW, Washington, DC 20008, Home Phone (202) 333-2682, Office Phone (301) 763-7475, U.S. Department of Commerce - Bureau of the Census, Washington, D.C., Mathematical Statistician, Design, implement and monitor surveys; write procedures discussing how to conduct the surveys, create forms and questionnaires; write results of various surveys in statistical reports; use various software packages (extensive computer usage).

Melanie Tarbell married Ralph Ford on May 19, 1990. Melanie is employed at CALDOR, Inc., as an information Center specialist and Ralph (Clarkson '86) is employed at IBM in East Fishkill, NY. They reside in Danbury, CT. (Best wishes!)

1988

Scott Barnett, 340 Woodlake Manor Dr., Lakewood, NJ 08701, Home Phone (908) 364-9570, Office Phone (908) 870-7008, AT & T Bell Laboratories, W. Long Branch, NJ, Scott is a member of the Technical Staff currently leading a small software development team. His primary responsibility is to do development and coordinate the releases of their product. Scott got married in June '92, he is enjoying life in New Jersey and invites anyone to come down and visit him and the shore! He recently completed his master's in Computer Science at Columbia University. (Thanks for the nudge, Scott, on Nancy's and Barre's (Seguin) wedding and Dan Voce's too; Jim Reitano has not told us yet!) (Best wishes!)

Maryann Bingham, 227 Old Post Road, Ulster Park, NY 12487, Home Phone (914) 658-8097, Office Phone (914) 382-2960, Kingston City Schools, Kingston, NY. Maryann says "Right now I'm teaching Computer Literacy courses through the Adult Education office at Kingston City Schools. Despite New York's budget difficulties, I'm holding my own. My son, James Edward, was born December 10, 1991 and he's the highlight of my life. The Newsletter is great. Keep up the good work. I'm glad to see the department is still keeping up its quality of educating students to 'think mathematically'". (Thanks, Maryann and congratulations!) **William Broderick** married **Heidi Learned** ('90) on July 27, 1991. They are both programmers for IBM in Poughkeepsie. They reside in Wappingers Falls, NY. (Best wishes!)

Eric C. Lohr is currently enrolled in the MBA program at the College of Insurance in Manhattan (101 Murray Street, NY, NY 10007-2132) where he also works as a Graduate Assistant. Eric sent information on Actuarial Science (thanks!); he has passed Part One of the Actuarial Exams after reviewing his Calculus and Linear Algebra. (Congratulations! We are proud of you!) (Yes, we do remember you Eric!)

Barre R. Seguin and Nancy A. Wilson got married October 19, 1991. They reside at 9070A Frazier St., Laughlin AFB, TX 78840, Home Phone (512) 298-3239. (Best wishes!)

Scott Rajeski and Cynthia Guyette ('89) were married on June 29, 1991. Scott received his master's degree in business administration from Clarkson University recently. Cynthia, who received her master's degree from Potsdam College, is a special education teacher for BOCES in Ogdensburg. (Best wishes! Congratulations! We are proud of you!)

Karen (Schautz) Van Wright, 152 Oregon Trail, Pine Bush, NY 12566, Home Phone 744-5784, Office Phone 744-2031, Pine Bush High School, Pine Bush, NY, Mathematics Teacher 7-12 (Computer Science classes 6 period daily including AP). Karen married Thomas in June, 1991. (Best wishes!)

1989

Ron Bousquet has some big news for us: he just bought a house! His new address is 844 Maria Lane, #1, Sunnyvale, CA 94086.

Lisa L. Carte, Donnelly Rd., RR 1, Box 15D, Olmstedville, NY 12857, Home Phone (518) 251-4306, is teaching French and Mathematics at the Minerva Central School.

Dean Kimball and Michelle Tarzia ('90) were married on August 4, 1991. Dean is employed by the EDS Corporation. They are residing in Plano, TX. (Best wishes!)

Alan Marciano, 5625 W. Flamingo, Apt. 2093, Las Vegas, NV 89103, Home Phone (702) 876-4950, Office Phone (702) 877-0040, Lebenson Actuarial Services, Inc., Las Vegas, has dual responsibilities, primary job is a pension plan consultant, other responsibility is to maintain both hardware and software at Hewlett Packard Computer System. Alan says "Unfortunately, my mathematic abilities have not helped me very much at the Black Jack tables." (Sorry, Alan!)

Andrea L. Newhouse, 101 Skyview Dr., Liverpool, NY 13088, Home Phone (315) 457-2192, Office Phone (315) 471-1121 x 2218, American General Life Insurance Company of New York, Syracuse, Collection Service Assistant - billing and collections department.

Daniel Voce and Christine Bartolotti ('90) were married on August 3, 1991. Daniel is attending SUNY Albany where he is pursuing his Ph.D. in mathematics. They reside in Delmar, NY. (Best wishes!)

1990

Tonya Avanzato married Paul LaBrosse on May 25, 1991. Paul is a 1990 graduate of Clarkson University. They reside in Amherst, NH. (Best wishes!)

Nelson W. Chase, III, Hudson Falls, NY, is a substitute mathematics teacher in the Washington/Warren/Saratoga County area. He is also a YABA junior bowling coach.

Phoebe Cheung writes to us from the University of Chicago where she is pursuing a Ph.D. degree in economics. Phoebe writes "Graduate School doesn't only require hard work and intelligence; it takes a great deal of maturity and commitment as well".

Darwyn Cook is working toward his Ph.D. degree in mathematics at Louisiana State University. He has passed his written exams in Algebra/Linear Algebra and Analysis/Topology. He will be writing his dissertation in Harmonic Analysis. On July 27, 1991 Darwyn got married to Rose Marie Chrysler, a 1989 Potsdam graduate. They reside at 375 West Roosevelt A, #1238, Baton Rouge, LA 70802-7820. (Best wishes!)

Heidi Learned (see William Broderick ('88))

Scott A. Smith, 308 S. Main St., Apt. 3, Oxford, OH 45056, Home Phone (513) 523-3957, Office Phone (513) 529-6539, Miami University, Oxford, OH, Teaching Graduate Assistant, teaching a five hour Calculus class while taking approximately ten hours of graduate level mathematics. Scott says "If all goes as planned, I will be graduating with an M.A. in Mathematics in early May, be getting married on May 23rd (to Jessica Lowe - a '91 Potsdam graduate), and continuing my education in the fall. (Congratulations, we are proud of you and best wishes!)

Robert "Rob" L. Welcher, 316 Belevue Ave. E. #204, Seattle, WA 98102, has managed to end up in Seattle where he will stay for a while, after having been almost everywhere.

1991

Deborah E. Davidson, 29 Northwood Dr., Windham, ME 04062; 3500 Sutherland Ave., Apt. F-314, Knoxville, TN 37919, Home Phone (207) 892, 8427, School Phone (615) 558-7412, Office Phone (615) 974-67093, University of Tennesee, Knoxville, Knoxville, TN, graduate student in Statistics, graduate assistant. Deborah says "Potsdam teaches you to think/reason. It's invaluable, take advantage of it. It will take you a lot farther than you think it will". Deborah hopes to graduate in May '93 with an MS in Statistics. Her career objective is "Apply statistical and analytical skills in an industrial setting for the purpose of process improvement". She'd like to return to the Northeast to stay, that is if the economy recovers enough for her to find a job. She feels that she was very well prepared for graduate school even though she chose a different field of study. Deborah was quite impressed with the Newsletter and pleased that she could "give directly to the Math Department". (Thanks, Debbie.)

Paula J. Golding, 8551 Richmond Hwy. #204, Alexandria, VA 22309, Home Phone (703) 780-4783, Office Phone (703) 685-3457, Analytic Services, Inc. (ANSER), Arlington, VA, Mathematician. Paula is currently a programmer in SQL windows at ANSER, developing the appropriation management support system data base for their clients in the Pentagon. This system will enhance their financial tracking capabilities that are used to manage and report funds. Paula is also working towards her Ph.D. in Mathematics Education at the American University in Washington, D.C. Paula and Mike Maida will be getting married on August 8, 1992. (Best wishes!)

Sarai Hedges, 709 Fifth Street, Apt. #10, Bowling Green, OH 43402 is studying for her Master's Degree in Applied Statistics at Bowling Green State University where she received a teaching assistantship.

Michael Maida, 8551 Richmond Hwy. #204, Alexandria, VA 22309, Home Phone (703) 780-4783, Office Phone (703) 549-3542, St. Stephen's & St. Agnes School, Alexandria, VA. Mike teaches Math to 6th and 8th graders at their middle school. He also is a 6th grade advisor in charge of ten 6th graders. Mike is the creator and head of their Recycling Club. Mike says "My first year of teaching was a wonderful experience!". Mike and Paula Golding will be getting married on August 8, 1992. (Best wishes!)

Kathleen K. Reape was married to Gary L. Noftsier on June 1, 1991. Gary is employed by Climax Manufacturing in Lowville, NY. They reside in Castorland, NY. A baby boy, Joshua, was born on April 20, 1992. (Best wishes and congratuations!)

CONTRIBUTIONS

We wish to thank all the alumni, faculty and friends of our Mathematics Department that contributed to the Annual Fund (restricted to the Math Department) for 1991-1992. The names are those who contributed as of June 1992.

As of June 1992 the alumni and friends of the Mathematics Department have contributed over $7,000 to our program. We can put this money to good use. Some of the ways these funds are used by the Department are: to produce and distribute the Newsletter to over 2,000 alumni and high schools from which the mathematics graduates of 1992 came; for cash awards to recognize our students for their high achievement in mathematics; to pay the dues for the students we nominate to membership in the Association for Women in Mathematics and the Association for Mathematics Teachers of New York State; to pay for the Math Lab when this becomes necessary due to state financial constraints (it is getting to be more so); to purchase computers when this becomes necessary due to scarcity of local funds (again it is getting to be more so). As money for education gets tighter in the State of New York, we need your support even more. Please continue to remember us; we appreciate every contribution you make.

Mrs. Susan M. Bailey
Mrs. Patricia A. Beaulieu
Mrs. Karen W. Beck
Ms. Lori Blaha
Ms. Anne E. Bonnet
Mr. Robert Brenner
Mr. & Mrs. Paul J. Brunetto
Mr. Leonard J. Burdick
Ms. Lisa L. Carte
Dr. Vasily C. Cateforis
Mr. William J. Cavanaugh
Mr. & Mrs. Michael L. Cescon
Mr. Nelson W. Chase, III
Mrs. Mary C. Cuzzupoli

Ms. Wendy D'Ambrosi
Ms. Deborah E. Davidson
Mr. & Mrs. Michael D. Deady
Ms. Mary Ann Dermady
Mr. Kenneth W. Diller
Mrs. Penni L. Farrington
Mr. Thomas Finnegan
Mr. Paul A. Fioramonti
Dr. Hector B. Foisy
Mrs. Anne Marie Freitas
Mrs. Phyllis R. Furman
Ms. Natalie Gilbert
Mr. George J. Gillen, Jr.
Ms. Eileen Weischedel Goettel

Capt. Matthew L. Halpin
Ms. Sarai A. Hedges
Mrs. Rebecca H. Himmelstein
Mrs. Ana R. Hubbard
Dr. & Mrs. Harold K. Hughes
Charles & Margaret Johnson
Mr. J. Kevin Kivlin
Dr. John Koker
Mr. & Mrs. Michael J. Komar
Mrs. Joyce Kopcik
Ms. Linda Elaine Krencik-Drace
Mrs. Eileen C. Krick
Mr. William Krick, Jr.
Ms. Diane E. Lamon
Mrs. Barbara J. Law
Mrs. Marsha J. Lewicke
Mrs. Regina Lubniewski
Mr. Werner K. Maass
Miss Alice J. Mansfield
Mrs. Wilhelmina Marsh
Mr. William J. Martin
Mr. Mark W. Metzger
Mrs. Jean Michaelsen
Dr. Cheryl Miller
Mr. John Harris Moore
Mrs. Nora B. Myers
Mrs. Suzanne U. Orlando
Mrs. Linda F. Ormsby
Mrs. Joan J. Osborne
Ms. Alice J. Ostanek
Dr. James M. Parks
Mrs. Kim M. Perilli
Dr. Laura Person
Mr. & Mrs. David J. Readyoff
Mr. John M. Rey
Mr. & Mrs. Jeffrey T. Roberts
Mr. Timothy Allen Rumph
Mr. Thomas A. Saunders
Dr. Irene Schensted
Dr. Harris Schlesinger

Mrs. Karen H. Schuh
Lt. Barre R. Seguin
Mrs. Susan J. Selvek
Dr. Charles L. Smith
Dr. David Spellman
Dr. & Mrs. Clarence Stephens
Mr. Peter A. Swakopf
Ms. Darlene S. Tegza
Mrs. Katheryn F. Thurston
Mrs. Nancy J. Tomanek
Mr. Donald J. Toomey
Mrs. Karen S. Trimm
Mr. David John Valois
Ms. Panagiota Vamvakitis
Mrs. Barbara Sullivan
VanYserloo
Ms. Linda A. Welch-Joseph
Mrs. Faye W. White
Mr. Darryl Willette
Mr. James P. Willey
Miss Karen A. Witting
Mr. Paul D. Wright

AROUND THE DEPARTMENT

There were papers and books submitted for publication, or accepted or in progress:

Dr. James Magee

Reviewed the papers titled:

1) Some properties of Set Ck in 1p- Space by D. K. Ganguly and S. Ray for the Mathematical Reviews.

2) The Hahn Space by Chandrasekhana Rao, K for the Mathematical Reviews.

Reviewing a paper titled: Strong Boundedness and Strong Convergence in Sequence Spaces by Martin Buntinas and Maza Tanovic-Miller for the Mathematical Reviews.

Dr. Kazem Mahdavi

1) Has submitted a paper titled On lattice isomorphism of mixed abelian groups (joint with John Poland) to the Archiv der Mathematik.

2) In preparation: Education of Mathematics.

Dr. Cheryl C. Miller

Had an article titled "Imprimitive Automorphism Groups" appear in the Quarterly Journal of Mathematics (Oxford) No. 43, March 1992, pp. 23-44

Dr. Laura Person

Has reviewed a book titled Linear Algebra for William C. Brown Publishers. Has had a paper titled "The Thurston Norm is the Singular Norm" accepted for publication in Topology and its Applications.

Grants received:

Dr. Cheryl C. Miller

Association for Women in Mathematics (AWM) grant to attend Conference on finite and infinite Combinatorics in Sets and Logic, Banff, Alberta, 4/22-4/26/91.

Papers presented and invited talks given:

Dr. Kazem Mahdavi

Invited talk:

1) Education of Mathematics; workshop on fostering the success of underrepresented groups and minority in Mathematics, Pomona College, CA, December 7-8, 1991.

2) On lattice isomorphic Abelian group, AMS Annual Meeting, Baltimore, MD, January, 1992.
3) Lattice isomorphic Abelian group, Regional Group Theory Conference, Bucknell University, Pennsylvania, May, 1992.

Dr. Cheryl C. Miller

Gave a talk titled "A New Structure Whose Automorphism Group Has Equal Orbits on 4- and 5- Sets" at the Institute for Mathematics and its Applications (IMA) conference in Model Theory in Chicago on October 11.

Dr. Armond Spencer

Invited talks:

1) At the Seaway Section, Mathematical Association of America, meeting in Fredonia: "Why Not Just Teach Math", November 2, 1991.
2) On the Potsdam Program at Watertown Rotary, February 27, 1992.

Conferences attended:

V. Cateforis, J. Parks, and I. Schensted attended the Summer Joint Meetings of the American Mathematical Society and Mathematical Association of America, August 7-11, 1991, University of Maine, Orono, Maine.

J. Parks attended a MAA Minicourse on "Julia Sets and the Mandelbrot Set" at summer meeting AMS/MAA, U. Maine, August 7-11, 1991.

Laura Person and Vasily Cateforis participated in the SUNY Mathematics Workshop on stategies to improve the success of minority students in mathematics, October 4-5, in Syracuse.

J. Magee attended the April 11-12, 1992 meeting of the American Mathematical Society, Special Session on Sequence Spaces, held at Lehigh University.

Kazem Mahdavi and I. Schensted attended the Algebra Day at Carleton University, Ottawa, Oct. 5.

C. Miller attended the IMA Model Theory Conference, Chicago, Illinois, October 1991. She also attended the conference on Finite and Infinite Combinatorics in Sets and Logic in Banff, Alberta, April 22-26, 1991.

Kazem Mahdavi attended the winter national meeting of the American Mathematical Society (AMS), January 6-10, Baltimore, Maryland. At the meeting he gave a talk on lattice isomorphism of abelian groups (Jan. 8), took a short course on New Scientific Applications of Geometry and Topology (Jan. 6-8) and was one of fifteen mathematicians invited to participate in a meeting to discuss the goals and services of the AMS (Jan. 10).

James Parks attended the winter Joint Meetings of the American Mathematical Society and the Mathematical Association of America (AMS/MAA), Jan. 7-11, Baltimore, Maryland. At this meeting he attended a minicourse on Mathematical Modeling with a Spreadsheet.

A. Spencer attended the Seaway Section of the MAA meeting at Fredonia, November 1-2, 1991.

J. Parks and V. Cateforis attended the Associated Colleges of St. Lawrence Valley supported talk on "Understanding Today's Students: A Review of Twenty-five Years of Data" by Dr. Eric Dey, Asso. Survey Director, UCLA Graduate School of Education (Clarkson University, Friday, 3/6/1992).

K. Mahdavi, C. Miller, J. Parks, L. Person, D. Spellman, A. Spencer, and (student) Tina Bergdorff attended the 18th Annual New York Regional Graduate Mathematics Conference, March 20-21, 1992 at Syracuse University.

Other news...

Faculty engaged in other professional activities:

Dr. V. Cateforis has been appointed a member to an Ad Hoc Committee on Advising of the Mathematical Association of America.

Dr. Kerrith Chapman
Directed a seminar in Orthomodular spaces and additive measurement for a BA/MA student (Fall 1991 - Spring 1992).

Dr. James Magee
Participated in a year long seminar in Duality Theory with M. Armstrong.

Dr. Kazem Mahdavi
   1)   Directed seminars in Differential Geometry, Universal Algebra, Relativity Theory and Category Theory for four BA/MA students (Summer 1991, Fall 1991, Spring 1992) and
   2)   Also took a course on new scientific applications of Geometry and Topology.

Dr. Cheryl C. Miller

Participated in Joint SLU - Potsdam Logic Seminar: presented "Imprimitive Automorphism Groups" as a weekly seminar, Fall 1991
Attended weekly, Spring 1991.
Attended Graduate Student Seminar on Posets, 1991-92 school year.

Dr. Laura Person
Directed a seminar in Tiling Groups for a BA/MA student (Fall 1991 - Spring 1992).

Dr. Irene Schensted
Co-directed a BA/MA student's seminar in Relativity Theory and directed another BA/MA student's seminar in Topics in Probability Theory.

Dr. Armond Spencer
1) Mathematical Association of America Lecturer;
2) Participant in year long seminar on Ortho Modular Spaces;
3) Consultant to Radford University Mathematics Department (Visit April 17-21).
4) Vice President for Academic Affairs Lecture Series Presenter "My Semester at York University (And What I Learned About Teaching at Potsdam)".

Members of the Mathematics Department serve the college through participation in committees and governance:

Faculty Assembly
K. Mahdavi
C. Miller (alternate)
A. Spencer (Departmental Representatives)
J. Parks, Graduate Affairs Committee
L. Person, Hearing Officer for campus judicial system
W. Sloan, Business Affairs Committee
A. Spencer, Dean's Search Committee

School of Liberal Studies
V. Cateforis, J. Parks, A. Spencer, Members of the Liberal Studies Council
H. Foisy, Curriculum Committee
L. Person, Interdepartmental Programs Committee

Other
> V. Cateforis, A. Spencer, Presidential Scholars Council
> C. C. Miller, K. Mahdavi, Potsdam College Phonathon Fall and
> Spring 91-92
> J. Parks, Academic Computing Advisory Committee, Member and
> District Representative of the Association of Mathematics Teachers
> of New York State (AMTNYS).

Admissions Saturday Open House:
> V. Cateforis (9/21 and 3/21)   J. Parks (10/19)
> H. Foisy (11/16)   A. Spencer (12/7)

Dr. and Mrs. Dunn have been enjoying their first year of retirement
traveling, visiting and doing those things that a working schedule
often precludes. September found them in Margaree Forks, Nova
Scotia, catching Atlantic salmon with the new retirement fly reel
from the department (which had been broken in on the Dartmouth
and York rivers of Gaspé, Quebec during a two week summer trip).
October, November and December were hunting, fishing and visiting
months back home. January and February were sun, golf and fishing
in Tampa Bay and Panama City, Florida. March was grandchild
number four in Tarrytown, NY, their own Patrick Mahon, 7 lbs. 12
oz., whose father was born in Galway Bay, Ireland, a place they
expect to visit soon with parents, Eugene and Lynn. April found the
Dunn's in Chicago, with son Michael, watching the Cubs lose
again. May found them back at the annual Mathematics Dinner in
Potsdam. With future plans including Russia, Alaska and New
Zealand, Professor Dunn says he will probably have to find another
job. He asks "Any leads?".

Professor and Mrs. Daniel Kocan are enjoying their retirement
in Central Florida. They appreciate the urban lifestyle and yet are
only 50 miles from the Atlantic coast beaches. The fair weather and
international airport make for easy travel. In addition to local trips,
they are planning European holidays. They just returned from three
weeks in England. They hope to visit Paris in November.
Professor Kocan has tutored in the Mathematics Lab and has given
calculus courses as an adjunct in the local community college.

Dr. Smith wishes to be remembered to all his past students who
collectively have made his professional career so enjoyable and
memorable. In good health, he continues to live in Potsdam at 39

Bay St. with Sasha, his chocolate lab. Although he retired in 1990, he has been teaching two mathematics courses each semester and loving it. His daughter, Sarah, married Daniel Cullen this past October and his son, Fred, graduated from Purchase College with a degree in English Literature and a writing concentration this past May.

Dr. Wesley Mitchell has resigned his position with our Department. We can share some of his thoughts with all our alumni and friends: "I have the highest regard for my colleagues in the Department, and have enjoyed a professional relationship with the Department that would be difficult to duplicate at another institution. I have the highest regard, as well, for the students of the College, in particular, those that choose to educate themselves in the Department." "I am having fun working in industry. I was fortunate to obtain a position where I am constantly challenged."

"I have enough time to pursue interesting topics, and can very directly influence products and strategies with my work. I'm well-enough rewarded to be able to put aside a substantial amount of money each month for investment." "I will always think fondly of my many friends in Potsdam, and will always be interested to hear of my colleagues and students." Dr. Mitchell resides at 1614 Martin Ave., Sunnyvale, CA 94087 and works at Sunsoft, A Sun Microsystems Company.

Dr. Dilip Datta, Professor, Department of Mathematics, University of Rhode Island, Kingston, RI 02881 spent his sabbatic with us for most of 1991-1992. He wishes to thank everyone for making his stay here very fruitful and enjoyable. Dr. Datta really accomplished a lot during his sabbatic here. He says his stay here has been of benefit to him in more ways than he had expected. Two of the papers that he wrote here have already been accepted for publication. The papers are entitled *Arithmetic Matrices and the Amazing Nine-Card Monte (jointly with R. S. Clark) and Some Entertaining Matrices.* Dr. Datta learned a great deal about the humanistic environment for teaching and learning mathematics that the people here have created. He learned more about the art of teaching mathematics from the people here during the past year than he had learned as a math teacher for a quarter of a century. The love shown for math, the sense of display in teaching math and the respect that we have for our students he says is truly admirable. Above all, he realizes now more than ever before that the teachers hold the key to a successful math program. He is so convinced that the present and the future math teachers have so much to learn from our example, that he is determined to publish his observations in the form of a book. He thanks us all for a most enjoyable and educational experience.

A Departmental Dinner was held May 3, 1992 at the French's 1884 House. Dr. Richard Del Guidice, Dean of the School of Liberal Studies was the honored guest as he is stepping down after eight years as Dean of the School. He was presented with a pen set, Black Italian Marble Double Desk Set from Sheaffer.

PROFILE OF JUNIOR AND SENIOR MATHEMATICS MAJORS

JUNIOR MATHEMATICS MAJORS – APRIL, 1992

AN ANALYSIS OF ABILITY AND ACHIEVEMENT
   Potsdam College of the State University of New York/Potsdam, New York

Average	Total	Cum. Total	Cum. Pct.	Mean	COLLEGE CUMULATIVE AVERAGES Median	Max.	Min.	Below 3.0	Cum. Total
HIGH SCHOOL AVERAGES									
95 and Above	3	3	3.8	3.82	3.80	3.86	3.76	0	0
90 - 94.9	18	21	26.9	3.29	3.33	3.82	1.96	3	3
85 - 89.9	31	52	66.7	2.77	2.80	3.77	1.52	22	25
80 - 84.9	10	62	79.5	2.70	2.71	3.09	2.29	9	34
Below 80	7	69	88.5	2.36	2.24	3.02	1.96	6	40
Don't Know	9	78	100.0	3.14	3.33	4.00	1.94	3	43

COLLEGE CUMULATIVE AVERAGES

Average	Total	Cum. Total	Cum. Pct.	Mean	Median	Max.	Min.	Below 3.0	Cum. Total
MATH SAT SCORE (1991 AVERAGES: National - 474 , New York - 468)									
700 and above	6	6	7.7	3.41	3.76	3.86	1.96	1	1
650 - 699	9	15	19.2	3.24	3.31	3.67	2.67	3	4
600 - 649	12	27	34.6	2.78	2.64	3.43	2.18	7	11
550 - 599	13	40	51.3	2.31	2.80	3.61	1.52	7	18
500 - 549	11	51	65.4	2.86	2.92	3.45	2.38	9	27
450 - 499	2	53	67.9	2.68	2.59	2.78	2.59	2	29
400 - 449	3	56	71.8	2.57	2.39	2.93	2.29	3	32
350 - 399	0	56	71.8	0.00	0.00	0.00	0.00	0	32
Below 350	0	56	71.8	0.00	0.00	0.00	0.00	0	32
Don't Know	22	78	100.0	2.98	2.89	4.00	1.94	11	43

VERBAL SAT SCORE (1991 AVERAGES: NATIONAL - 422 NEW YORK- 413)

	Total	Cum. Total	Cum. Pct.	Mean	Median	Max.	Min.	Below 3.0	Cum. Total
700 and Above	0	0	0.0	0.00	0.00	0.00	0.00	0	0
650 - 699	1	1	1.3	1.96	1.96	1.96	1.96	1	1
600 - 649	3	4	5.1	3.39	3.17	3.82	3.03	0	1
550 - 599	8	12	15.4	3.26	3.12	3.83	2.47	3	4
500 - 549	13	25	32.1	3.07	3.10	3.86	1.96	6	10
450 - 499	14	39	50.0	2.77	2.59	3.45	2.30	10	20
400 - 449	10	49	62.8	2.94	2.85	3.40	2.29	6	26
350 - 399	7	56	71.8	2.54	2.55	3.33	1.52	6	32
Below 350	0	56	71.8	0.00	0.00	0.00	0.00	0	32
Don't Know	22	78	100.0	2.93	2.89	4.00	1.94	11	43

COLLEGE CUMULATIVE AVERAGES

	NUMBER	CUM. NUMBER	CUM.PCT.
3.75 - 4.00 Summa cum laude	8	8	10.26
3.50 - 3.75 Magna cum laude	5	13	16.67
3.25 - 3.49 Cum laude	12	25	32.05
3.00 - 3.24	10	35	44.87
2.75 - 2.99	13	48	61.54
2.50 - 2.74	10	58	74.36
2.00 - 2.49	16	74	94.87
Below 2.00	4	78	100.00
Don't Know	0	78	100.00

SENIOR MATHEMATICS MAJORS – APRIL, 1992

AN ANALYSIS OF ABILITY AND ACHIEVEMENT

Potsdam College of the State University of New York/Potsdam, New York

COLLEGE CUMULATIVE AVERAGES

Average	Cum. Total	Cum. Total	Cum. Pct.	Mean	Median	Max.	Min.	Below 3.0	Cum. Total
HIGH SCHOOL AVERAGES									
95 and Above	6	6	5.2	3.58	3.48	3.92	3.31	0	0
90 - 94.9	17	23	19.8	3.30	3.34	3.93	2.44	5	5
85 - 89.9	42	65	56.0	2.93	2.81	3.72	2.24	29	34
80 - 84.9	16	81	69.8	2.74	2.69	3.37	2.05	13	47
Below 80	4	85	73.3	2.73	2.75	2.86	2.50	4	51
Don't Know	31	116	100.0	3.02	2.92	3.88	2.23	16	67

MATH SAT SCORE (1991 AVERAGES: NATIONAL - 474
NEW YORK - 468)

COLLEGE CUMULATIVE AVERAGES

Average	Total	Cum. Total	Cum. Pct.	Mean	Median	Max.	Min.	Below 3.0	Cum. Total
700 and Above	8	8	6.9	3.39	3.48	3.93	2.63	1	1
650 - 699	11	19	16.4	3.06	2.82	3.90	2.40	7	8
600 - 649	15	34	29.3	3.03	2.83	3.69	2.24	8	16
550 - 599	16	50	43.1	3.08	2.94	3.92	2.38	8	24
500 - 549	11	61	52.6	2.84	2.70	3.71	2.05	8	32
450 - 499	7	68	58.6	2.60	2.54	2.84	2.24	7	39
400 - 449	4	72	62.1	2.94	2.83	3.26	2.80	3	42
350 - 399	2	74	63.8	2.82	2.69	2.94	2.69	2	44
Below 350	0	74	63.8	0.00	0.00	0.00	0.00	0	44
Don't Know	42	116	100.0	3.01	2.91	3.88	2.23	23	67

COLLEGE CUMULATIVE AVERAGES

Average	Total	Cum. Total	Cum. Pct.	Mean	Median	Max.	Min.	Below 3.0	Cum. Total

VERBAL SAT SCORE (1991 AVERAGES: NATIONAL - 422
*   NEW YORK - 413)*

Average	Total	Cum. Total	Cum. Pct.	Mean	Median	Max.	Min.	Below 3.0	Cum. Total
700 and Above	1	1	0.9	3.60	3.60	3.60	3.60	0	0
650 - 699	2	3	2.6	3.32	3.03	3.61	3.03	0	0
600 - 649	2	5	4.3	3.65	3.58	3.72	3.58	0	0
550 - 599	4	9	7.8	3.55	3.44	3.90	3.38	0	0
500 - 549	18	27	23.3	3.05	2.93	3.92	2.40	10	10
450 - 499	19	46	39.7	3.02	2.77	3.93	2.24	11	21
400 - 449	16	62	53.4	2.90	2.80	3.71	2.24	11	32
350 - 399	7	69	59.5	2.60	2.59	2.94	2.05	7	39
Below 350	5	74	63.8	2.75	2.76	2.94	2.41	5	44
Don't Know	42	116	100.0	3.01	2.91	3.88	2.23	23	67

COLLEGE CUMULATIVE AVERAGES

	NUMBER	CUM.NUMBER	CUM.PCT
3.75 - 4.00 Summa cum laude	8	8	6.26
3.50 - 3.75 Magna cum laude	17	25	21.55
3.25 - 3.49 Cum laude	16	41	35.34
3.00 - 3.24	8	49	42.24
2.75 - 2.99	28	77	66.38
2.50 - 2.74	22	99	85.34
2.00 - 2.49	17	116	100.00
Below 2.00	0	116	100.00
Don't Know	0	116	100.00

REFERENCES

1. Bauer, Sue A.,*Thoughts on the Real Value of a Mathematics Education*, Department of Mathematics,SUNY Potsdam, 1988.
2. Cominsky, Lynn R. *What I Learned from Clarence Stephens, Teaching &*, Sonoma State University, February, 1988.
3. CUPM Report 19810. *Recommendations for a General Mathematical Sciences Program*, Mathematical Association of America.
4. Datta, D.K. and Scarfpin, J.A., *Types of Math Anxiety,* Math Notebook, The Center for Teaching/Learning of Math, Vol. 3, No. 9 & 10, 1983.
5. Datta, D.K., *Finite Mathematics* (second edition), Ginn Press, Needham Heights, 1991.
6. Davidson, Neil (ed.), *Cooperative Learning in Mathematics A Handbook For Teachers,* Addison-Wesley, 1990.
7. Feichtner, Susan Brown and Davis, Elaine Actis, *Why Some Groups Fail: A Survey of Students' Experiences with Learning Groups,* The Organizational Behavior Teaching Review, Vol. 9, No. 4, pp 75 - 88.
8. Finizio, N. and Ladas, G. Ordinary Differential Equations with Modern Applications, Wadsworth, 1989
9. Gillman, Leonard, *Teaching Programs That Work,* FOCUS, MAA, Vol. 10, No. 1, Jan-Feb, 1990, 7 -10.
10. Gilmer, Gloria ans Williams, Scott, *The Person Behind The Amazing Story,* UME Trends, Vol.2, No. 1, March 1990.
11. Gould, Lawrence I., *The SUNY Potsdam Miracle? Soound Lessons for Physics,* Journal of College Science Teaching, vol. XXI, 1992, 348 - 351
12. Halmos, P.R., *The Teaching of Problem Solving,* American Mathematical Monthly, Vol. 82, No. 5, 1975, 466-470.
13. Hilton, Peter, *Mathematics and its contribution to Education,* UME TRENDS, December 1990, p. 1.
14. Johnson Kenneth, *Potsdam State's Math Program Praised in Speech to National Groups,* Watertown Daily Times, Monday, March 12, 1990.
15. Luttmann, Rick, *The Basis for the Success of the Potsdam Program,* manuscript available at Potsdam College.

16. Madison, Bernard L. and Hart, Therese A. *A Challenge of Numbers: People in the Mathematical Sciences.* Committee on Mathematical Sciences in the Year 2000, National Research Council, National Academy Press, Washington, D.C., 1990.

17. Murphy, Derek, *Grad unusual, statistically speaking,* Greece Post (Rochester Market Area), Pittsford, NY, Oct 29, 1991.

18. National Research Council, *Everybody Counts A Report to the Nation on the Future of Mathematics Education,* National Academy Press, Washington, D.C., 1989.

19. National Research Council, *Moving Beyond Myths, Revitalizing Undergraduate Mathematics* , National Academy Press, Washington, D.C., 1991.

20. Newsreporter, *Past MAA Head Visits SUCP,* Daily Courier-Observer, Wednesday, October 11, 1989.

21. Notices of the American Mathematical Society, *Moving Beyond Myths*, vol. 38, No. 6, pp. 545 - 559.

22. Poland, John, *A modern Fairy tale*, Amer Math monthly, vol.94, N0. 3, 1987, 291 - 295

23. Rogers, Pat and others, *An Experiment in Teaching Mathematics*, manuscript available at Potsdam College.

24. Rogers, Pat, *Thoughts on Power and Pedagogy*, manuscript available at Potsdam College.

25. Spencer, Armond E., *The Potsdam Experience,* Proceedings Spring Conference on the First Two Years: Teaching the Mathematical Core, March 31 - April 1, 1989, University of Hartford, Department of Mathematics/Physics Computer Science, 205 - 212.

26. Stephens, Clarence F., *Developing Mathematical Maturity and Understanding,* Department of Mathematics, SUNY College at Potsdam, 1975.

27. Stephens, Clarence F., A Humanistic Academic Environment for Learning Undergraduate Mathematics, Department of Mathematics, SUNY College at Potsdam, 1981.

28. Stephens, Clarence F., *A Letter to Mathematics majors,* Department of Mathematics, SUNY College at Potsdam,1981.

29. Stephens, Clarence F., *Effective Teaching Strategies,* Presented at the workshop on Wednesday May 18, 1988, Spellman College, Atlanta, Georgia, circulated by the Department of Mathematics, SUNY College at Potsdam.

30. Stephens, Clarence F., *Identifying and Nurturing Mathematical Talent,* Department of Mathematics, SUNY College at Potsdam, 1982.
31. Stephens, Clarence F., *Present Status of our Department and Prospects for the Future,* Department of Mathematics, SUNY College at Potsdam, 1981.
32. Stephens, Clarence F., *A Humanistic Academic Environment for Learning Undergraduate Mathematics,* Department of Mathematics, SUNY College at Potsdam, 1981.
33. Stephens, Clarence F., *The Pending Death of the Mathematics Major,* invited talk at the joint summer meeting of the American Mathematical Society and the Mathematical Association of America, Toronto, 1982.
34. Tucker, Alan, *Redefining the Mathematics Major,* Mathematics Tomorrow, ed. L. Steen, Academic Press, New York, 1981, 47 - 55.
35. Weimer, Maryellen (Editor), *Why Groups Fail: Student Answers,* The Teaching Professor, Vo. 5, No. 9, November 1991.
36. Weld, Kathryn, *Why do Mathematics,* Department of Mathematics, SUNY Potsdam, 1984.

INDEX

ABOUT THE AUTHOR

Dilip K. Datta hails from Assam, in northeast India. After spending 11 years in various colleges (4 years for his B.A. degree from Cotton College, Assam; 5 years for his M.A. and the Ph.D. degree from the University of Delhi; 2 years as a Commonwealth Fellow at the University Southampton, England), he dreamt of becoming a professional student and applied for fellowships at different universities.

He had to give up his dream of becoming a professional student when the University of Calgary, Canada wrote to him saying that they could not give him a fellowship but they could give him a job. He joined its faculty in 1965. In 1967 he joined the University of Rhode Island, where he became a professor in 1981. His interests are in geometry and math education. He has published two previous books, *Concepts of Geometry,* and *Finite Mathematics.* He has published papers on Differential Geometry, Linear Algebra and Math Anxiety.

CENTER FOR TEACHING/ LEARNING OF MATHEMATICS

PROGRAMS AND SERVICES

At the Center for Teaching/Learning of Mathematics (**CT/LM**) we look at the nature of children's mathematics problems, diagnose their causes and then plan remedial instructional techniques.

Participants in **CT/LM**'s programs study approaches to mathematics' learning problems, examine existing techniques and learn to design diagnostic and assessment instruments for learning problems in mathematics.

The programs at **CT/LM** are especially useful to teachers, curriculum supervisors, parents and diagnosticians who work with children with learning problems in general and mathematics problems in particular.

CT/LM has developed programs and materials to assist teachers, parents, therapists, and diagnosticians to help children and adults with their learning disabilities in the area of mathematics.

At **CT/LM**, we are conducting and synthesizing research in order to develop materials (monograph, papers and concrete materials) useful for people working with children with learning problems in mathematics and to improve mathematics education.

Services:

- Regular workshops, seminars and lectures on topics such as: How children learn mathematics, why learning problems occur, diagnosis and remediation of learning problems in mathematics
- Individual diagnosis and remediation services for children and adults with mathematics problems.
- Consultation with and training for parents to help their children cope with their anxieties and difficulties in learning mathematics.
- Consultation services to schools and individual classroom teachers to help them evaluate their mathematics programs and help design new programs or supplement existing ones in order to minimize the incidence of learning problems in mathematics.
- Assistance for the adult student who is returning to college and has anxiety about his/her mathematics ability.

Contact our office for fee schedules.

P.O. Box 3149, Framingham, MA 01701 Fax (508) 788-3600
Tel: Mornings (508) 877-7895, Afternoons (617) 235-7200